PRAISE FOR

STARTUP VIETNAM

Andrew has done a fantastic job putting it all together in *Startup Vietnam*! I'm impressed by the statistics and knowledge that he's accumulated over the years in Vietnam, which flows well throughout the text. *Startup Vietnam* is definitely more insightful than the typical business-in-Asia book. A must read if you want to know about modern Vietnam.

Rachel Bui
cofounder and inaugural CEO, Australia-Vietnam Young Leadership Dialogue

Andrew Rowan has the kind of deep insight into the Vietnamese society and psyche of its people that makes *Startup Vietnam* a must-have guide for anyone looking to conduct business in Viet Nam, including the Vietnamese themselves. It is the combination of Western training needed to succeed in expanding global markets and Eastern sensibilities required to make business inroads that allows Andrew Rowan to masterfully walk us through understanding the nuanced economic culture of Viet Nam. The broad range of information presented, as well as the golden nuggets given in a gripping narrative style, are some of the many reasons I consistently teach *Startup Vietnam* in my international development courses.

Kiều-Linh Caroline Valverde
associate professor, UC Davis, Asian American Studies Department; author of *Transnationalizing Viet Nam*; director, New Viet Nam Studies Initiative (NVNSI)

Andrew Rowan is an oracle of insight into the complex yet compelling nation of Vietnam. Andrew's understandings that he shares with the reader in *Startup Vietnam* go beyond the business world and peer into the culture and energy that make Vietnam the heartbeat of development in Southeast Asia. A must read for anyone with an interest in modern Vietnam.

Stephen Conroy
secondary school assistant principal / humanities teacher, Concordia International School Hanoi

This book comes out timely and packed with useful information (including caveats) for people who are interested in doing business in Vietnam or with Vietnam, especially with its dynamic private sector and its even more dynamic startup companies. It's also a thought-provoking read for current startup founders, investors, and community developers in Vietnam. My startup team changed some of our behaviors based on Andrew Rowan's honest observations.

Đậu Thúy Hà
cofounder, KidsOnline

STARTUP VIETNAM

"A must read if you want to know about modern Vietnam."
- RACHEL BUI, COFOUNDER AND INAUGURAL CEO, AUSTRALIA-VIETNAM YOUNG LEADERSHIP DIALOGUE

STARTUP VIETNAM

INNOVATION AND ENTREPRENEURSHIP IN THE SOCIALIST REPUBLIC

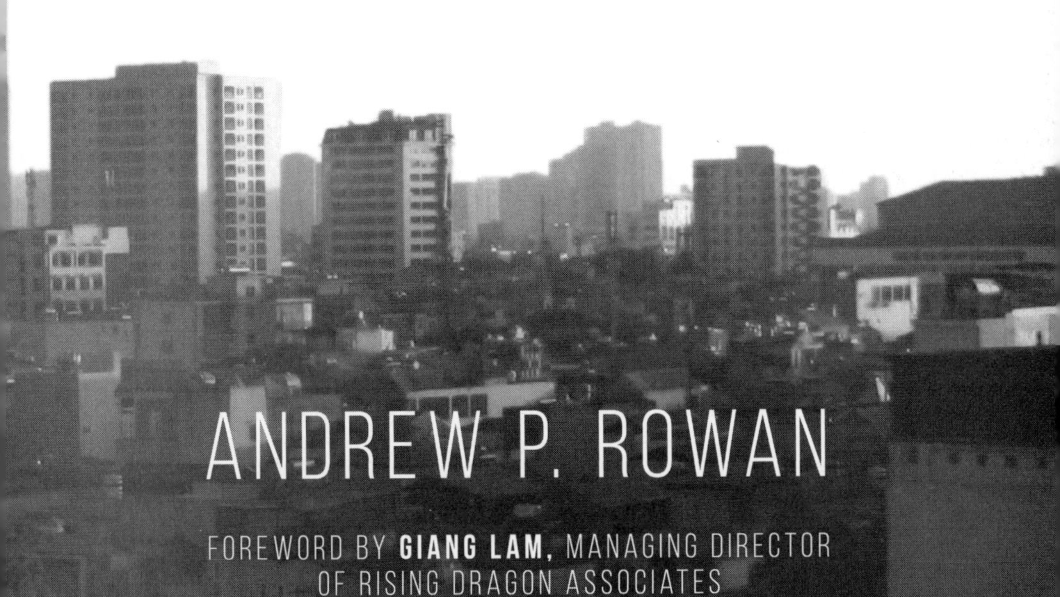

ANDREW P. ROWAN

FOREWORD BY **GIANG LAM,** MANAGING DIRECTOR OF RISING DRAGON ASSOCIATES

www.mascotbooks.com

STARTUP VIETNAM

https://andrewprowan.com/
Cover photography by Andrew P. Rowan
Author photo by Aleksandra Arefieva
Cover design by Zoe Wilson

For more information, please contact:
Mascot Books
620 Herndon Parkway #320
Herndon, VA 20170
info@mascotbooks.com

Library of Congress Control Number: 2018908952

CPSIA Code: PRFRE0119A
ISBN-13: 978-1-64307-260-9

Printed in Canada

For *Việt Nam*'s youth, the nation's future.
And for David, who is of the same generation.

A NOTE ABOUT
VIETNAMESE WORDS IN THE TEXT

AUTHOR'S NOTE

ALTHOUGH IN THE ENGLISH LANGUAGE, we write "Vietnam" to identify the country, it is actually two words in Vietnamese: Việt Nam. So the Socialist Republic of Vietnam in Vietnamese would be Cộng hòa xã hội chủ nghĩa Việt Nam. Similarly, words such as Hanoi, Da Nang, and Ho Chi Minh City would be Hà Nội, Đà Nẵng, and Thành phố Hồ Chí Minh respectively in Vietnamese. Where possible, efforts were made to preserve the original Vietnamese without disrupting the flow of the text or confusing readers who might be completely unfamiliar with Vietnam or the Vietnamese language. Vietnamese names have been preserved in their original Vietnamese format: family name followed by middle and/or first name. (Unless otherwise noted, people with the same family names are not related.) The only exceptions made for these policies were for members of the diaspora or for the most commonly used city names. (Saigon, i.e., Sài Gòn, is used interchangeably with Ho Chi Minh City throughout the manuscript.)

CONTENTS

CHINA
HANOI
HAI PHONG
LAOS
THAILAND
QUAN DAO
HOANG SA
HUE
DA NANG
HOI AN
CAMBODIA
HO CHI MINH CITY (SAIGON)
QUAN DAO
TRUONG SA
CAN THO
PHU QUOC
CON DAO
VIETNAM
Note: Approximate distances

FOREWORD

Energy. This is the word most often used by newcomers to characterize the atmosphere in Vietnam. I used it myself ten years ago when I began working here. There is an undeniable energy in the air; however, it seems particularly significant that so many people from so many different backgrounds would independently choose the same word to describe the country. Today, after being in Vietnam for more than a decade, I am surprised, when I first meet a newcomer, if I don't hear that person mention the word *energy* within the first few sentences.

If you've never been to Vietnam, the energy here is a little difficult to explain.

First, there's the traffic. Motorcycles, pedestrians, and automobiles navigate through the city, all on the same roads, with no dividers. It sounds chaotic. However, once you're here, it actually feels like a well-rehearsed orchestra. The motorcycles don't yield to pedestrians. They go around them. The timing is perfect. Neither the motorcycle drivers nor the pedestrians think twice about what is going on. Further, to show that this orchestra can deal with syncopation, every now and then, a street peddler will enter the scene, pushing his cart on the same road with the pedestrians, motorbikes, and cars, and stop to make a quick bowl of noodles for a passing customer. The pedestrians, motorbikes, and cars all adapt quickly and simply go around the new player without missing a beat.

Up from the road, between the curb and the row of townhouses, are makeshift shopping areas, cafes, and eateries. Sometimes merchants may combine all three services and offer snacks and drinks while customers peruse the goods. iPhone cases, belts, sneakers, and fresh avocados can all be bought on the curb, depending on the season and the current fashion trends. Again, it sounds chaotic, but it really is a well-rehearsed orchestra. A customer stops in with his scooter, hangs up his safety helmet, and plops into an open plastic chair. The vendor hands out a product, or sometimes a few, and the customer considers the goods for a while. Then a deal is struck, and the customer is on his way. It is so well orchestrated that a deal is normally made within a few minutes, and even small stands can serve dozens of customers an hour. At curbside cafes or restaurants, where customers come to hang out longer, there is even a scooter-parking service. When the customer arrives, he or she drops off the scooter and receives a parking slip. When the customer leaves, the slip is exchanged for the scooter. Not exactly premium valet service, but definitely not what you'd expect from a roadside eatery.

Beyond the curbside vendors are more upscale establishments. *Upscale*, here, means house-stores, which are more permanent than the curbside vendors. The front portion of the first floor of almost every house on every street in Vietnam is a storefront. Upper floors of the house may be used for living space or sales, but the first floor is almost always reserved for commerce, or at least rented to someone who will use it for commerce. Curbside vendors typically have a cart or a large tarp on the ground outside, and commerce is more or less conducted in the open air. Therefore, curbside sales are heavily influenced by weather, as well as city events that require the use of the curb. Vendors in a house do not have to set up and clean up each day. As a result, the house-store can be decorated more nicely. The house-store is more permanent than the curbside shop; however, the landscape is still continually moving and dynamic; therefore, very few are permanent beyond a few years. Storefronts change as fast as market trends in Vietnam. In fact, many times people may recognize a new storefront but can't recall what was there before.

Now consider the people in all this. National statistics indicate the median age in Vietnam is thirty-one years. Picture that for a second, if you will. Every other person in Vietnam was born after 1988. Vietnam is a very young country with plenty of energy, much of which can be seen openly as entrepreneurial energy. The street peddler pushing his cart on the street, the curbside merchant with his tarp of goods, and the house-store businessman all contribute to the entrepreneurial energy that is palpable in Vietnam. Every street in Vietnam, from the major cities such as Hanoi and Ho Chi Minh City to small towns such as Hue and Dalat, will exhibit a similar energy. Given the amount of activity everywhere across the country, I would say the Vietnamese are born entrepreneurs. From my perspective, it has always been like this. A decade or two decades ago, there were fewer products to sell and less disposable income to buy products; however, the energy that has grown to be so palpable today was always there, albeit on a smaller scale.

I was born in Hanoi. I grew up and was educated in America. Ten years ago, I came to Vietnam with a wave of foreign investors looking to capitalize on the best-performing stock market in the world. Nine years ago, when the Vietnam stock market crashed, most of those foreigners withdrew. I decided to stay.

Even though modern Vietnam is nothing like the Vietnam that I remember as a kid, I felt an energy here that was not anywhere else in the world. From an investment perspective, I believed the country had nowhere to go but up. So I stayed and learned how the country worked. I wanted to confirm firsthand what I had understood from the macroeconomic analyses. Basically, I wanted to be able to see Vietnam as the locals do.

Having both an American and Vietnamese view of Vietnam, I quickly recognized a few things that are often understated in the global macro reports on Vietnam. For example, one factor that influences the energy in Vietnam quite heavily but is very understated in macroanalyses is the foreign factor: expatriates and diaspora (often referred to as Overseas Vietnamese). Vietnam was a very conservative country that was basically closed to foreigners about twenty years ago. Unlike China, Vietnam did not have a long list of students overseas who could be recalled to help with rebuilding. As smart and hardworking as the local people were, the population was very young and didn't have the ideas or experience to start scalable businesses. Since the country opened up after normalizing relations with the United States, many foreigners and diaspora have come to Vietnam. Some came to work and decided to stay. Others came for holiday and settled down quickly after. Some diaspora came to visit family and decided to stay.

These foreigners contributed greatly to Vietnam's growth by bringing in new ideas and management expertise. Many have helped to start and grow businesses in Vietnam that are market leaders today. One thing is for sure: foreigners have helped to make the energy in Vietnam more dynamic.

Andrew Rowan, the author of this book, is a great example of a foreigner contributing to a new area in Vietnam. I met Andrew in 2016 at Techfest, a startup event in Hanoi. My first impression of him was of an even-mannered and very centered person. Being an American in the capital of Vietnam, Andrew was very considerate of both the political and economic factors that could affect his work. As centered as he seemed, Andrew had an entrepreneurial drive that was common to New York City. He had to be driven. Andrew was a foreigner evangelizing entrepreneurship in a country full of entrepreneurs. That sounds a little bit funny, but what he was doing was valuable. He was helping entrepreneurs with issues that were very basic in the United States but were new and difficult to Vietnamese entrepreneurs. He was helping people to be more structured in their thinking so they could avoid common mistakes. He was bringing global ideas and lessons to Vietnam. In a way, he was bringing the New York drive to Vietnam as well. Andrew's work is with startups and innovation, two topics that are very new to Vietnam. Without Andrew and his efforts, the country would understand these topics only from the perspective of someone reading the history of Yahoo! or Google.

Andrew's work in Vietnam brings forward another factor that is understated in the macro analyses: the effect of widespread internet usage and, more generally, technology usage, in Vietnam. Technology analysts already understand this, but it is important to note that nontech sectors in Vietnam have benefited enormously from the internet. Just recently, as Vietnam has accelerated the transition from agriculture to industry, young entrepreneurs are learning about innovation and how to build businesses based on innovation and technology as opposed to commodities. They want to be like Facebook, Apple, and Google. These companies all started humbly in a garage and now are multibillion dollar companies. As a result, there has been a surge in demand for entrepreneurship education in Vietnam during the past few years. I have witnessed it firsthand.

One Sunday afternoon in 2015, a couple of my friends, MIT alumni, sat together at a cafe in Hanoi to organize a small workshop to share with local entrepreneurs about entrepreneurship at MIT. We thought maybe ten people would come. If word spread, then maybe we'd have twenty people show up. We set the date for Wednesday evening, three days later. That Sunday night we put a post on Facebook to advertise the event. On Monday morning we had over two hundred registrations! On Tuesday morning we had over a thousand registrations! On Wednesday we scrambled and were lucky to borrow the main auditorium of the Ministry of Science and Technology, which had a seating capacity of four hundred.

It was a major feat to get the auditorium on such short notice; however, we had to turn away the majority of the almost two thousand online registrations. What we thought would be a workshop for a maximum of twenty people turned out to garner interest a hundred times that size.

The internet and social networking undoubtedly had a huge effect on the turnout of that event. It was an offline event, and it was not a tech event necessarily. The energy in that auditorium was truly amazing. There were over four hundred enthusiastic young entrepreneurs who were trying to grow their dream businesses in Hanoi. I was able to meet successful entrepreneurs from many industries. As expected, there were people working on e-commerce and social networking. However, there were also people from the food-and-beverage industry, education, construction technology, and finance. The majority of businesses were simply copycats of businesses already running in the United States. Groupon and Uber are two US businesses that have many copycats in Vietnam. However, there were some interesting new ideas, including new medications based on time-tested herbal remedies in Vietnam. There were also businesses that targeted real issues in Vietnam, including the demand to learn English and the demand to study overseas. I was able to confirm that in Vietnam, a country that started from a low base, just about any business, if executed well, could be successful.

I believe the key to Vietnam's growth so far has been the initial low base. I encourage entrepreneurs who are thinking about going into business in Vietnam to consider in detail the ramifications of growth from a low base. On the positive side, the country needs everything; therefore, anything will sell. Consider the millions of plastic tables and chairs that are needed by the curbside merchants across the country; the company that manufactures them is wildly successful. Furthermore, because the local labor rate is inexpensive, potential profits are huge. Consider the many outsourcing businesses that simply arbitrage the difference between labor rates in Vietnam and abroad. The challenge to operating a business in this environment is quality. First, recruiting and keeping high-quality staff is difficult. Sometimes, because of the imbalance in supply and demand in the local employment market, high-quality staff in Vietnam may even be more expensive than the same-quality staff in the United States. Second, because of the low base in Vietnam, revenue (and quality) per unit product sold locally may be lower than similar products sold outside Vietnam. The net result of starting from a low base with huge potential but with challenging operations is a high opportunity cost. At the simplest level, picking the right opportunity increases the probability of success dramatically.

So what should entrepreneurs focus on in Vietnam? This is a question I get asked a lot by entrepreneurs who are weighing competing opportunities. Opportunity cost is high, yes, but there are many opportunities. Sometimes, there are too many opportunities. This is the major issue in Vietnam currently. The local population is so young that they haven't seen many real-world problems. Therefore, they don't necessarily consider problems in industry or society that need to be solved. Instead, they tend to follow opportunities that have been marketed to them through Western media. Groupon and Uber, as mentioned before, as well as Facebook and Amazon, for example, are high-profile companies that have a large following and many copycats in Vietnam. Besides copycat businesses, however, there hasn't been a major movement to catch the imagination of the entrepreneurial masses in Vietnam.

I normally advise entrepreneurs to look at problems that are currently in Vietnam or coming to the country in the near future. For example, previously, the country was poor and inefficient. However, people ate fresh meat and vegetables every day. People didn't make a lot of money, but they were generally healthy. Today, as the country has grown, people earn more money and, because of better technology, pay less for their food. Also, because of growth, increased wealth, and opportunity, people are also able to enjoy expensive food from overseas such as KFC and McDonald's. As a result, as people become wealthier, they are becoming less healthy. Some entrepreneurs might focus on how to provide more healthy food to the population. Others see the opportunity in pharmaceuticals, reasoning that Vietnam has imported Western foods but has not imported Western pharmaceuticals to treat diseases associated with "unhealthy Western foods." Continuing along this line of thinking, manufacturing, regulation, finance, software, and services all could be improved in the healthcare and pharmaceutical industries. Apart from healthcare and pharmaceuticals, as the country moves from agriculture to industry, there is a plethora of issues in both agriculture and industry that need to be addressed. Starting from a low base, each issue is a major opportunity. These are opportunities that should seem obvious to any Vietnamese analyzing the country's growth; however, I am often surprised that many young entrepreneurs find this information new and interesting.

Andrew and I sometimes reflect on the cultural differences between American entrepreneurs and Vietnamese entrepreneurs. One issue that I keep coming back to is identity. Prior to President Bill Clinton's visit to Vietnam two decades ago, Vietnam was basically closed to the outside world. The country was branded internally, as well as from abroad, as a poor third-world country ravaged by war and colonialism. Today, the young population has largely forgotten the old brand. The people are restless and working hard to create a new brand for Vietnam. Russia is known for its math geniuses. India has information technology (IT) talent. China has its factories. What will Vietnam be known for? This is a major psychological hurdle for the young entrepreneurs in Vietnam; however, it is also an indication of the vast amount of freedom that the country currently has to decide its own future brand. Perhaps Vietnam could be a fusion of Russia, India, and China, all in a smaller package. Perhaps Vietnam will be known for its successful local execution of copycat business models. At this point, it's not clear what brand the people want to adopt.

Perhaps Vietnam is not yet ready to choose an identity. Perhaps change has been so fast and exciting that the people want to wait and explore other options before deciding on a new brand. Everyone knows that change has been fast in Vietnam; however, sometimes I'm impatient with how slowly things are improving or how slow growth seems recently. Then I realize that the country has improved tremendously over the past twenty years, and the economy has actually been growing at a blistering pace compared to other fast-growing countries. For example, it took only a year for the central government to implement the one business ID program. Previously, business registrations were managed by one department, and tax registrations were managed by another department in the central government. The two departments could not communicate effectively, due to the different IDs. As a result, regular business operations were extremely inefficient because businesses had to go back and forth between the two interdependent but separate departments. The one ID program effectively reduced inefficiencies by half. I was surprised to learn that in a government as inefficient as Vietnam's, the implementation of this national program, which required converting all existing businesses to the new system before allowing new registrations, was implemented in only a year.

When talking about fast-growing countries, people normally think about China. Many compare Vietnam today to China of twenty years ago. Indeed, China's growth has been remarkable; however, I believe the two countries are different because Vietnam has the benefit of seeing China's growth and learning from China's mistakes. Furthermore, Vietnam now has access to newer and cheaper technology than China did twenty years ago. With no legacy infrastructure to replace, Vietnam can directly deploy the latest technologies without considering sunk costs or political red tape. For example, Vietnam's mobile-phone system largely skipped 2G technology and has been using 4G for a couple of years now, already catching up to US standards. If anyone thinks that because Vietnam is an emerging country, mobile coverage is spotty, that person would be very wrong. In fact, I've been happier with my emerging-market 4G coverage in Vietnam than with my first-world 3G coverage in the United States.

Some days I feel Vietnam's growth is too slow. Other days, I think things are changing too fast. Normally, ten years in a place makes you a local and someone who knows his way around. My decade in Vietnam has made me an old local, but I am continually challenged by this rapidly changing and emerging country. New roads, buildings, and neighborhoods are the obvious changes in Vietnam. However, new laws, businesses, and technologies are the real major changes in this dynamic economy. Locals, diaspora, and foreigners all contribute to a positive energy that is absolutely palpable. Ten years ago, as a newcomer, I felt this energy and didn't quite understand it. One muggy evening, I plopped myself down at the last plastic table at a crowded curbside cafe in Ho Chi Minh City to cool down. The traffic was intense. The air was suffocating. Most of the tables were occupied by groups of four to six customers. There were Vietnamese customers as well as foreigners. I had expected to hear conversations about the muggy weather or the bad traffic. Instead, some people were talking about the growth of the stock market. Others were talking about buying land for a new factory. There were also people talking about opening a new mobile-phone store.

I sat by myself, happy to have a cold Coke in such hot weather. After serving all the tables, the proprietor came to sit with me, since there was nowhere else to sit. We struck up a conversation about his plan to open another cafe. He wanted the next cafe to be bigger, since his current one filled up easily in the evenings. He wanted to have background music to deal with the traffic noise. He wanted better lighting, and he wanted to hire staff. It quickly occurred to me that the proprietor, and just about everyone else at that curbside cafe, was super optimistic about the economy. The proprietor was exuberant about his individual income potential. He had good reason to be. Five years earlier, he had borrowed money from friends to open the cafe. His income was barely thirty dollars per month then. It grew three times in five years. While a hundred dollars per month is nowhere close to being rich, if your income started at thirty dollars per month and it has been consistently increasing by thirty dollars per month every two years, there is good reason to be exuberant. Probably everyone at that curbside cafe had the same energy and exuberance. It's easy to understand now the reason behind this excitement and positive energy that is so characteristic of Vietnam.

Giang V. Lam
Managing Director of Rising Dragon Associates
Boston, Massachusetts, 2018

SECTION I

MORE THAN MEETS THE EYE

CHAPTER 1

WHY VIETNAM?

DURING THE TWENTIETH CENTURY, VIETNAM was host to revolutionary, civil, proxy, and/or conventional wars—depending on your perspective—involving foreign soldiers from countries such as France, the United States, Japan, South Korea, Australia, New Zealand, Thailand, Taiwan, the Soviet Union, Canada, the Philippines, and China. Today, those nations send businesspeople, investors, and skilled workers instead of battalions to Vietnam.[1] Still, to many foreigners, Vietnam is a place that has a war named after it—and when mentioned, it conjures up scenes from *Apocalypse Now*, *Platoon*, or *Full Metal Jacket*.

But Vietnam is more than just a war. And we are in a new century. Today, things are different, perhaps in ways unimaginable after the Fall of Saigon (or Reunification of Vietnam, again, depending on your perspective) in April, 1975. Currently, there are more than thirty thousand Vietnamese students at institutions of higher education in the United States,[2] Vietnam's former enemy. Vietnamese students are the fifth-largest group of students in the United States from any country. Vietnam sends more than just students to America; the United States is Vietnam's largest export market.[3] Trade between the two countries increased one hundred-fold—from USD $451 million in 1995, the year relations were normalized, to USD $45 billion in 2015. In 2016, Vietnam exported USD $177 billion worth of goods,[4] placing it in the top thirty exporters in the world. Total goods export-import turnover for Vietnam reached a record USD $425 billion in 2017 as agricultural export turnover reached USD $36 billion.

Almost ten years before the normalization of relations between Vietnam and the United States, Hanoi's leadership implemented Đổi Mới (renovation) under the Communist Party leadership of General Secretary Nguyễn Văn Linh in 1986. In the more than thirty years since the renovation policy took effect, Vietnam has created and experienced remarkable economic growth and a meteoric development story. In fact, Vietnam's economic success has been so robust, it has experienced the "world's second-fastest growth rate per person since 1990,"[5] behind only China, according to *The Economist*. Since the Communist Party, and subsequently the state and the people of Vietnam, embraced Đổi Mới as its official policy in 1986—the Year of the Fire Tiger—Vietnam has steadily integrated its economy into the global marketplace, most notably by the country's accession into the World Trade Organization (WTO) in 2007 with its then USD $77 billion economy. Ten years later, in 2017, Vietnam's economy was USD $238 billion, skyrocketing from USD $6.3 billion in 1989 due to a 6.6 percent average gross domestic product (GDP) growth rate since 1986.[6]

The results of these liberalization efforts were that by 2010, poverty in Vietnam had been reduced to around 20 percent from 60 percent in the early 1990s. As of 2017, according to the Asian Development Bank (ADB),[7] the poverty rate in Vietnam is 7 percent—even lower than some of its regional neighbors, including Thailand and Indonesia.[8] These statistics alone are a testament to the incredible economic transformation that has taken place in Vietnam.[9]

For its efforts, international organizations such as the World Bank and the International Monetary Fund (IMF) have recognized Vietnam's development success. In 2013, the World Bank acknowledged Vietnam's path from one of the world's poorest countries to a lower-middle-income country in the span of twenty-five years. In 2016, Christine Lagarde, managing director of IMF, delivered remarks in Hanoi about Vietnam "gearing up for the next transformation." If Vietnam is able to avoid the middle-income trap—when a country's growth slows after it reaches middle-income levels—it can then provide a blueprint for similarly sized developing countries. It won't be an easy accomplishment; Vietnam is still in the midst of a transition between modernity and tradition, and it needs to confront new and unknown social, economic, and political challenges head-on in this century. It will truly be uncharted territory for Vietnam's development arc—but the country has the momentum of largely positive change on its side.

In the span of thirty years, Vietnam has gone from a subsidy economy (in the period before 1986) to a "startup economy," with thousands of potentially high-growth enterprises. While late to the party, Vietnam has managed to catch up—in part due to massive influxes of official development assistance (ODA), foreign direct investment (FDI), and overseas remittances—and is well-poised to benefit from shifting global and regional economic trends. Today, Vietnam's market is a far cry from the centrally planned and isolated economy of the 1980s in the pre-Đổi Mới period. Remarkably, Vietnam's economic growth hasn't slowed down in recent years—it was the top economic performer of the ten member states of the Association of Southeast Asian Nations (ASEAN) in 2016 with a 6.21 percent growth rate. For 2017, Vietnam attained a 6.8 percent GDP growth rate, a ten-year high, with a per capita income of USD $2,385 and 127,000 newly formed companies, according to the *VnExpress*.[10] In 2018, the economic momentum continued as Vietnam's GDP growth rate in the first quarter exceeded 7 percent, the highest in ten years.

Undoubtedly, entrepreneurs have played a significant role in the development of Vietnam. The Vietnam Young Entrepreneurs Association (VYEA), founded in 1993, has nine thousand members across sixty-six chapters throughout the country. In 2011, the VYEA members had total gross sales of USD $25 billion, representing nearly 20 percent of Vietnam's economy that year.[11] However, it was only the year before VYEA's founding, in 1992, that Vietnam recognized the role of the private sector in the national economy via an amended constitution.[12] The result of its ascending market economy—which a 2014 Vietnam Chamber of Commerce and Industry (VCCI) survey found that 89 percent of Vietnamese prefer—is that GDP per capita soared to USD $2,200 in 2015 from USD $100 in 1990, according to the *Nikkei Asian Review*.[13]

While Vietnamese leaders—notably the late prime ministers Võ Văn Kiệt and Phan Văn Khải—have embraced economic reforms and liberalization, the pillars for new, inclusive, and sustainable elements of the private sector to prosper must be strengthened in order to level the playing field, increase transparency, and quickly seize upon emerging opportunities in the coming decades of development—not in the conventional sense of depending on foreign aid, but in developing competitive strategies to financially, socially, and environmentally thrive with a foundation of sustainability. These future commitments and reforms have to encompass social and governance dimensions in addition to economic goals if they are to last well into an unknown and rapidly changing future.

What marks this period of Vietnam's history as different from others is the faster, greater flow of new ideas, enabling solutions for global challenges to come from anywhere, including Vietnam. Vietnam's ninety-six million[14] citizens have more access to the outside world than ever before via social media and direct interactions with—or as—tourists, students, or expatriates.[15] The youth are at the heart of Vietnam's transition in the twenty-first century, coming of age at a time when the facade of Vietnam's urban centers are literally changing overnight.

Today, the median age in Vietnam is thirty-one, with almost 70 percent of the population under forty years old as recently as 2015[16] and with over a million babies born each year, even with a recently loosened two-child policy. Furthermore, the Organization for Economic Cooperation and Development's (OECD's; 2012) Programme for International Student Assessment (PISA) reveals that Vietnam's fifteen-year-olds perform on a par with those in Austria and Germany.[17] In 2012, Vietnam broke through the top-ten rankings in science for the first time,[18] a place it maintained in the 2015 PISA, done every three years. (In the 2015 PISA, Vietnam ranked 8th out of 72 participating countries, even ahead of some OECD countries such as Germany and the Netherlands.[19]) Remarkably, about a quarter of Vietnam's population is fourteen or younger, with nearly 70 percent of the population between the ages of fifteen and sixty-four. The fact that a quarter of Vietnam's population is fourteen or younger means that by 2021, 15.5 million new consumers will enter the market, according to a TNS Global Analysis.[20] However, not everyone in today's Vietnam has the means to participate in the formal economy—or the ability to join the growing digital economy.

In the United Nations Development Programme's (UNDP) *Human Development Report 2016*, which examines the "opportunities and empowerment necessary to realize the full potential of their lives" for everyone, Vietnam ranked 115th in medium human development classification, maintaining its 2014 rank. "Everyone" includes ethnic minorities, of which there are fifty-four officially recognized groups in Vietnam. As the *Human Development Report 2016* outlines, "There are gaps between the capabilities of ethnic or linguistic minorities and the Kinh-Hoa majority," so not everyone has benefited from Vietnam's economic success in the past few decades. Economic inequality in Vietnam could increase in the future, as those who are well placed to reap the growing opportunities "suck the oxygen out of the room," so to speak.

As Vietnam's population reaches one hundred million and beyond, the middle and affluent classes are expected to increase to thirty-three million by 2020, more than double the number from 2012 (fourteen million), according to BCG.[21] Nielsen's estimates are even more aggressive; those earning USD $714 or more per month are expected to number forty-four million by 2020 and ninety-five million by 2030.[22] According to a Knight Frank report,[23] by 2025, Vietnam will see the largest creation of ultrahigh net worth (USD $30-plus million) individuals in the world. With increased purchasing power, these consumers will desire new products and services as their values of self-expression are reinforced by their buying decisions and purchasing habits.

In addition to consumption, air travel is also on the rise in Vietnam, allowing Vietnamese to build vital interpersonal networks in addition to digital social networks. Vietnam's aviation market is growing at the third-fastest rate in Asia-Pacific, according to the Civil Aviation Authority of Vietnam. In 2016, the number of air travelers increased by 29 percent, from 52.2 million passengers in 2015. Over the next twenty years, Vietnam will be in the top five fastest growing air travel markets, according to the International Air Transport Association (IATA).[24] In particular, the route between Hanoi and Ho Chi Minh City (still colloquially known as Saigon) is the sixth-busiest in the world, with up to 6,769,823 passengers annually, comprising 35 percent of the total air traffic in Vietnam, according to the IATA. (In 2018, Bamboo Airways, a new airline, was announced by FLC Group and set to join Vietnam Airlines JSC and Vietjet Aviation JSC in the ranks of Vietnam-based carriers.[25])

To make room for the additional passengers and cargo expected to arrive in and depart from Ho Chi Minh City, plans for a second airport, the Long Thành International Airport, have been unveiled. When construction is completed, expected to be in 2050 at a cost of USD $16 billion,[26] the airport will have capacity for a hundred million passengers and five million tons of cargo per year. However, the first phase, which includes one terminal and a runway, is aimed to be completed by 2025 and is estimated to process 25 million passengers per year.

Ho Chi Minh City's current international airport, Tân Sơn Nhất, is not forgotten: it will receive an upgrade in the form of two new terminals accommodating forty to fifty million passengers per year. The 32.5 million air travelers who passed through the airport in 2016 already exceed the designed capacity of 28 million passengers. Currently, USD $847 million[27] is the projected cost for all the upgrades and expansions associated with the airport's master plan through 2030. These infrastructure investments are necessary to tap into future economic opportunities in Vietnam, which would enable the country to avoid the middle-income trap.

Presently, Vietnam has what is referred to as a "socialist-oriented market economy," which is a mix of state-owned enterprises (SOEs), joint stock companies, and private enterprises—the most successful of these often have close ties to local, provincial, or national governments. While there is some ambiguity around a precise, current definition of a "socialist-oriented market economy," with each Party Congress (held every five years), more arguments and clarifications are put forth[28] to constantly improve the baseline understanding of the term. What is abundantly clear is that Vietnam is one of the most procapitalist nations in the world, according to a 2015 Pew Research Center survey.[29] About 95 percent of Vietnamese respondents agreed with the following statement: "Most people are better off in a free market economy, even though some people are rich and some are poor."

Hanoi seems to have reacted favorably to the burgeoning private-sector attitudes and activities; 2016 was declared by policy makers as the Year of the Startup and there are a number of efforts at all levels of Vietnam's government fostering the formation of a startup economy. Departments in Ho Chi Minh City, ministries in Hanoi, and public-private partnerships (PPP) in Da Nang are all mobilizing—albeit at different paces—to ride the "startup wave" into the next phase of development for Vietnam. At the same time, the SOE reform process is underway as equitization plans are put into effect, however slowly. ("Equitization" is what the rest of the world calls privatization.)

The implications of such efforts across the country are clear: Vietnam is indeed "gearing up for the next transformation," as Managing Director LaGarde alluded to in 2016. In what shape that transformation will manifest is yet to be seen, but in our lifetimes, there won't be another moment like this in Vietnam's history. In other words, the startup economy will be what follows the "socialist-oriented market economy" in Vietnam for the foreseeable future—and the final product is currently in the making.

Thus, this period in Vietnam's history is an extraordinary opportunity for visionary policy makers, private-sector advocates, and even non-Vietnamese to contribute to and shape Vietnam's future. As a fellow New Yorker put it, "There are people who will become fabulously rich in Vietnam—and they don't even have Vietnam on their radar yet." Beyond financial gains, Vietnam is at the forefront of several industries and grand challenges—so industry leaders can take advantage of their positions to pioneer solutions and export or license the resulting technologies abroad. Within the coming challenges of sustainability and sovereignty lie these kinds of opportunities—that is, there are many problems, so someone (or many people) will need to come up with many solutions. For now, the question is, will you be a part of Vietnam's story?

AT THE FOREFRONT

Globally, there are over four million members of the Vietnamese diaspora in countries including the United States, Canada, France, Russia, Poland, Germany, and Australia. Some Overseas Vietnamese (or Việt Kiều, as they are known in Vietnam) are migrants, and others are immigrants or refugees—or the descendants of refugees. As a result of this global network, inward remittances to Vietnam totaled more than USD $12 billion in 2015, planting Vietnam firmly in the top ten countries receiving remittances from abroad. (In 2007—the same year Vietnam joined the World Trade Organization—remittances totaled USD $6.18 billion.)

To put this capital influx in perspective, Vietnam received USD $24.4 billion in FDI in 2016[30] and nearly USD $36 billion in FDI in 2017,[31] according to Hanoi.[32] Combined remittances and FDI accounted for almost USD $30 billion in Vietnam in 2016, contributing to Vietnam's second year in a row of surpassing 6 percent GDP growth. According to an analysis by

JLL, the cumulative total registered FDI in Vietnam reached approximately USD $320 billion in the ten years preceding the end of 2017. Almost 60 percent went into manufacturing, followed by approximately 17 percent into real estate activities.[33] Looking ahead, *The Economist* projects an average real GDP growth rate of 6.5 percent through 2021—without impact from the currently halted Trans-Pacific Partnership (TPP; now changed to the Comprehensive and Progressive Trans-Pacific Partnership without the United States), the proposed twelve-nation trade deal from which Vietnam was expected to gain the most. Despite this setback, interest in Vietnam's economy only seems to be increasing from abroad.

In recent years, manufacturing contracts that traditionally went to Chinese companies have shifted to Vietnamese enterprises, partly due to rising labor costs in China. Additionally, IT outsourcing projects that have typically gone to Indian firms have also turned to Vietnam, prompting one local investor in Hanoi to declare, "We make 'shirts and shoes' for tech." Global firms have taken notice: in 2015, Cushman and Wakefield[34] declared that Vietnam was the top pioneering business process outsourcing (BPO) destination in the world in terms of attractiveness, driven partially by raw and hungry talent; Vietnam retained its spot for 2016. These years are a key time for the software industry and software developers in Vietnam.

The chief operating officer (COO) of a Hanoi–based IT outsourcing firm that specializes in content moderation believes that by 2020, his firm's work can be done with 10 percent of his current staff (currently over two hundred), and by 2025 the content-moderation process could be fully automated. The implications of such comments are twofold: (1) since Vietnamese firms are at the forefront of these industries, they are in a position to develop these automation technologies locally, and (2) Vietnam's labor force is not impervious to automation technologies, despite its currently low wages. Thus, Vietnam's economy will be challenged by technologically driven productivity growth at a time when 1.5 million new jobs are needed annually to keep up with population growth, according to experts at the Vietnam Summit 2016, produced by *The Economist*.[35]

Simply, Vietnam's low-wage manufacturing advantages won't last forever. As wages in Vietnam rise, the garment industry will seek greener pastures, such as Myanmar. Manufacturing is already transitioning away from countries such as Bangladesh in South Asia to Ethiopia in East Africa. But select manufacturing is also shifting back to the West: in 2016, Adidas announced[36] that it would start making shoes again in Germany—with the exclusive aid of robots, beginning in 2017. (Vietnam is the world's third-largest shoe exporter in the world and it is Nike's and Adidas's main footwear producer.[37][38])

Thus, garment jobs could either be outsourced or automated out of existence in the near future. This shift means that over the next decade, 86 percent of Vietnam's two million jobs in the clothing and footwear industries are at risk due to disruptive technologies, according to the International Labor Organization (ILO).[39]

Confronting these challenges—which are not unique to Vietnam—will require coordination with regional and global institutions such as the East Asia Summit (EAS), ASEAN, and Asia-Pacific Economic Cooperation (APEC). APEC, in particular, has significantly impacted Vietnam's economic development. From 1998 through 2006, APEC members invested USD $49.5 billion in 6,527 projects in Vietnam, according to the Vietnam Chamber of Commerce and Industry (VCCI).[40]

In November 2017, the central coastal city of Da Nang hosted the APEC Summit, which brought the heads of twenty-one member economies together during Leaders' Week. During this time, all eyes were on Vietnam as agendas, joint statements, and plans were finalized and delivered. This major event was also an opportunity for Vietnam to showcase its homegrown innovation as well as promote some of its startup success stories as more than eight hundred senior business executives descended upon Vietnam during the APEC CEO Summit 2017. With the theme Creating New Dynamism, Fostering a Shared Future, there were many points of convergence—literally and figuratively—since ten APEC members are among the top fifteen investors in Vietnam. (In September

2018, Vietnam had the opportunity to host a record number of regional heads of state or government at the World Economic Forum on ASEAN in Hanoi with a theme of *ASEAN 4.0: Entrepreneurship and the Fourth Industrial Revolution*.)

Currently, Vietnam is at the intersection of manufacturing and IT outsourcing, and it is also well positioned to benefit from increased trade in the region. As of January 2018, Vietnam had ten free-trade agreements (FTAs) with countries such as South Korea, India, New Zealand, and Australia—with six more FTAs in negotiations. With sixteen FTAs coming online or already implemented, Vietnam has fully embraced free trade and foreign direct investment. Of note is the EU–Vietnam Free Trade Agreement (EVFTA), which is expected to come into effect in 2019.[41] Moreover, thousands of goods will have their tariffs reduced to zero as part of ten decrees stipulating preferential import tariffs between 2018 and 2023.[42] Vietnam has also turned to opportunities in the region. Publicly, Hanoi has announced its intention to become a "top-five" investor in Myanmar, while Vietnamese workers and companies already have significant presences in neighboring Laos and Cambodia.

Today, Vietnam is the world's largest producer of pepper, the second-largest exporter of coffee, and the third-largest exporter of rice. However, Vietnam's largest export is not agricultural. It is digital—that is, electrical machinery. One in ten smartphones in the world are produced in Vietnam, according to the Brookings Institution.[43] Samsung is Vietnam's largest exporter, contributing more than 22 percent of USD $175.9 billion in export revenue in 2016, up from 18 percent in 2014, according to *Viet Nam News*.[44] In 2017, exports from Samsung totaled USD $54 billion, according to *Tuoi Tre News*.[45] Samsung's largest smartphone production base is in Vietnam, where 140,000 workers make up about one-third of its global workforce.

Since 2009, Samsung has invested USD $17.3 billion into Vietnam's economy, setting up operations across the country, including USD $2.5 billion in factories in the northern province of Bắc Ninh (producing cell phones, smart phones, tablets, and vacuum cleaners); USD $5 billion in a hi-tech assembly plant in the northern province of Thái Nguyên (in Yên Bình Industrial Park); and USD $1.4 billion in a plant in Ho Chi Minh City. Furthermore, Samsung Vietnam's research center is located in Hanoi, making Vietnam an essential part of Samsung's global supply chain—and Samsung an integral part of Vietnam's economy as its largest foreign investor. (Other multinationals, such as LG and Intel, have made cumulative multibillion dollar investments in Vietnam as well.)

Outside of industrial parks and assembly plants, in urban areas, Vietnam's dynamism has been recognized, most recently in 2017. According to JLL's 2017 City Momentum Index, (CMI),[46] Hanoi and Ho Chi Minh City are the second- and eighth-most dynamic cities in the world, respectively. No other developing economy had two cities in the top ten, with the exception of India (Bangalore at first place and Hyderabad at fifth place). The index identifies change and highlights "which cities or metropolitan areas may be best at positioning themselves to compete in today's ever-changing economic landscape." As one might expect, innovation hubs such as San Francisco, London, and Shanghai are included on the list. High-potential cities, such as Hanoi and Ho Chi Minh City, "continue to attract capital from foreign investors betting on their transition from low-wage manufacturing to high-value activities."

Similar conclusions were echoed in a 2017 report by Oxford Economics, which projected Ho Chi Minh City to be the second-fastest-growing city in Asia through 2021 (partly due to its manufacturing and services sectors)—the only non-Indian city in the top seven.[47] In 2017, Vietnam also held the distinction of having the third-fastest-growing stock market in the world (and best performing in Asia),[48] the VN-Index, which was launched in 2000 with a base index value of 100 and broke through one thousand points in early 2018 after a 52 percent return[49] for 2017.[50] Finance, banking, real estate construction, and consumer goods were among the most profitable stocks,[51] as foreigner investors anticipated the long-awaited equitization process among SOE giants such as Vietnam Dairy Products

JSC (Vinamilk), Saigon Beer Alcohol Beverage Corp (Sabeco), and Hanoi Beer Alcohol and Beverage Joint Stock Corp. (Habeco), reflecting the nation's beer industry as being one of the last to privatize. The relaxation of ownership restrictions in these kinds of firms is prompting record interest from foreign investors.

At the 2018 Vietnam Economic Forum, organized by the Central Economic Commission of the Vietnam Communist Party, Natasha Ansell, the 2017 American Chamber of Commerce (AmCham) chair and country officer of Citibank Vietnam, made the following remarks:

> Speaking about capital markets in Vietnam…We see investors today, in particular foreign investors, looking less at the index, looking more at the individual targets…they look at the quality of the company, they look at the quality of the management and invest on that basis. But [the] good news for Vietnam is that in this last, say, three years, and in particular last year, the number of companies that are sizable and that are of quality that are traded on the local stock exchange has increased, and that continues to grow.

Indeed, foreign investors have been paying more attention to Vietnam in recent years due to emerging markets pioneers and their comments on Vietnam's potential. Private equity firms, such as Warburg Pincus and KKR, have cumulatively invested more than USD $1.3 billion into Vietnamese companies. In late 2017, Dr. Mark Mobius, the former emerging markets fund manager at Franklin Templeton Investments, advised an audience member at a conference in Jakarta to invest "a third in commodities, a third in African stocks and a third in Vietnam" of USD $100,000.[52] These comments followed an October 2017 interview where he presented his "single best idea right now" to Reuters: "Probably, Vietnam…it's really doing a terrific job."[53] In 2015, Franklin Templeton committed to investing USD $3 billion into Vietnam,[54] and in a 2017 blog post, Dr. Mobius noted,

"As services (including tourism) represent more than 40% of Vietnam's GDP, it is the area we are most interested in."[55]

However, Vietnam is not only at the forefront of economic growth and investor interest. As a country among the first to be impacted by climate change, Vietnam will serve as a litmus test—a top-five country "likely to be most affected by climate change"[56]—for how a rising sea level[57] and weather volatility[58] will impact countries globally. In 2017, Vietnam experienced sixteen typhoons during its annual season (including one the week before the APEC Summit in central Vietnam)—a record.

The cost of climate change may be more than Vietnam can afford if business as usual continues. In a World Bank report, *Transforming Vietnamese Agriculture: Gaining More from Less*,[59] Vietnam's agricultural sector was recognized for its success in food security, albeit at increasing environmental costs. For example, Vietnam's mangroves in coastal areas rapidly decreased from 408,500 hectares in 1943 to 155,290 hectares by 2000, partly due to aquaculture activities, of which Vietnam is a top global producer.[60] Vietnamese agriculture is now at a "turning point," according to the report; "it must generate more economic value—and farmer and consumer welfare—using less natural and human capital and less harmful intermediate inputs." In other words, Vietnam's future growth in its agricultural sector "can rely primarily on increased efficiency, innovation, diversification, and value addition" at a time when "climate change is expected to give rise to more erratic weather patterns." Adding to this increasing danger is the fact that parts of southern Vietnam are sinking due to encroaching seas, according to the Wetlands Management Research Center at Ho Chi Minh City University.[61]

Increasing saltwater intrusion is not the only environmental challenge Vietnam faces.[62] Air pollution is on the rise in major cities such as Hanoi and Ho Chi Minh City, according to a study[63] by Vietnam's Ministry of Natural Resources and Environment (MONRE), which examined air quality from 2011 through 2015. In Yale University's 2016 Environmental Performance Index,[64] Vietnam ranked 170th out of 180 countries in air quality, and 131st in its overall ranking. Remarkably, according to Green Innovation and Development Centre (GreenID),[65] a Vietnamese nongovernmental organization (NGO), the air quality in Hanoi did not violate World Health Organization (WHO) standards on only twelve days in the first quarter of 2017. The WHO has repeatedly issued warnings that Vietnam is among the most air-polluted countries in Southeast Asia, with Hanoi among the "more polluted"[66] cities in the world.

Each day, 140 new cars and 750 motorbikes are registered in Ho Chi Minh City, according to *VnExpress International*,[67] which will only further contribute to traffic density, air pollution, and associated health and economic costs.[68] In 2017, Ho Chi Minh City had 7.5 million motorbikes and 790,000 cars, up from 4.5 million motorbikes and 420,000 cars in 2010, according to *Vietnam Net Bridge*.[69] Combined with plans[70] to develop additional coal-powered plants to meet its growing energy needs, Vietnam could find itself at the forefront of pollution effects—potentially on a par with China.

While there are plans to incorporate new forms of mass transit, such as metro systems in both Hanoi and Ho Chi Minh City, it remains to be seen if the rising middle class in Vietnam will forgo automobiles—and the convenience, status, and protection they afford.

Hanoi's first operational line will be the thirteen-kilometer Cát Linh–Hà Đông line (known as Line 2A), which underwent testing in late 2017. Construction for this line, which runs from Đống Đa District to Hà Đông District along twelve stations, began in 2011 with an initial investment of USD $552 million. It is scheduled to become operational in early 2019 with a total investment of USD $868 million, according to the *Viet Nam Net Bridge*.[71]

Hanoi Metro Line 2, originally scheduled to begin operations in 2015, had its deadline extended to 2023 and its estimated cost increased to USD $1.57 billion from USD $861 million for the 11.5-kilometer line.[72] Hanoi Metro Line 3,[73] the third of eight lines planned for the capital, is expected to open by the end of 2021. By 2025, Hanoi is expected to diversify investment capital for three additional priority metro lines or expansion sections to the tune of USD $15 billion, with total investment demand reaching USD $40 billion for all metro lines running a length of 417.8 kilometers when the final vision is implemented.

Ho Chi Minh City's first metro line, covering 19.7 kilometers from Bến Thành in District 1 to Suối Tiên in District 9, began construction in 2012 and was supposed to be completed in 2017 and operational by 2018, with an original estimated cost of USD $1.2 billion.[74] However, due to delays, funding problems, and ballooning costs, it won't be completed until 2019 at the earliest—and possibly as late as 2020—with an updated cost of USD $2.49 billion.[75]

The city's second metro line, proposed to run forty-eight kilometers from Bến Thành to Tham Lương in District 12, seems to be facing similar challenges. The original estimate called for USD $1.34 billion in funding—but the new estimated cost in 2015 was USD $2.07 billion, according to *Tuoi Tre News*.[76] The line is scheduled to be completed in 2019, according to the *Vietnam Investment Review*.[77]

These are the states of just two of six planned lines for the southern metropolis; these costs will likely increase in proportion to project delays. Vietnam needs USD $480 billion through 2020 for infrastructure investment, including 1,380 kilometers[78] of highways and eleven power plants with a total capacity of 13,200 megawatts, according to Hanoi.[79] If Vietnam does not meet its future power production targets, then it could face power shortages beginning in the early 2020s, according to the Ministry of Industry and Trade.[80] Overall, Vietnam is the second-highest spender on infrastructure in Asia, sandwiched between China and India, according to the ADB.

In addition to roads and power generation, Ho Chi Minh City and Hanoi need USD $4.6 billion to invest in metro lines and bridges, aiming to reduce traffic congestion and safeguard the environment, according to *VN Express International*.[81] Thus, innovative financing techniques such as blended finance, which strategically uses public-sector and philanthropic funding to increase private capital flows into bankable projects, can be pioneered or piloted in Vietnam with support from multidevelopment banks and institutions such as OECD, the World Economic Forum (WEF), and the ADB. Publicly, Vietnam has already called for foreign investors,[82] especially from Japan, to use PPPs to help satisfy USD $400 billion in infrastructure needs over the next decade.

As we'll see in the next section, although Vietnam's prospects are bright, it will be the Vietnamese people, along with diasporic and foreign allies, who will determine the actual trajectory of the country as it confronts a rapidly changing environment and world.

A PROMISING FUTURE

Vietnam's advantageous place in the hyperglobal economy of the future isn't assured—not by a long shot. It does have strong potential to make its mark on the world and export Vietnamese solutions and innovations during the next phase of its rapid economic development. Vietnam's greatest strength—its human capital—has thus far tapped into the benefits of globalization via low-wage manufacturing and the low cost of mobile computing, complemented by increasing access to the internet. However, this manufacturing and outsourcing model is reaching its limits: in the not-too-distant future, Vietnamese entrepreneurs and companies must find new ways to create and add value at home and abroad. Simply put, Vietnam must move up the value chain and increase productivity in order to remain competitive in the global economy. Whether this happens relies largely on the foresight, vision, and commitment of leaders in the public and private sectors.

For now, macroeconomic trends are favorable for Vietnam. In particular, the youth have embraced international education experiences as well as the latest cultural trends from South Korea, Japan, and the United

States. Presently, there are more than 130,000 Vietnamese students studying at institutions of higher education outside Vietnam—at a collective price tag of over USD $1 billion,[83] mostly in Japan and Australia. These young Vietnamese are bright, optimistic for the future, talented, eager to learn, and focused on improving their socioeconomic conditions. It might be this generation that unlocks the full potential of Vietnam's human capital resources—understanding both local and international norms and seamlessly transitioning between them (at least, more easily than previous generations). Those who studied abroad are bringing back different mind-sets for problem solving and sharing them with local organizations and new foreign networks plugged into Vietnam. However, it would be wrong to assume that students who exclusively study in Vietnam are any less interested in "going global."

In 2015, 4.42 million students graduated from Vietnamese universities, a 40 percent increase from 2010 figures, according to the *Nikkei Asian Review*.[84] These graduates are interested in working with and learning new techniques, best practices, and new skills from foreigners and, more importantly, are generally more candid about the challenges ahead for Vietnam, having witnessed the priorities of other societies in relation to their own—especially through travel, foreign contacts, or the internet. These are largely positive signs—especially attitudes toward the daunting and unknown challenges—as not everyone benefits from the effects of globalization.

Until now, Vietnam has benefited immensely from the increase in global trade and labor arbitrage. In the future, it has the potential to continue its incredible development story for the next thirty years and beyond. However, it will require real efforts and a genuine commitment from employer and employee alike to realize the nation's full economic potential. With more than a hundred thousand new engineers trained in Vietnam per annum, according to the UNESCO Institute for Statistics,[85] Vietnam has a comparative advantage that places it in the top ten countries for engineering output. It would stand to reason that some of these engineers will go on to found companies, perhaps even adding disproportionate value to Vietnam's economy—and becoming wildly successful in the process.

For now, these engineers are fueling Vietnam's "app economy," as outlined in a 2015 policy brief by the Progressive Policy Institute (PPI). In "Vietnam and the App Economy," Vietnam was declared as "the top-rated App Economy in Southeast Asia (including Singapore, Indonesia, Malaysia, Thailand, and the Philippines)" based on an analysis of technical job postings throughout the region. This advantage may give Vietnam the opportunity to build a larger portion of its economic growth on the creation of apps by keeping Vietnamese employed or by developing home-grown intellectual properties, which offer a greater value capture than outsourcing projects. It's less capital intensive to become a mobile applications hub than a manufacturing hub, after all. Thus, according to the PPI, Vietnam may be in the "early stages of a virtuous circle, where increased demand for App Economy tech personnel leads to more Vietnamese workers getting app development training."

Suffice it to say, growth has been the main driver of Vietnam's story, and it looks to stay that way in the future. In a recent PwC report, *The World in 2050,*[86] Vietnam was identified as potentially one of the three fastest-growing countries in economic terms (along with India and Bangladesh) between 2017 and 2050. It could potentially climb twelve places—the greatest movement—in the rankings to twentieth place by 2050. By 2030, Vietnam is expected to be a top-thirty economy, valued at USD $1.303 trillion, up from approximately USD $595 billion today (on a purchasing-power parity), where it stands at thirty-second place. The Atlas of Economic Complexity, developed by Harvard University's Center for International Development, projects 5.9 percent annual growth for Vietnam's economy to 2026, making it "the 9th fastest growing economy for the coming decade."[87]

The Economist Intelligence Unit[88] projects that by 2020, new wealth builders (NWBs) in Vietnam—that is, households with financial assets of USD $100,000 to USD $2 million—will increase to 347,000, up from

16,000 in 2010. In this regard, Vietnam's growth statistics lag behind only India and Indonesia—countries whose populations far outsize Vietnam's ninety-six million people. Given these increases in disposable income, it should come as no surprise that Vietnam's Ministry of Industry and Trade projects that annual Vietnamese retail sales will exceed USD $480 billion by 2025 and reach nearly USD $1.94 trillion by 2035.[89] In 2017, Vietnam's retail sales reached a record USD $129.6 billion, with 10.9 percent growth over the previous year.[90] (In 2016, management consulting firm AT Kearney again ranked Vietnam in the world's top thirty retail markets as part of its Global Retail Development Index, a list that Vietnam has been on since 2008.[91])

In the Global Innovation Index[92] (GII) 2017 Report, which focuses on innovation in agriculture and food systems, Vietnam placed twelve rankings higher than its 2016 status, marking the highest rank to date. Vietnam ranked tenth in its Innovation Efficiency Ratio (IER), showing that Vietnam is "punching above its weight," according to the Economist Intelligence Unit's former lead analyst for ASEAN.[93] Moreover, Vietnam ranked forty-seventh out of 127 economies (third in ASEAN, behind Singapore and Malaysia) with a score of 38.3 in the GII, published by Cornell University, INSEAD, and the World Intellectual Property Organization (WIPO, an agency of the United Nations).

Additionally, the World Economic Forum's *Global Competitiveness Report 2017–2018*[94] listed Vietnam as fifty-fifth (up from sixtieth place the year before) on its Global Competitive Index (GCI) of 137 countries. The GCI has three subindices encompassing basic requirements, efficiency enhancers, and innovation and sophistication factors. Vietnam has seen other positive movements on indices: the World Bank ranked Vietnam eighty-second out of 190 in its 2017 Ease of Doing Business measurement.[95] This ranking is a nine-spot improvement from ninety-first place in 2016.[96] For the 2018 survey, Vietnam was ranked sixty-eighth, partly because it "made exporting and importing easier by upgrading the automated cargo clearance system and extending the operating hours of the customs department," the World Bank noted. (In the *Connecting to Compete 2018* report by the World Bank, which contains the Logistics Performance Index, Vietnam was the top-performing lower-middle-income economy with an overall rank of 39,[97] up from 64 in 2016.[98])

Furthermore, Vietnam has some of the fastest-growing cities in the world in population metrics; for example, each year 130,000 migrants arrive in Ho Chi Minh City in search of work and a new life.[99] Ho Chi Minh City, with an official population of 7.3 million in 2015, is already the fourth-largest city in Southeast Asia, behind Manila, Jakarta, and Bangkok. However, according to local officials, Ho Chi Minh City's population surpassed 13 million people in 2017, as the 7.3 million figure only accounted for registered residents.[100] (In 1975, Saigon's population was 2.5 million, while in 1994, the city reached a population of 4.5 million permanent residents with 500,000 temporary residents, according to the *New York Times*.[101])

Despite differences in population accounting, Vietnam's cities are poised for massive population growth: by 2025, Ho Chi Minh City will be home to 9.2 million official residents, a population increase of 27.4 percent. Hanoi is expected to officially increase its population to five million in 2025, up from 3.6 million in 2015, marking an incredible 37.5 percent change, according to the United Nations World Urbanization Prospects.[102] Additionally, Vietnamese cities such as Cần Thơ, Biên Hòa, Hải Phòng, and Da Nang will experience double-digit population increases by 2025, ranging from 45.9 percent to 29.2 percent. At some point in the next decade, Vietnam's population will surpass one hundred million, maintaining its position as the third-largest population (behind Indonesia and the Philippines), as ASEAN's population crosses the seven hundred million threshold. These extra millions of digital natives will eventually become consumers of online content, part of what Google calls the "Next Billion" internet users.

In Google's *Mobile Apps in APAC: 2016 Report*,[103] Vietnam was identified (along with Thailand) as a country that experienced "high smartphone

penetration but low average installs…presumably due to low-spec devices with limited memory and functionality." As outlined in a TNS/Google "Mobile App Usage Study" survey referenced in the report, 94 percent of smart phone users in Vietnam use social networking apps, followed by 91 percent for messaging/communications, and 77 percent for search. Vietnamese users spend approximately 150 minutes per day using social networking apps, second only to Thailand in Asia-Pacific (APAC) among the eleven countries surveyed.[104]

According to the *Asian Nikkei Review*, Facebook was used by forty million people in Vietnam as of early 2017. By mid-2018, the country had fifty-eight million users,[105] making it the seventh-largest market for the social network; Ho Chi Minh City alone had fourteen million users. Adding the number of Zalo users (a local chat app by VNG) brings the number of social network users to seventy-four million, or more than three-quarters of the country. The large increase in smart phones—especially prized iPhones—has been a major driver of social media access and adoption. (According to Reuters, during the first half of 2014, Vietnam was Apple's fastest-growing market in the world.[106])

The smart phone has risen across Vietnam over the last few years. According to IDC, 11.6 million smart phone units were shipped to

Vietnam in 2015—a 57 percent increase from 2013.[107] By the end of 2016, smart phone sales accounted for 67 percent of all mobile phones sales in Vietnam, according to Euromonitor International.[108] About one-third of the population accesses the internet via mobile, a number that will increase as more handsets are purchased by a growing population. Already, Vietnam had 128 mobile cellular subscriptions per one hundred people in 2016, according to the World Bank.[109] Internet penetration in Vietnam has grown from 12 percent in 2005 to 44 percent of the country's ninety-one million people in 2015, according to the *Wall Street Journal*.[110] Today, more than 60 percent of Vietnam's population is online, according to the *VnExpress*.[111] (Of note is Cốc Cốc, a hyper-localized browser that is native to Vietnam; currently it has almost 24 million monthly active users.) To prepare for the growing number of internet-connected devices, the Ministry of Information and Communication expects to have 3G and 4G coverage available for 95 percent of residential homes by 2020, according to *Viet Nam News*.[112]

Viettel Telecommunications (owned by the Ministry of Defence), Vinaphone (owned by Vietnam Posts and Telecommunications Group), MobiFone Telecommunications Corporation (under the Ministry of Information and Communication), and GTel Mobile (with links to the Ministry of Public Security) were the first telecoms to be granted 4G licenses by the Ministry of Information and Communication in 2016, according to the *Nikkei Asian Review*.[113] Although the first 4G pilots were held in Vietnam in late 2015, the service became widely available for consumers in 2017, according to *VN Express International*.[114]

Some Vietnamese companies, such as BKAV, an IT firm, have even attempted to create a Vietnamese luxury phone to compete with the Apple iPhone, but sales of its Bphone were not encouraging.[115] Viettel, the military-run telecom, is following in BKAV's footsteps, as it has announced plans to release the Viettel Luxury Phone—Smart Phone 4G with a retail price of over USD $1,000, according to *Vietnam Net Bridge*.[116] Unlike BKAV, Viettel has a built-in user base—and can compel its employees to use certain products, as was the case with its Mocha chat application. (Vingroup, Vietnam's largest conglomerate, is also gearing up for smartphone production under the Vsmart brand in addition to artificial intelligence research.[117])

Yet Vietnamese firms' aspirations in telecommunications aren't limited to domestic expansions and upgrades; Viettel is active in nine international markets, and entered Myanmar in June, 2018. Additionally, in 2017, the company announced its intention to enter Indonesia and Nigeria, which would help boost its current subscriber rate of ninety million global customers, according to the *Vietnam Economic Times*.[118]

Continued investment in Vietnam's telecommunication networks—projected to be more than USD $10 billion by 2022[119]—will be vital to fostering communication, commerce, and collaboration between Vietnam and the world, as well as among different regions in Vietnam: the urbanization rate (33 percent in 2016) is projected to reach 50 percent by 2025, according to the Vietnam Institute for Architecture, Urban and Rural Planning (VIAP),[120] Ministry of Construction. As the World Bank notes, "No country has achieved high income status and strong economic growth without first urbanizing, and nearly all countries become at least 50% urbanized before fully reaching middle income status."[121]

Along the path toward the future, new business models—with an emphasis on transparency—and technological innovations such as blockchain-based applications will accelerate the leapfrogging of Vietnam's economy as people continue to flock to urban centers. In particular, Financial Technologies, or Fintech, has the power to enable the participation of underbanked and unbanked consumers in Vietnam's formal economy. This focus on financial inclusion, combined with systemic reforms and investments in education, innovation, and best practices, could further propel Vietnam's GDP growth rate beyond even the most favorable current projections—or at least avoid the middle-income trap.

CHAPTER 2

FIRST IMPRESSIONS

In 2016, over 10 million tourists visited Vietnam, contributing USD $18 billion, or 7.5 percent of GDP, to Vietnam's economy, a record[1] bested only by the number of tourists who visited Vietnam in 2017: 12.9 million. Additionally, Vietnam ranked sixty-seventh in the *Travel & Tourism Competitiveness Report 2017*,[2] published by the World Economic Forum. Vietnam—along with Brunei, Thailand, and Myanmar (in Southeast Asia)—is among the "ten fastest growing destinations for leisure-travel spending" between 2016 and 2026, according to World Travel and Tourism Council (WTTC) research. By 2020, Vietnam's tourism industry is expected to contribute 10 percent of national GDP as it aims to welcome seventeen to twenty million foreign visitors per year. A decade later, Vietnam wishes to position itself as a leading tourism destination in Southeast Asia—a goal it can accomplish if it addresses lax regulations, high levels of emissions, deforestation, and limited water treatment to promote environmental stability and sustainable tourism practices, according to the report.

Another area of concern is the tourist experience, which can involve numerous scams—beginning at the airport with dodgy taxis, continuing with tricky street vendors, and potentially running into nefarious characters—both local and foreign—in certain areas. YouTube video bloggers Lynn and Noah Camp began their fourteen-part video series on Vietnam in 2014 with a video titled *Backpacking Vietnam Part 1: Shocked and Scammed in Hanoi.*[3] In the video, the Camps are swindled out of approximately five US dollars for bananas—with a midtransaction price change by the local fruit vendors. Another common scam involves tourists paying for a "hop on, hop off" bus pass to travel the country, only to find out (after the first leg) that the ticket was actually for a single journey. These experiences have driven some travelers to document why they will never return to Vietnam, such as a 2010 blog post by Nomadic Matt,[4] who delivered one of the harshest criticisms of the tourist experience in the country. Polish blogger Anna Lysakowska shared a similar experience online (limited to Hanoi) in her 2015 post "Why I Won't Be Visiting Hanoi Again."[5] As Lysakowska explains,

> As a white person in Hanoi you're being scammed pretty much all the time, it's just that sometimes you might not know it, or you don't want to know it. The worst part of it is that when you actually do pay attention to the behavior of the locals, you'll notice that after they charge you three times as much as the others, they'll laugh about it in Vietnamese in front of you.

To be fair, that's not representative of every interaction in Vietnam as a tourist or foreigner (and even hotels and restaurants are susceptible to being scammed themselves as the *Rusty Compass* travel guide has documented).[6] Yet, even if you're an expat in Vietnam, local vendors will assume you're a tourist and even offer you the standard spiel: "Hello, my friend—where do you go?" These aggressive sales tactics (mostly hard selling) and lackluster customer experiences cost Vietnam: only 5 percent of first-time visitors—who make up 90 percent of all visitors—return to Vietnam, according to the Pacific Asia Travel Association (PATA).[7] A 2013 opinion piece[8] by Briton Tim Russell, who lived in Vietnam for ten years, sums it up: "You can market a tourism destination all you like, but if people go there and have a negative experience, they simply won't go back."

For those who make it past the initial culture shock and tourist stage in Vietnam, diving into the entrepreneurial scene is a whole different story. A 2016 article, "Opening Up to International Investment and Diversification—A Case Study of Vietnam,"[9] published by the Maastricht School of Management, summed up foreign entrepreneurs' experiences:

> In a nutshell: Vietnam is young, dynamic, cheap, and a land full of opportunity, but finding the right product and people is absolutely critical. Entrepreneurs may not lose their shirts, but they might lose their patience.

Which city you arrive in first can shape your initial feel for the business landscape. Finding the right people on the ground can be tough to achieve, especially when many are quick to say yes and even quicker to accept credit—and to shift blame when it's convenient. In the beginning of your Vietnam experience, you won't even know how necessary it is to know what you don't know. For many expats and tourists, Ho Chi Minh City is usually the first stop. (In fact, the number of foreign arrivals to Ho Chi Minh City have increased more than 14 times in the past 25 years, according to the city's Department of Tourism.[10]) According to Swiss national and cofounder of SoNice.vn, Raphael Wilhelm:

> Saigon [Ho Chi Minh City] is home to an incredible [number] of talented entrepreneurs, designers, and tech talents whereby like-minded people from all over the world join forces and build a company. Cost of living, food, and beers are cheap, and [it's] 30 degrees [Celsius or 86 degrees Fahrenheit] warm weather all year around.

Today's Vietnam can be very different from foreigners' preconceived notions—despite the increasing availability of Vietnam-centric content on YouTube, Twitter, and Facebook. Even consuming this niche content might not be enough to prepare for the Vietnam experience: Vietnam can surprise, frustrate, humble, and charm one to wild extremes—sometimes in the same day or hour. Yet, there is something enchanting about this complex environment—almost as if one is embarking on a time-traveling journey and ending up in another dimension—which can take some time to understand, even on a simplistic level. On one hand, the shift in Vietnam continues toward the West. Consumers seemingly crave Western and foreign brands, products, and experiences—or what they perceive those experiences should be.[11] Simultaneously, there is no full grasp of the associated customs and values to reel in conspicuous consumption or ostentatious displays of wealth. For example, in the middle of the private unveiling of the Oriental Sun at the first Rolls-Royce dealership in Vietnam in 2014, a VIP guest stood up and pointed at the USD $1.8 million model, shouting, "Muốn! Muốn!" (Want! Want!). Whereas the up-and-coming Vietnamese consumer might opt for an entry-level bottle of wine, purely for the image of sophistication it affords, the Vietnamese elite can afford to embark on wine-tasting tours in France—and they do. So, in a paradoxical fashion, as more Vietnamese consumers continue to move into the middle class, they will be able to afford and acquire products and services that they previously could not have while striving to maintain nostalgic connections with Vietnam's past.

This inevitable scenario will require time to fully pan out. However, time is sometimes hard to utilize effectively in Vietnam. Two years in a monochronic society are not equivalent to two years in Vietnam on a linear scale—in part due to approaches to time, follow-ups, preparation, and other requirements taken for granted in the West. Even after one has lived for a year in one of Vietnam's major urban areas, there will be a learning/adjustment period for the next stop in Vietnam—if there is one. There will be some commonalities, but mind-sets and approaches to situations are quite different in Ho Chi Minh City compared to Hanoi. In some ways, it's like traveling to a different country. To put it more accurately, Vietnam is a collection of villages—in a tribal sense more than anything else.

The challenges you'll face as a foreigner working in Vietnam are a culmination of differences—differences of visions, standards, expectations, languages, culture, and, ultimately, opinions. Perceptions of good design, aesthetics, and fashion are very different from the West's version. That's neither good nor bad, so explore these arts with an open mind but be aware of the limitations in terms of technologies (for manufacturing or software development), varying skill and consistency levels, and acceptable content (from sociopolitical perspectives).

Trying to explain the general differences across Vietnam to someone who has never been here can be quite challenging. For many expats in Southeast Asia (with more than ten distinct markets), the region and its various cultures can be difficult to understand and navigate, let alone effectively explain to family, friends, or readers in another part of the world. Research, while helpful to understand context, is not a substitute for direct experience.

In a 2015 article, "Sizzling Saigon: Here Comes the Middle Class!,"[12] Yale University lecturer Dr. Vikram Mansharamani described his experience visiting Ho Chi Minh City:

> During my short trip, I had the chance to meet with business and government leaders, local and foreign investors, artists, farmers, and several taxi drivers. I ate at a restaurant that made [New York City] look cheap, with Vietnamese who regularly spend six figures on custom-designed jewelry featuring imported gemstones. Inequality was palpable in almost every walk of life, even if the tide appeared to be lifting all boats. There were also contradictions galore. An attendant at a roadside noodle stand beamed a broader smile than I've ever seen after receiving my tip of less than USD $1. But

> one thing was absolutely certain: consumption is booming. The middle class is using its newfound income to emulate a Western lifestyle.

Even though Vietnam is changing and modernizing, an element of "traditional Vietnam" still exists—and may remain long after the cityscape has transformed. It should go without saying that Vietnam has many faces, shapes, forms, and settings. Don't try to stereotype or label what you see, but instead, try to understand why things are the way they are—that's far more important than criticizing or condemning the status quo. Once you understand something, you can see where the opportunities lie—even across cultures.

For now, one of the grand questions facing Vietnam is, how willing is the young generation to keep and practice all their parents' traditions? It will certainly be a wire act between social and international pressures for them—but reaching an equilibrium they are comfortable with will help the rest of the world understand Vietnam's global role for decades to come. Zdravko Tumbovski, a Macedonian businessman who came to visit Hanoi in 2014, had this to share:

> In particular, this next decade will be crucial for Vietnam as the country transitions to increased trade with more global partners, the middle class continues to grow, and more foreign investment pours into the economy. Vietnam has many natural resources, a lot of talented people, and a willingness to exceed economic indicators but it will not be without some development friction, conflict between traditional and modern Vietnam—and addressing some major investor concerns. However, the long-term benefits will be far greater than what the shortcut rewards of today will provide.

Creating aligned incentives to achieve long-term benefits such as additional value capture, deep and lasting relationships, and an improved global reputation will not be easy—but nothing worthwhile ever is.

PERSPECTIVES OF VIETNAM

Examining present-day Vietnam from afar happens through the eyes of individuals—those who have come here for the first time, longtime locals, or those who have adopted this crossroads of development and tradition as their home or temporary base. No matter which category you fall into, Vietnam will be a wild and crazy ride at first, filled with extreme high points. It will also leave you dazed and confused at other times.

However, the Vietnam experience is not uniform—it is different for everyone who lives, works, or travels in Vietnam. Perhaps the most complex perspective is that of the Việt Kiều (generally understood as Vietnamese born or raised overseas). Thousands of people fled Vietnam during the Second Indochina War (also known as the Vietnam War in the United States or the American War in Vietnam), and hundreds of thousands more fled after Vietnam was reunited in 1975, resulting in millions of people creating the Vietnamese diaspora, primarily throughout North America, Europe, and Oceania. Many Việt Kiều families left Vietnam with just the clothes on their backs and settled into a new country to call home, usually starting over with almost nothing. Countless others perished during the journey of the "boat people," succumbing to sea conditions, Thai pirates, or other elements along the way.

In the 1990s, the Vietnamese government called for the Việt Kiều to return to Vietnam to reintegrate and afforded them special property and business rights (compared to foreigners) in order to help speed up Vietnam's economic development.[13] Some Việt Kiều have been willing to sign up for the opportunity to help develop Vietnam, while others have remained steadfast in their political and national convictions despite the natural cultural and language advantages they would have in present day Vietnam. Today, half of Overseas Vietnamese live in the United States and contribute approximately 60 percent of all incoming remittances to Vietnam, according to the *VnExpress International*.[14]

If you're not a member of an Overseas Vietnamese community and you've never traveled to Vietnam, then you're largely relying on primary or synthesized accounts of other people's experiences. The good news is that the number of perspectives and the media conveying those perspectives are increasing; only by opening up to differing perspectives can we begin to understand the world around us and how we fit in it. The point here is that everyone has something to add to the tapestry of the Vietnam (*not* Vietnamese) experience—but those experiences should be scrutinized (even the one you are currently reading) until the consumer has had the chance to get on the ground and come to his or her own conclusions. There is no substitute for direct experience, but short of that, the account, analysis, or opinion that you entertain should be sound, relevant, and contextual. Viewpoints on Vietnam will only grow as more foreigners visit and Vietnamese people create content to share with family and friends, and with the world.

Yet one encounters many contradictions while navigating Vietnam. Even firsthand experiences can be misleading on a superficial level and without the context of prior experience. Moreover, statistics, though they sound promising, can be hard to apply on a relevant level—that is, from macro to micro. For example, what are the incentives for a Vietnamese business owner to invest in training for his or her workers with current economic growth north of 6 percent? (It's much easier to replace workers, who might jump ship after an initial training period.) Furthermore, there always is a gap between design and implementation, especially for programs or initiatives that are reported on in Vietnam. The devil is in the details, as the saying goes.

Data, especially reliable open-source data, can be hard to come by in Vietnam, especially as of a few years ago, but additional sources have been increasing since then. Today, there's sometimes conflicting data and its credibility depends on the source and any potential spin on the topic. It's no surprise, then, that what one sees in Vietnam is not always what one gets—in a literal or figurative sense, or both, sometimes. Thus, it's helpful to bounce theories and feelings off locals, Việt Kiều, and expats alike without making assumptions at the onset. (Such open and honest dialogue requires an element of trust, which can take time to build.)

Most importantly, don't believe what you see or read—even this account. Talk to as many people as possible, get as many different points of view as possible, and then make your own decision about what is really going on. One thing is sure: prepare to forget any preconceived notions, conceptions, or stereotypes that you might have about Vietnam. But keep in mind that the urban metropolises are not wholly representative of Vietnam; the rural areas are where upward of 70 percent of the population live. In some cases, seeing something for yourself is not representative of most of the country's experience.

Ultimately, Vietnam is what you make of it—through good times, bad times, or whatever you experience in between. It's not always easy to live here, but after some time you may come to enjoy it—or perhaps even thrive in the environment. If not, the alternatives available are to go back to wherever you came from or to move on, in which case there is no shame, since Vietnam is not for everyone.

In Vietnam, the only thing that you can directly control is your attitude: toward others and the situation that you are in, because Vietnam is not static. Vietnam has different meanings for different people—some of these perceptions change every day, every year, or every visit, while others remain frozen in time. Some of those meanings include tradition, an untapped opportunity, a glorious past, increasing competition, the fatherland, independence, echoes of war, a bright future, a rising dragon, the Party, people of the sea, resilience, freedom, children of the mountains, liberalization, home, and happiness. Other meanings can be deeply personal, depending on initial orientations to the country and its history.

Thus, the answer to the question What is Vietnam? can only be answered individually, depending on one's biases. However, the more interesting question—for everyone to look toward—is, What will Vietnam become? And determining that answer will require a collective effort at several salient points in the nation's future.

Besides the original Việt Kiều, who were born in Vietnam and grew up elsewhere, multigeneration reverse migration is on the rise as well. In 2016, BBC Radio 4's *Today* program held a three-hour live broadcast from Ho Chi Minh City as it documented the phases of Vietnam's migration patterns and their economic effects, beginning with refugees from Vietnam settling into a new land, then looking at international Vietnamese economic migrants sending back remittances to their families, and finally with people returning to start new lives in Vietnam—or reconnecting with their heritage.[15] These new waves of immigrants and expats include the second generation of Overseas Vietnamese arriving in Vietnam, as well as those who have no preexisting ties to Vietnam and are curious about life in the young and dynamic country.

One millennial Vietnamese American (born in the mid-1980s) who traveled to Ho Chi Minh City in late 2016 and spent two months there exploring investment opportunities compiled a list of everything that stood out in the southern metropolis to someone familiar with the culture. This Vietnamese American's note is reproduced here—in two sections—under the condition of anonymity:

PROS

1. Passionate people/youth—sometimes too passionate, but this is a good thing.
2. Everyone is eager to start or build something.
3. Growing middle class.
4. Increase in mobile penetration/usage.
5. Large youth population.
6. Rise in mobile and digital demands.
7. Lack of regulations, clear rules, and guidelines provides opportunities for entrepreneurs to be creative in their business models. Entrepreneurs, business personnel, or investors with experience can benefit from this unclear playground (with the right team).
8. Individuals with an appetite for operations in unknown and unclear territory with malleable business models will do well here.
9. Influx of foreigners and returnees.
10. Business professionalism, acumen.
11. Financial understanding.

CONS

1. A lot of hobby angels, no serial entrepreneurs.
2. Business plans and models have not been thoroughly thought out prior to execution.
3. Too many family members and friends working on projects together. I met a group, and between them they are working on multiple ideas and multiple startups. None are really driving revenue. The team isn't carefully selected, and it ultimately breaks down.

4. Baseless startup—everyone has one. Most don't have revenue, just ideas. Ideas are not startups.
5. Labyrinth of relationships/paperwork/layers/networks for foreigners to dig through and try to understand—delays and extends the due diligence process.
6. Unwillingness to trust people they don't have an existing relationship with—which is fair to some degree, but business is business. We don't have to be drinking buddies to conduct business. We don't need to be friends for years to do business, either.
7. Pitch events and conferences all have the same speakers, same content, and same startups. Too many events are saying the same thing. It's frustrating and partly a waste of time. All smoke, but very, very few fires.
8. Need an absolute understanding of Vietnamese business practices and very strong ties to influencers to get things done or done quickly. Need to account for "discretionary" government fees. Not sure if it happens in tech, but miscellaneous fees cover miscellaneous items plus bribery fees.
9. Ego or cultural difference—possibly a combination of both—they don't ask for help.
10. Lack of appreciation for the service industry, perhaps because they don't see the true value of it.
11. A reactive mind-set and approach to problem solving as opposed to risk mitigation and a proactive mind-set to prevent problems.
12. Unwillingness to share information—very hard to identify a problem.
13. Copycats—"next Uber"—instead of trying to innovate to solve an existing problem or anticipate a solution to a forthcoming problem.
14. Unwillingness to give up ownership.
15. Not very good at asking questions—not sure if they're shy or just don't want to ask.
16. Varied talent pool.

17. Passive talent—maybe it's a cultural thing, but most don't say much. Capable, good talent lacks business confidence; it ultimately hurts them.
18. Willingness to listen: very one dimensional in approaching problems.
19. Western education doesn't mean Western experience.
20. Very short sighted, with short-term solutions.
21. Why are there so many coworking spaces?
22. No dedicated mentor group to advise startups on the proper business model. If this exists, we might see better quality startups. Fewer startup ideas and wannabes.
23. Response time via email is slow. They call when they need something, but when you ask them for a clear email or write-up, they say yes, and then you never hear from them.
24. They don't plan ahead or respect your time. Instead of saying "No, I'm not interested" or letting you know they'll be late, they'll delay, and then there'll be radio silence. What's worse, they'll ask you to email them and then completely ignore you. This bothers me to no end.
25. Family problems come up a lot as a reason for saying no. For example, [my partner] and I sat with three groups of developers. Regardless of how excited they were at the meeting or over email, all of them eventually said, "Sorry, due to family issues, we can't commit."
26. Traffic, infrastructure, and pollution are (the latter one of the major reasons) why I don't think I can live in Vietnam for an extended period of time.

A few months later, this tidbit was shared: "I think Vietnamese people have a problem saying 'no.' From my [exchanges] with people in Vietnam, 'no reply' is equivalent to 'no,' but if they want something, then it's 'reply, reply, reply.'"

It's one thing to read about Vietnam in a book or listen to a professor talk about it during a lecture; it's completely different to live it. You can't fully know[16] Vietnam by reading about it, but it does help to accelerate the understanding process once you jump into it, hopefully feet first.

SEEING IS BELIEVING—OR IS IT?

What does Vietnam look like today? Encapsulating daily life in a major city in Vietnam—as a snapshot of the most common sights, sounds, and experiences in Vietnam—is a challenge and would only scratch the uppermost layer of a superficial, cosmetic surface. Some items on this list are not exclusive to Vietnam (or even Asia), but they are noticeable in daily life in major cities such as Ho Chi Minh City or Hanoi.[17] Vietnam is the land of…

1. CAFÉS

The café is an important part of life for the Vietnamese. They are used for a number of core activities, including meetings, relaxing, literally sitting around, playing tabletop and digital games (multiplayer and single player), and communicating status (e.g., "I don't need to work, so I can hang out here all day"). Some common drinks are cà phê sữa đá, sinh tố xoài, and trà đá. The café culture here is strong, rich, and all encompassing, but different in parts of the country.

2. IPHONES

Not just smart phones, but Apple iPhones. These devices are ubiquitous and are used by celebrities along with a growing number of shopkeepers and street vendors. One way that the number of iOS devices increases in the country is through family: as people upgrade their handsets to the latest models, they pass on their older models to family members. There are millions of iOS devices in Vietnam due to consumers willing to spend months of their salaries on the latest iPhone, but the app marketplace has been largely fragmented in recent years.

3. HONKING AND MOTORBIKES

Rush hour in a major Vietnamese city comprises a sea of traffic, clouds of exhaust, and incessant honking—loud enough to hurt your ears. Many Vietnamese drivers seemingly use the horn simply because it is there. Another large portion seems to use the horn like sonar by sending out "pings." Vietnam is the world's fourth-largest market for motorbikes (after India, China, and Indonesia). During rush hour, motorbikes form rivers, which larger vehicles attempt to ford through impatiently. Trying to navigate an intersection with other motorbikes is akin to being in a mechanized cavalry phalanx. Although the Vietnamese dream is to drive to work in a car, cars will never fully replace motorbikes due to physical space limitations, such as the alleys in Hanoi's Old Quarter.

4. WI-FI

There is no need to ask if a venue has Wi-Fi. It's easier to ask for the password (usually 12345678, 88888888, 68686868, or a variation). Almost every café or restaurant provides free Wi-Fi (that works when an undersea cable isn't damaged).[18] The widespread availability of unsecured Wi-Fi could pose a cybersecurity risk in the future, especially if the lax attitude toward privacy continues.

5. NEW CONSTRUCTION

Drive around Hanoi after a twenty-minute ride from Nội Bài International Airport, and you can hear and see the future of Vietnam in the form of demolition work and scaffolding. Fly into Ho Chi Minh City's Tân Sơn Nhất International Airport, and from above, you'll see cranes dotting the city. Some future projects will be added to an already large real estate inventory (with outrageous prices), while smarter developers will differentiate their projects via advanced automation, control, and integration technologies in buildings to benefit end users (and, ultimately, to increase return on investment).

6. RECYCLING

The mantra "Reduce, Reuse, Recycle" is "Resell, Reuse, Repurpose" in Vietnam. Empty water bottles are collected and sold or given to door-to-door recyclers. Anything that is not completely destroyed is used or repurposed until it falls apart—frugal innovation, if you will. It's one of the most efficient aspects of Vietnam—especially when contrasted to some Western habits of instantly replacing or upgrading appliances à la "throwaway" culture.

7. NAME BRANDS

The nouveau riche are rising in status and increasing in numbers, flocking to established luxury brands, although some lack the sophistication that usually comes with style. As they say, "money doesn't buy class," so there is opportunity for etiquette schooling and manners training, especially in parts of the north.

8. YOUTH

Young people are everywhere, and although there are seemingly far too many banking and finance majors, the youth are the future of Vietnam (clichéd as it may sound). A segment of them are break dancing; rapping; and popping, locking, and dropping their way into adulthood while those studying science, technology, engineering, and mathematics (STEM) subjects seem to be diving headlong into startups and IT outsourcing. Many young Vietnamese idolize K-pop stars, consume Japanese manga, and are hungry for American culture[19]—but they will all eventually craft their own styles.

9. TOUCH

Personal space does not exist in Vietnam. Touching, sometimes inappropriately (from a Western point of view), is a way to communicate, since much of the Vietnamese language relies on context. Couples (not just romantic ones) can be seen walking together in a semidrunken stagger while talking loudly, laughing, or sharing some inside joke. Be prepared to "pinball" off people in crowded public spaces, as space is a luxury. Coworkers regularly and playfully slap each other; a sign of affection or budding romance if opposite sexes are involved (usually women slapping men).

10. DRINKING

Drinking alcohol and Vietnam go hand in hand. Bia Hà Nội, Bia Sài Gòn, Bia Trúc Bạch (the "finest beer in Vietnam"), Bia Hạ Long, Bia Huda (Huế)—you get the idea (those are all beer brands). Then there is rượu đế, rice alcohol, which comes in a variety of flavors—there's nothing like rượu dừa nóng (hot coconut rice wine) during the Hanoian winter. In 2016, Vietnam joined the top ten global consumers of alcohol, with more than 3.4 billion liters of beer and 342 million liters of spirits consumed, a recognition it retained for 2017, according to the Vietnam Beverage Association.[20] Drinking is an occasion for bonding and building relationships with counterparts, and it functions as social (and professional) lubrication. Basically, make sure you bring your drinking shoes or a nominee to drink for you.

11. SMOKING

Cigarettes, traditional pipes, and hookahs: nonsmokers are in for a rough time in Vietnam. There's always someone smoking nearby (usually Marlboro or Thăng Long brands). Smoking is allowed indoors and is encouraged in nightlife spaces. Air quality is already poor in major cities such as Ho Chi Minh City and Hanoi—and the long-term health implications of these combinations are alarming. Purchasing air and water filtration systems will become more common as Vietnamese seek to protect their children from increasing pollutants.

12. STARES

Everyone stares here, especially if you are an attractive or "exotic" woman, a foreigner, or different in any way, shape, or form—in the latter case, folks stare at you as if you were an alien descended from the heavens. A simple smile or wave can break the ice, but if coming from a culture where staring is considered impolite, then it may be jarring to some.

13. RIDE SHARING

Until March 2018, Uber logos were visibly plastered on helmets and track jackets throughout Vietnam's major cities. Uber Vietnam launched in Ho Chi Minh City in 2014 and soon thereafter in Hanoi. Grab, which is based only in Southeast Asia, launched in Vietnam in early 2014 and acquired

Uber's Southeast Asia operations in early 2018. In June 2018, Go-Jek, an Indonesian startup, announced the launch of Go-Viet as part of its Southeast Asia expansion plans.

14. MASH-UPS

Vietnam is host to several up-and-coming music festivals, including Quest, now in its fifth iteration as of 2017, and Equation, which debuted in 2017 with a three-year growth plan. Furthermore, Hanoi is "the hub for Vietnam's burgeoning techno scene," according to Boiler Room, a premier electronic music event series. Hanoi was also the home of Zone 9, an experimental and (former) entrepreneurial art-space complex embodying "Paris meets Berlin meets New York" in Southeast Asia. Saigon has too many notable venues to list.

15. CHANGE AND STREET LIFE

Everything is done on the streets, from eating to reading to sleeping—even haircuts. In Vietnam, sidewalks are not for walking; they are for living—or for parking your motorbike. Attempts to "clean up" or "reclaim" sidewalks have thus far been unsuccessful in the long term. Food, trinket, and fruit vendors litter the streets, as do ubiquitous plastic chairs and tables.

If you find a favorite restaurant or coffee shop, enjoy it as long as possible because it might not be there six—or even three—months later. Double-check before scheduling that meeting if you haven't popped in for a while.

TWENTY YEARS (+/-)

Twenty years ago, this list would have been radically different except for a few items. Most vehicles on the roads were bicycles at that time. Imagine what a snapshot of Vietnam will be like in the 2030s, with approximately 105 million people. Unrecognizable? Some parts Bangkok and other parts Hong Kong or Singapore? Sustainable ecotourism as a major industry? A center for innovation in Southeast Asia?

The technology and infrastructure for consumer-centric startups to be successful is already present; for example, the economic gap between the United States and Vietnam is huge, but there are iOS devices, Wi-Fi infrastructure, and mobile phones everywhere. (And the 4G speeds are even faster than in the United States, sometimes![21]) Overall, there is growing opportunity in Vietnam. Some people might even say that the region's future is here.

In the early twentieth century, the population of Vietnam was about twenty million. Today, Vietnam has close to a hundred million people. Vietnam is rapidly changing; some changes are positive, while others are unclear. What will Vietnam's role be as we continue deeper into the twenty-first century? Only time will tell, but one thing is certain: the pace of change here will surely increase.

CHAPTER 3

VIETNAM UP CLOSE

At times, the Vietnam experience can be absolutely crazy. Things are slow until they are not. Sit on the side of any road and observe: Vietnamese rush through traffic on motorbikes as if their lives depended on getting to their destination as soon as possible—only to sit and casually sip coffee or tea once they arrive. Cars move in slow motion as they make U-turns in the middle of a busy street—or they careen down the wrong side of the road. City and coach buses barrel through the streets, driven as if they were sports cars. In all, rush-hour traffic can be a wild city-wide production—or it can stay close to a standstill—that is, taking forty-five minutes to go five kilometers (about three miles) in a car. But for yours truly, Vietnam is a gem in Southeast Asia. However, it's not without its challenges as you start to notice jarring contradictions.

One of the first things that you might notice in Vietnam is a completely covered person—usually a woman—zipping along on a motorbike, looking somewhat like a Pac-Man ghost. (And probably looking left while turning right, if at all.) There's an obsession with staying out of the sunlight for fear of darkening one's skin—and it's difficult to find any skincare products without whitening agents. (As in other societies, light skin signifies that one doesn't have to work outside performing manual labor.) After some time in Vietnam, you might realize that the Vietnamese men have a pretty sweet deal when it comes to household responsibilities, which usually consist of drinking and smoking with their buddies, due to the patriarchal society structure and traditional attitudes toward gender roles. (To be fair, they do have other familial responsibilities, depending on their birth order, such as taking care of their parents financially.)

With these two concepts in mind, it should be no surprise that the experience of a white male in Asia may be unrivaled in its totality. Everything from preferred treatment to exclusive access is available for the taking—and sometimes you are ushered into the role by service workers. Constant discrimination (against the local populace) can be real and ugly, akin to a second-class, tiered system where—in a professional environment—locals may "sabotage" one another in order to curry favor with foreigners in one instance and then band together to shift blame onto foreigners the next moment. Some locals might even seek to "collect" foreign friends for the prestige and status they bring.

This preferential treatment can make it difficult to forge connections with young Vietnamese, who are sometimes intimidated when speaking English with foreigners. It's also hard to know exactly what the motivations of individuals who latch onto foreigners might be. It's dangerous to operate in Vietnam with a superficial knowledge of the culture—in doing so, one runs the risk of being a "white face"[1] promoting various projects. At the worst and most basic level, foreigners are viewed as "walking ATMs" and treated as such when buying items like fruit in the streets—but these experiences apply to tourists most of all. (No matter how long you've been in Vietnam or how proficient your Vietnamese language skills are, you'll always be a foreigner.)

However, Americans traveling to Vietnam should feel reassured that this discrimination is not based on their passport (or twentieth century history). Quite the opposite is true: according to a 2014 Pew Research Center survey,[2] 76 percent of Vietnamese "expressed a favorable opinion" of the United States—in 2017, 84 percent of Vietnamese respondents[3] said they now have a "very or somewhat favorable view." For some foreigners, this dual spirit of infatuation with race (white) and sex (male) can go to their head: being treated "like a king" can become addictive. Sadly, it can get out of hand, as arrogant and hedonistic tendencies may develop, especially in places such as Saigon, where the limits of excess during a night out on the town seem hard to identify and even harder to reach. (In recent years, coworking spaces in Saigon have sprung up almost as quickly as posh rooftop bars.)

The risk of overstimulation is real, especially with several strongly caffeinated Vietnamese iced coffees during the day and copious drinks containing (real or fake) alcohol late into the night. Visiting Vietnam for the first time is almost a primal release where anything is possible—shocking in some ways, exhilarating in other ways. But that's Asia: the illusion of freedom in the streets because your input doesn't matter in matters of state.

"Freedom" includes public drinking, public intoxication, and general lawlessness…if you can get away with it. Drunk driving is punished by a fine (paid on the spot) or by injury (including death), whichever comes first. Foreigners sometimes succumb to these dangerous local mentalities when explaining away otherwise reckless behavior. In a less extreme example, existing biases may cloud one's ability to appreciate progress—of developing relationships, standards, and quality—within the local context. Vietnamese American Christopher Zobrist, a pioneer in innovation and entrepreneurship in Vietnam, expands on these kinds of challenges:

> Coming from a developed country that churns out high-quality products as well as infrastructure (roads, public buildings, etc.), Americans as well as people from other developed countries have a natural expectation to see and make things at a high standard of quality. Vietnam is still a developing country, so many things are made with what little resources were available, and so the expectation for quality coming from domestically produced goods is not high.

Foreigners and locals can have completely different ideas of a given subject or context, further compounded by limited communication skills on both sides. A foreigner might keep hearing yes, but nothing may happen as a result of the conversation. When one is a guest in Vietnam, it can be difficult to square what one sees with what one hears—and in fact, neither may be completely accurate. Asking the same thing in different ways might shed some additional light on the situation, but the generally accepted approach to "doing things" might only suit Vietnamese startups within the country's borders, especially for those who wish to expand regionally or internationally.

European American entrepreneur Stefan Van Der Bijl, former managing director of Cofounder Venture Partners, a venture builder in Ho Chi Minh City, shares his initial impressions of Vietnamese startups and whether or not they can go global:

> I think they can, but have not found their mojo yet. Most of the startups I see are blatant copies of others outside [Vietnam]. If they copy, [then] they lose first-mover advantage, [they] are a 'me-too' play. Few have original ideas. Translating something that worked abroad does not mean [it] will work in [Vietnam] or vice versa. [Vietnam] has [96 million] people, they should only need develop internally, see from there about expanding abroad. The time zone difference is a real problem for anything involving direct communications—best would be for them to have offices outside [Vietnam]—few can afford [this]. ([Would] be nice to have [Vietnam] government-sponsored office space abroad for Vietnamese startups). Only some Vietnamese startups really have an idea what it's like to work at startups that have clients round the clock—they tend to be comfortable. Haven't had [international] exposure, their experience is only [Vietnam]. Vietnamese startups can get 90% of the way, the remaining 10% fit and finish is where they fail.

Even foreigners from Asia-Pacific might have some trouble acclimating to the way things are done in Vietnam. Koreans and Japanese definitely have advantages based on similar business and cultural rituals, but even for other Asians, it can take some time to get used to the challenges. In a 2017 BBC article,[4] couple Yosuke and Sanae Masuko, cofounders of Pizza 4Ps, a wildly popular establishment that has expanded rapidly, shared their story of how the institution came to be in 2011—and the challenges along the way. On working styles in Vietnam and Japan, Ms. Masuko said, "We found the gap [in] working culture between Vietnamese and Japanese… difficult to bridge…but things are improving."

While there are advantages to having been in Vietnam long-term, being a fresh-faced foreigner can be an asset as well—especially when identifying opportunities. John Wise and Wombi Rose, cofounders of Lovepop, were inspired by something they saw while traveling in Vietnam. According to the duo,[5] "We found ourselves on a school project in Vietnam, [and] we fell in love with the unique art form of beautiful, hand-crafted, paper cards. Our inner engineers came to life with the world of possibilities—we wanted to create everything as a delicate paper sculpture!"

At the time, the Lovepop founders were students at Harvard Business School and launched the company from the Harvard Innovation Lab in 2014. The team went on to join Techstars in 2015 and was featured on *Shark Tank*, raising over USD $9 million in six rounds along the way. All because of a trip to Vietnam.

Besides innovators, Vietnam also attracts pioneers such as Aigerim Zhangozina, the first woman from Kazakhstan who managed a technology company abroad. Zhangozina is among the relatively few expats who have worked and lived in more than one major city in Vietnam:

> After working in Ho Chi Minh City for four years, I moved to Hanoi in 2013. I immediately noticed the differences in the business environment. First of all, there was far less international exposure for business at the time, especially for tech

startups, so it took some time for me to build a network. Most of the time, I had to use my connections in Ho Chi Minh City to get introduced in Hanoi. Luckily, such startup incubators as Hub.IT and HATCH! were launched, and once they started organizing industry events, things moved faster.

Meanwhile, the fact that local businessmen were not that "spoiled" by foreigners' attention in Hanoi compared to Ho Chi Minh City helped me to establish many meetings with C-level executives: they were eager to at least see me and talk to me. Our startup was based on a B2B2C model, so it was quite challenging to acquire partners. I'm very grateful to everyone in Hanoi who supported me during that period. Some of them helped me to connect to big players through social networks (e.g., LinkedIn), although they had never met me before.

In addition, thanks to historical connections between Vietnam and my home country, Kazakhstan, (part of the ex-Soviet Union), I received great support from governmental organizations and media in Hanoi such as the Vietnam E-commerce Association, the *VnExpress*, and Vietnam Internet Association. At the press conference organized by the latter and where I was a spokesperson about Internet marketing in 2012, I was sitting next to the vice minister of information and communication and discussing with him the latest trends (which is hard to imagine back in my home country!).

The second challenging difference I faced in Hanoi was human resources. It was harder to find English-speaking talents in Hanoi, especially in digital marketing. Either they had already moved to Ho Chi Minh City or had been

> employed by big companies. Again, I was lucky to hire some real "gems" for my team through connections.
>
> What surprised me the most about Vietnam was an overall positive attitude to female leadership and entrepreneurship, especially in the startup industry. I'm from a country where men still dominate in business and tech, but in Vietnam I never felt uncomfortable during business meetings. There's an interesting cultural norm here: as a woman you won't be allowed to pay if you have a business lunch or meeting in coffee shop.
>
> Openness to innovations, support for foreign investment companies, and a highly entrepreneurial spirit, especially among women, are the factors contributing to a positive image of Vietnam as a future technological leader. In addition, general friendliness to foreigners makes one want to contribute to this wonderful country more and more. Did I mention how much I love Vietnam?

While it's clear that Zhangozina has made the most of her time in Vietnam, not everyone who comes to Vietnam is ready or able to add value and contribute to Vietnam's development aspirations. Being a foreigner in Vietnam is an opportunity to reinvent oneself—but not everyone appreciates this reality, instead embracing and promoting newly discovered attitudes toward time, customer service, and standards. Thus, culture shock may cut in two ways: first, as a minority in Vietnam, especially if you are not used to being one; and second, making sense of expat society, especially whom to trust and socialize with, while potentially growing tired of meeting a stream of new expats only to have them disappear months—or weeks—later. Such is the steep learning curve in Vietnam, especially when some friendships eventually evolve into business relationships.

Yet, Vietnam is a place where—if you stick it out for a year or two—you may be able to make a blend of the foreign and local benefits. But there are many challenges along the way, and people will come and go. Having real local friends helps—not just people to drink with and who may want to practice English with you. Only then will you see the deeper aspects of Vietnam up close.

EXPECTATIONS, SOCIAL CONTEXT, AND MISCOMMUNICATION

Coming to Vietnam and doing things the way they are done back home is a recipe for a long and hard haul that produces suboptimal results. In other words: disaster. First, there are many pitfalls in Vietnam. Here, it's easy to have hours turn into days, and eventually weeks, without anything tangible to show for it. Bad habits can develop quickly and are often hard to break. Ask for perfectly acceptable things as you would in any other country (such as a dry napkin in certain parts of the country), and the likely response is a variation of "Your requirements are too high." If you are unlucky enough (Vietnamese are highly superstitious) to get scammed—and you will, one way or another, so anticipate it—the scammer will be smiling the entire time, even long after the transaction has concluded.

In this context, it's easy to remain within the expat community, bypassing many misunderstandings. But for those who have long-term plans involving Vietnam, living in a country without experiencing it is a wasted opportunity. Alternately, some expatriates (also known as immigrants) and Việt Kiều go too deeply into Vietnam. That is, they have been in country for so long that they begin to adopt local practices—and not the best ones. They see how low the bar is for some practices and gravitate toward the bar instead of trying to raise it. After all, Vietnam is not a best-practices paradise (except for public vices such as smoking and drinking), although some guests fool themselves into believing the opposite is true. Because of these gaps, it's possible to make an impact on an individual or communal level—if you are willing to put the time into mentorship and training.

The majority of business relationships between locals and foreigners begin over coffee and usually progress toward the bottom of a bottle of alcohol (among men, especially) near the end of the night over subsequent meetings—or from day one. Facebook (once banned in Vietnam) is the preferred social network for business opportunities—not LinkedIn—and double opt-in introductions are rare. More often than not, the lines between personal and professional relationships are so blurred that life becomes a series of interactions to help one another in every aspect of the actors' respective livelihoods.

If you are still interested in Vietnam, then read on: everything here is built on relationships—with whom and how strong. From an enforcement perspective, contracts—which Westerners often love to reference—are essentially worthless. When push comes to shove, litigation is handled behind the scenes, as the outcome largely depends on which party has deeper pockets. In reality, contracts (Memoranda of Understanding, more likely) serve as acknowledgments that there is an existing relationship between two people or organizations—but it's up to both parties to keep that relationship in good standing. As one might imagine, proximity to and goodwill with government officials is a competitive advantage—but not without some risk, depending on the nature of the relationship. For some foreigners or Việt Kiều, this means marrying into a powerful family (war hero, legacy, or public sector) in order to cut through the reams of red tape that blanket every aspect of Vietnamese society.

Some expats choose to marry into Vietnam, routing everything through their local spouses. This option works with a solid foundation and mutual understanding, as in any genuine relationship. But the less time an expat has spent in country, the higher the chances for cultural misunderstandings. For one, relationships and responsibilities take on different meanings in urban and rural Vietnam. Furthermore, the roles of men and women are quite different from the modern, Western interpretation of equality, romance, and social obligations. Scroll through any Vietnamese expat-oriented Facebook group, and you will find that it is full of these misunderstandings, which (naturally) can only be resolved in the court of public opinion.

Yet, having a trusted local by one's side can be the difference between success and failure, as Vietnam has a steep learning curve; who and what is right is not always clear in the local context. This is true in many Asian and Confucian cultures, so it can take some getting used to, coming from the West. Dr. Everett Myers, a former Fulbright professor at Vietnam National University, moved to Vietnam in January 2015. Previously, Dr. Myers was a professor at the Center for Global Affairs at New York University, with prior experience in Japan. He notes, "Significant ambiguity [exists] in the rules and regulations and most importantly in their implementation and enforcement. [Foreigners] should expect a heightened degree of scrutiny in any of their business dealings. As such, a local partner to help navigate the local territory is a must for many foreign enterprises in Vietnam."

Triangulating who and what is the "real deal" can take up a great deal of time, even expanding into more than one city. Expats may experience scams from their leasing agent or even from fellow expats, but figuring out why things are the way they are—that is, understanding the explicit and implicit set of cultural rules that dictate what happens in daily life—helps to minimize risk. Dr. Myers observes, "The principal pitfall to avoid is falling into the 'value trap' i.e., making value judgments on Vietnamese society as contrasted with the West. Once one enters this trap, they will find themselves in a ten-foot hole with a five-foot ladder...tough to get out of. Avoid the value judgments and simply recognize the differences... this will help reduce the anxiety and enable one to better navigate the Vietnamese landscape."

Newly arrived foreigners sometimes complain about locals not being straightforward, or even lying. Locals might consider this "bending the truth," as white lies are usually perfectly acceptable (to them). One of the biggest contributions to failure is not setting the right expectations on both sides. There's an often-repeated saying in Vietnam: "The longer you stay in Vietnam, the higher your patience, and the lower your effectiveness." While that may be true for some segments of expats (or immigrants), many foreigners in Vietnam would disagree. But for all the successful or prominent expats in Vietnam, there are others who were effectively driven out of the country—sometimes due to unforeseen circumstances, such as previously undisclosed conflicts of interest ranging from relationships to existing businesses.

The resource that is in the shortest supply is talent (this is true across Southeast Asia), as there are many examples of local organizations valuing perceived loyalty over competence. If loyalty is not a factor, then age dictates in every social situation. (The power distance between men and women in Vietnamese culture is substantial.) So if—like your author (at one time)—you are a twenty-six-year-old foreign consultant working with a fifty-year-old local manager, you will be wrong if you don't agree with the "facts" despite the clear and obvious reality. Imagine Vietnamese students working with local investors—who presumably have money and are significantly older. It creates an imbalance in every interaction, which can be even more pronounced with gender power distance.

Organizationally, Vietnam is not a place to learn best practices (except how to navigate in a developing economy—i.e., risk management): companies regularly use unlicensed software, employees display extreme examples of unprofessionalism (e.g., viewing pornography in the office during lunch), and many companies use a top-down, micromanaged approach, "confusing activity for productivity" as one foreigner put it.

However, Vietnam is great if you are trying to do something new. If you take a look at the West, everything is developed: industries, infrastructure, institutions. In markets such as Vietnam, you can create and shape new markets. Yes, it is labor, time, and capital intensive—but it is also a place where demographic and economic projections promise the creation of massive amounts of value well into this century.

This is a long-term approach—something that may clash with local counterparts. A perceived weakness in Vietnam is the short-term orientation that many people seem to take. Quick fixes and the like are preferred over fundamental solutions providing lasting improvements. Part of this attitude emerges from the educational system, which is based on Confucianism. "Saving face" is always touted as an Asian characteristic, which sounds sensible until you see it unfolding before you. Ask someone for directions, and instead of hearing "I don't know," you will be pointed in the wrong direction. Ask if a particular task has been accomplished, and you'll be met with a resounding "Yes, yes!"—only to find out it hasn't even been started yet.

Perhaps that is why it's not uncommon to encounter foreigners who have been in country for less than six months but have an obvious analysis for everything that is wrong with Vietnam, which usually includes some aspect of the north. Even within Vietnam (in places such as Ho Chi Minh City), Saigonese and expats alike will warn about the dangers of traveling to Hanoi. As the refrains go, "The weather sucks"; "Don't do business with the Hanoians; they will cheat you"; "They aren't friendly"; and "The traffic is worse than in Ho Chi Minh City." Some of this is true; the weather is indeed better in Saigon.

Pry a bit deeper, and you might be surprised to learn that the same locals who are giving you advice have only "visited Hanoi once a few years ago." And many of the foreigners dishing out tips to avoid the city have never visited Hanoi, since their local friends "advised against it."

Hanoi, Ho Chi Minh City, and Da Nang are all distinctly different in culture, language, jokes and slang, ways of thinking, and simply doing things. These major distinctions are lost on those who spend time in only one area of Vietnam. Of course, it's much easier for a northerner to do business in the south (and easier for a foreigner to operate in Hanoi than it is for a southerner), due to stereotypes and biases based on regional accents. (Again, unless there are family shortcuts.) But the key to better understanding Vietnam is knowing that the considerations used to develop your business model in Ho Chi Minh City probably won't work in Hanoi and might not work in Da Nang, due to cultural and regional differences. For those with a larger vision, the deeper you go into Vietnam, the harder it is to go regional.

A TALE OF THREE CITIES

Without a doubt, the three major cities in Vietnam are Hanoi, Ho Chi Minh City, and Da Nang (in terms of geographical distribution, Cần Thơ and Hải Phòng have economic and population significance as well). They are all incredibly different—from accents to governing styles and weather—and have varied strengths and weaknesses. Ho Chi Minh City seemingly aspires to acquire the commercial and cosmopolitan aspects of Bangkok or Singapore. There are more publicly visible expressions of art and creativity in the streets compared to Hanoi. On the other hand, Hanoi has a vibrant underground music and art scene, which is sometimes a merging of the local and foreigner communities. Of the three major cities' public sectors, the Ho Chi Minh City government tries to be progressive, the Da Nang city government is the most accessible, and Hanoi's city government may be the most conservative. (For those who like sleeping in, Hanoi may not be the city for you—the wartime speakers, which the city considered removing,[6] are still used, blaring propaganda twice daily starting around 7:30 a.m.)

It's not uncommon for young Hanoians to move to Ho Chi Minh City to escape family pressures and expectations in the north. In general, women are expected to live with their parents until marriage, usually before the age of twenty-five. At that point, they move in with their husband (and sometimes his family) and prepare to raise children. In Hanoi, the joke is that first comes the baby and then the marriage, to ensure that the grandparents will be pleased. However, in recent years, women are waiting longer to be married—until the age of thirty or later. But they also run the risk of being labeled *ế*, or "spoiled," by their communities. If a young woman does move out from her home before marriage, it's probably to live in another city (i.e., from a rural area to an urban center), although there are some exceptions to this "rule." So those who never leave Ho Chi Minh City (especially foreigners) may fall into the trap of believing that Ho Chi Minh City is Vietnam and vice versa. But it's not: almost 70 percent of Vietnamese live in rural areas.

During a 2015 meeting at the American Center at the US Consulate in Ho Chi Minh City, about sixty entrepreneurs, investors, and other community builders gathered to discuss the major challenges confronting the ecosystem. Led by a local and a Vietnamese American, the session attempted to identify the community's needs. There were three or four participants from Hanoi, most of whom were foreigners. As the conversation swirled around the room, it became clear that the "startup ecosystem" ended at Ho Chi Minh City's limits for the purpose of the discussion.

One of the complaints concerned the inability to access the right networks, as well as the lack of cooperation among members of the community—quite a different experience from working in Hanoi. Thus, some needs are local, and some needs are nationwide. Cooperation among players—or lack thereof—can make a major difference in developing initiatives on the ground, and it still has a long way to go.

As one Vietnamese Australian entrepreneur put it, "There are ten different communities in Ho Chi Minh City trying to do the exact same thing." This might be an exaggeration when it comes to efforts and events, but the overall atmosphere is different in Hanoi. To provide just one example, there are fewer Việt Kiều in Hanoi, especially American Việt Kiều. The diplomatic community is more obvious and accessible in Hanoi as well.

In short, the expats who are there genuinely like living in Hanoi or are building government relationships.

Contrast this to Ho Chi Minh City, which accounts for approximately a quarter of Vietnam's GDP. The focus is on all things commercial, nightlife, and glamor. Ho Chi Minh City's nightlife can certainly be dangerous for your liver and your wallet. Here, you can stay out until sunrise one night—and do it all over again the following night. On the other hand, Hanoi has a general closing time at midnight for drinking establishments—although for those in the know, the party moves to speakeasies. (Hanoians like to start drinking earlier, too.)

Saigon (the name is still used to refer to Ho Chi Minh City within its city limits and beyond) is a city that lives to party. Compare the local bia hơi in Saigon—wide open, colorfully decorated, and full of drinking chants and mirth—with those in Hanoi, which are more sparsely decorated and somewhat narrower, and you will definitely feel a difference. (Of course, you are not expected to tip in Hanoi, as you are in Saigon.)

Da Nang is almost exactly in the middle (in both geography and neutral setting—though spiritually closer to Saigon, despite being a favored destination for Hanoians) of Hanoi and Ho Chi Minh City and has qualities that neither Hanoi nor Ho Chi Minh City can match. It's a coastal city with fresh air, mountains, a river, and opportunities for biking, surfing, and hiking. With such appealing qualities, Da Nang has a great deal of potential to develop as a foreign startup hub, or at least as a base for a programmatic approach to targeting incoming foreign startups. Da Nang also perfectly embodies and reflects Vietnam's position at the center of globalization changes and has potential to lead the way in the future as it tries to determine its new identity. (However, cheap labor is not a sustainable comparative advantage, and Vietnam will have to move up the value chain to be competitive with other developing countries long term.)

What then, is the context for operating in Vietnam as a foreign entrepreneur or innovator? Foreigners can never compete with Vietnamese on a labor-rate basis—the minimum wage (in 2016) was somewhere between

USD $107 and $156 per month, depending on urban or rural areas. In addition, "commissions" (as considered in the West) aren't really commissions. Within some local organizations, different managers (finance manager, technical manager, etc.) vie for contracts, sometimes depending on the largest commission. These contracts are then fulfilled via a director's network from their staff all the way to the delivery drivers to pick up the equipment. Local partners usually handle similar "marketing fees" for foreign companies.

In such an environment, it can be difficult for an American to do business as a guest, without the same networks or experience of "traditional" Vietnam, such as "coffee money." (Younger Vietnamese are more likely to acknowledge coffee/tea money and the envelope culture that exists.)

Unless you want to do things "local style," you must find other ways to add or create value while being mindful of the Foreign Corrupt Practices Act (or similar laws; e.g., the United Kingdom Bribery Act).[7] Building relationships in Vietnam takes time: lots of (hours-long) coffee meetings can be compressed into several beer-drinking sessions. These (usually inebriating) sessions can be compressed into a karaoke lounge stop. Overall, people generally are quite accessible in Vietnam and willing to extend their networks and knowledge to newcomers. (Although it's easier to get "burned" in Hanoi if a prominent member of the community doesn't vouch for you.)

However, there are no shortcuts to building trust—unless via a trustworthy introduction that brings you into the fold. As with most things in life, credibility, authenticity, and reputation are everything.

Things are a bit more open minded in Ho Chi Minh City, but that just means that it takes longer to build rapport to a deeper level. The most likely places to build social cohesion and build out diverse networks are bars, restaurants, lounges, and clubs. Thus, it can sometimes be hard to tell if an engagement is a business meeting, a get-together among friends, or a mix of both. (The English comprehension levels are much higher in Saigon as well, compared to Hanoi.)

Anecdotally, Hanoians are a bit better at separating business and pleasure, but often not by much. However, they can be known for becoming "unleashed" in Saigon during a weekend getaway. For Westerners (especially newcomers), coming to Vietnam is like being plopped down in a place where there are no rules for conduct. No one will tell you to go home (except at midnight in Hanoi—although this rule is relaxing), and no one will refuse to sell to you. You are free to do whatever you want—and that's intoxicating in its own dangerous way. It's almost the opposite of a "nanny state" (with the exception of acceptable content), and it is definitely a capitalistic survival-of-the-fittest approach to see who can outlast whom.

Many local behaviors (which foreigners would classify as rude) are the result of this survival mode due to twentieth-century foreign influences in the nation's history. Vietnam is still in transition to a society of self-expression; Facebook has been one outlet, but, more often than not, opinions seem to be of extremes. Civics and civility have yet to be mastered online as well as in the physical domain—which can be frustrating when one is dealing with nuanced subjects. As we'll see in the next part of the book, there's more than initially meets the eye to Vietnam.

SECTION II

THE NEW VCs OF VIETNAM

CHAPTER 4

A MIND-SET SHIFT

Interpretations of Vietnamese behavior can be misleading; it can be quite difficult to fully understand the mind-set of a person who—from a Western perspective—opts for seemingly illogical decisions. Long-established ways of thinking are seemingly omnipresent: superstitions play an outsized role in Vietnam, relative to the West.[1] For the most part, a lack of focus on soft skills or interpersonal communication can be explained away, especially when recalling that "rudeness" is not a concept for many individuals perhaps still in "survival mode." Throw in a language barrier, and the cultural gap between foreigners and Vietnamese can increase even more. One perspective often used to view Vietnamese professional behavior is short-term versus long-term orientation—that is, Vietnamese people only plan for a very short time ahead, due to expectations of long-term plans going awry (because of historical instability, unreliable business partners, or plain bad luck, etc.). However, there is an additional framework that can also be applied to the Vietnamese decision-making matrix: results versus process.

During a span of two weeks near the end of 2016, two foreign-educated Hanoian businessmen separately laid out the same basic theory for your author. First, Nguyễn Trọng Khang, founder, chairman, and CEO of MK

Group, manufacturer of identification, SIM, and security cards, shared during a meeting in his office, "Vietnamese people are results-oriented—but for a company to be sustainable, it needs to be process oriented." Mr. Khang should know—he was awarded Entrepreneur of the Year in 2014 by EY, and his company currently employs four hundred people, leveraging "American technology, Japanese quality, and Vietnamese price" in its market niche. (Recently, MK Group expanded to South America.)

About a week later, Giang Trung Kiên, research director of MB Capital (Military Bank Capital), a local private equity firm, explained over dinner, "Vietnamese people are results oriented, but Westerners are process oriented." Both men studied abroad—the former in the United States and the latter in Australia—and were united in their thinking about results in relation to the process, despite their difference in age.

The framework of "results versus process" within the context of uncertainty about the future explains many seemingly questionable decisions in Vietnam. It explains why managers expect to "go from A to Z" without a feasible plan in between, why a landlord might spend an inordinate amount of time to "win" one million Vietnamese đồng (approximately USD $50; a real example) during an unreasonable negotiation, and why people seem to be taking shortcuts everywhere—shortcuts that don't scale in the long term.

While some stakeholders in Vietnam may want to see socioeconomic results more quickly, especially results related to private-sector development and startups, it's important to remember that Vietnam was largely a closed-off society until 1994, due to the United States–led trade embargo (and the journey toward full relations being restored lasted from 1995 through 2016). Thus, older mind-sets will need some time to subside or change as Vietnamese people increase their interactions with the rest of the world in the areas of commerce, cultural exchange, and collaboration. However, the clock is ticking as the region and other nations around the world attempt to make sense of the Fourth Industrial Revolution (also known as Industry 4.0) and what it means for their future prospects.

Of course, a quick-fix approach—opting to treat the symptoms rather than the cause—to problem solving (or not even acknowledging something is a problem) is not accepted by all in Vietnam. In recent years, "Western-style," often used as a euphemism for a more transparent and international approach, has been offered as an alternative to the "traditional" way of doing things. But the greatest potential difference lies in adopting new mind-sets and orientations such as lean startup methodology, design/systems thinking, and effectuation—all ways of validating decisions and utilizing feedback loops to make future decisions.

At the Finland-Vietnam Innovation Partnership Program (IPP2) Final Demo Day in Ho Chi Minh City in January 2016, Phạm Nam Long, founder and CEO of Abivin, a big data startup, declared during his pitch, "We happen to be in Vietnam, but our mind-set is global." Therein lies the most important shift in thinking among today's entrepreneurs in Vietnam: from local to global, with a long-term orientation coming into full view.

Trần Trung Hiếu, a former official at the Ministry of Industry and Trade (MOIT) and ASEAN Secretariat exemplifies this way of thinking when he said during our first meeting, "The world is changing, so we, too, must change with the world." Trần expands on his thoughts even further:

> We have witnessed a drastic change in all facets of life since the Đổi Mới [in] 1986, notably the perception shifting of the young people. When [the] living standard is significantly improved, [the] '8x onwards generation,' the term that today we usually refer to as [the] young generation, is more proactive and Western-influenced. They are liberalized, loosened up, and not mindful of living their own life with their own style. It seems that the traditional values or morals have not been appreciated as much as the older generation. They are open to novelty, bold ideas and willing to embrace the globe.

These aforementioned changes in thinking and orientations to societal roles don't have to be gargantuan. They can be as simple as a deeper appreciation for the value of new communities—not based in the traditional village sensibilities, but formed around shared values and goals. For example, one area where attitudes have visibly changed is the perception of coworking spaces in Vietnam. In 2013, there were fewer than a handful of coworking spaces in Vietnam. In Ho Chi Minh City, Vietnamese American entrepreneur Christopher Zobrist set up the Start Center in 2012—the first coworking space in Vietnam. The following year, Zobrist raised USD $100,000 in seed funding to open Saigon Hub above Highlands Coffee on the corner of Nguyễn Đình Chiểu and Đinh Tiên Hoàng Streets in District 1.

Today, the Start Center is still operational in an alley off Nguyễn Thị Minh Khai Street, under a different name (and owner Martial Ganière): Start Saigon. However, Saigon Hub did not fare as well; it shut down in 2014 because it was not financially sustainable, with too few paying members. At the time, the value of a coworking space in Vietnam was not appreciated—the general thinking among locals was, "Why pay for membership when I can buy a coffee in a café and spend the day there?"

Up in Hanoi, Singaporean entrepreneur Bobby Liu opened Hub.IT in Hanoi's Tung Shing Square (Hoàn Kiếm District) in late 2013. Situated on the second floor, the space was the only privately funded coworking space in Hanoi at the time. In November 2015, Hub.IT was acquired by Topica Edtech Group, and Liu became senior director and evangelist, helping to expand the Topica Founder Institute (TFI), as codirector, into Thailand in 2016.

The year 2015 was a pivotal time for coworking spaces as they gained mass appeal among Vietnamese users. It marked the first time that coworking space chains emerged across Vietnam, most notably, Toong (in Vietnamese, tổ ong means "hive"), with five locations across Vietnam; Dreamplex, with two locations in Ho Chi Minh City; and Up, with six locations and two more in the works as of January 2018. While coworking spaces globally have grown annually at a rate of 53 percent, in Vietnam they have grown at 58 percent per year, according to CBRE.[2] As of January 2018, there were at least seventeen coworking space providers with twenty-two different locations across Vietnam.

Finding the right business model for these coworking spaces was initially challenging. Toong's first location on Tràng Thi street in Hanoi's Hoàn Kiếm District was partially closed after opening. Toong's management team, led by founder and CEO Đỗ Sơn Dương, realized that it was more efficient to sell office spaces for teams of three to five people—at a higher price and for a longer amount of time—than it was to focus on freelancers. So during the closure, the fourth level of the building (the second floor of the space) was renovated to make room for more office spaces.

The American cofounder of another coworking space in Hanoi acknowledged that before a bistro was added to the space, it had not reached its break-even point. Basically, members were paying to stay in the space, but they still needed food and drinks, which they would buy elsewhere until the bistro was added.

Overall, the benefits of a coworking space—its community, a place to gather and exchange ideas, and an event space—were what drew Vietnamese and foreigners into proximity with one another. (It also helped that President Barack Obama and Google CEO Sundar Pichai both visited Vietnamese entrepreneurs in coworking spaces—the former at Dreamplex in Ho Chi Minh City, and the latter at Toong in Hanoi.)

These days, it seems as if a new coworking space is being unveiled or commemorated every few weeks in Hanoi or Ho Chi Minh City. (WeWork, the coworking space giant, set up its first Vietnam location in late 2018, opting for Ho Chi Minh City.) Even the public sector has entered the coworking space industry, such as Saigon Innovation Hub (SI-Hub) in Ho Chi Minh City or the Da Nang Business Incubator (DNES)—both launched in 2016. (Vietnam Silicon Valley, an incubator launched in 2013 by the Ministry of Science and Technology in Hanoi, has a coworking space for its portfolio companies.) There can only be benefits from more cross-cultural interactions between locals and foreigners—and intraregional exposure among Vietnamese—in order to learn from each other and cocreate new opportunities that will require new solutions based on new ways of thinking (i.e., "how we got *here* is not how we will get *there*").

The story of FPT might be one of the starkest examples of how Vietnam's companies are changing gears and preparing for the future. In 1988, thirteen cofounders launched the company, then named Food Processing Technology (FPT), demonstrating its original intent. Two years later, in 1990, the company's leadership board decided on IT as its core competency and changed the name to Financing and Promoting Technology (FPT). Less than ten years later, FPT decided to go global by focusing on providing outsourcing technologies. Today, FPT operates in twenty-one countries and has seven domestic subsidiaries operating across four industries: technology, telecommunications, distribution and retail, and education. It currently provides services to 10 percent of the Fortune 500.

In 2015, FPT launched FPT Ventures with a USD $3 million fund to foster intrapreneurship within its ranks and to tap into the growing interest in startups in Vietnam. FPT Ventures provides approximately USD $3 million in seed and early-stage funding (as well as technical resources) to Vietnamese startups with a minimum investment amount pegged at USD $50,000. Thus, FPT can become more involved in the creation of value-added products and services in order to capture a larger piece of the lifetime value of a startup in the local market. Initially, FPT was testing the venture-building model with some internal projects, allowing the conglomerate to explore different areas to innovate in. As we'll see in the next section, other forms of Vietnamese innovation have been in practice for decades.

LEAN AND AGILE BY NATURE

Innovation is not a word that is usually associated with Vietnam. More likely than not, when people hear "Vietnam," they think of conflict instead of the Southeast Asian country. Yet innovation is not confined to places such as Silicon Valley, Berlin, or Singapore. It's present in Guadalajara, Hyderabad, and yes, even in Ho Chi Minh City and other parts of Vietnam.

One aspect of innovation sometimes overlooked in developed countries is innovation by constraint—where, for example, you have to use every available resource such as the corn and the cob (for firewood, as is done in rural México). To outsiders, Vietnam may be a surprising source of innovation—but throughout Vietnam's history, adaptability and flexibility have been the underlying factors in overcoming seemingly impossible odds just to even exist.

It's this practical spirit that the Vietnamese seem to have embodied in their everyday lives that allows them to stack, strap, or slide seemingly impossible items onto the backs of their motorbikes and then take off. It should come as no surprise, then, that Vietnamese find clever ways around barriers and other obstacles—as they have always done in the past.

In February 2017, Ho Chi Minh City launched a campaign to "take back the sidewalks," which prompted the destruction of anything that obstructed a sidewalk, including walls, flower beds, house and ATM steps, and even small, free-standing structures. The deputy chairman of District 1, Đoàn Ngọc Hải, made a public promise to show how committed the city was to emulating Singapore: "If we can't take back the sidewalks, I pledge to resign," he said, according to the *VnExpress*.[3] This style of sidewalk reclamation seemed to be gaining steam, and similar efforts were underway in Hanoi as well. However, by May, Đoàn had been barred from leading the campaign by District 1's Party Committee and People's Committee, according to *Tuoi Tre News*.[4] And the sidewalks had returned to their natural state.

In June, he was brought back to continue his campaign, and in August, Đoàn asked for carte blanche to fully tackle the sidewalk issue.[5] Alas, it wasn't meant to be: in January 2018, true to his word, Đoàn offered his resignation[6] before withdrawing it in May after encouragement to stay on.[7] (Despite the clean up efforts, some might say the sidewalks are even worse off now than they were before in terms of safety.[8]) One community that had been hit particularly hard by the campaign was Vietnam's famed street vendors, who sell everything from food to trinkets and more. After their sidewalk spots were taken away, the vendors were forced to improvise, according to a video produced by the *VnExpress*.[9] In one instance, a vendor was "walking her fish," since she was not allowed to sit on the side of the road to sell it. In another example, an old bus was converted into a makeshift restaurant for customers to board and eat bún chả. Since stalls were not allowed, vendors hung their goods from trees or sold iced tea from their cars. In perhaps the best example, footage of a man grilling pork on a roof was shown, while presumably moments later, the final product was placed in a bucket and lowered onto the sidewalk level to serve. If there is a loophole, chances are that Vietnamese will find it and exploit it—such is human nature.

But these kinds of unintended consequences are nothing new in Vietnam. In April 1902, Hanoi, then capital of French Indochina, launched "the Great Rat Hunt," with mixed results.[10] At the time, the concern of the French administration was the potential threat of bubonic plague and its carriers—rats and fleas—on *le quartier européen*.

In response to the growing numbers of vermin, the French recruited the Vietnamese to eliminate rats in the sewers and set their wages based on the number of rats killed. On some days, the Vietnamese hunters produced over twenty thousand dead rats originating from Hanoi's sewers. By July, the native rat hunters were unhappy with their wages, and after work stoppages and slowdowns, they received an increase in fees: from one to two cents per rat. In 1904, the prevailing rate for a dead rat in Hanoi was four cents, thanks to additional early collective bargaining techniques.

Until this point, the French had used only local state workers, but with the rat problem persisting, they opened up the hunt: anyone bringing in a rat tail could collect a bounty of one cent. (Bringing in the entire body of a rat would have been too complicated and unsightly.)

As the French publicized this new reward program, rat tails came flooding in, to the delight of French authorities—while sightings of rats without tails in Hanoi increased. Eventually, the authorities realized that "less-than-honest but quite resourceful characters"[11] were catching rats, cutting off their tails, and releasing them. Even worse, health inspectors detected "more enterprising but equally deceptive individuals"[12] growing rats on farms on the outskirts of the city. The *dératisation* campaign had inadvertently incentivized rat farming, and, in the face of fraudulent schemes buoyed by entrepreneurial spirits, the hunt came to an end.[13]

Fast-forwarding several decades, Vietnamese ingenuity shone among its people once again as Vietnam's government and economy transitioned in 1975. In *Vietnam: Talking to the People*, documentarian Jon Alpert took a fascinating (and at times heart-breaking) look at Vietnam in 1984, as a follow-up to the 1977 release of *Vietnam: Picking Up the Pieces.* When Alpert revisited Vietnam in 1984, the country was still in its Thời Bao Cấp (subsidy economy) period, before the start of Đổi Mới in 1986. After the reunification of Vietnam in 1975, "Amerasians,"[14] or the children of American soldiers and Vietnamese women—of which there were as few as twenty thousand[15] and as many as three hundred thousand in total,[16] though the exact figure is widely disputed—and functionary and military remnants of the Republic of Vietnam (South Vietnam) were in orphanages and reeducation camps, respectively.

During this period in Vietnam's history, society was being transformed yet again under the guiding ideology of its political leaders. Yet black markets were ubiquitous in Hanoi and Ho Chi Minh City: you could buy whatever you wanted—if you could afford it. Levi's jeans, radios, and even counterfeit Coca-Cola were all available for purchase, but those who didn't have the means had to improvise with the resources they had.

In one segment of the film, Alpert shows gas stations that were closed due to the lack of gasoline. When a shipment of gas does come in, queues begin to form, and customers purchase only the bare minimum amount of gas needed to get to their next destination. In the next frame, Alpert shows a strange-looking bus and narrates: "Creative Vietnamese have invented a new way to run their vehicles." Alpert proceeds to shout at a man dumping a bag of something into a chute affixed to the side of the bus while standing on top of the clearly modified bus: "What's he putting in there?" After asking a second time, Alpert exclaims, "Charcoal?" In the following shot, Alpert asks, "So you mean this motor runs without gasoline?" The driver eventually proceeds to start the engine, and the final shot of the segment shows the bus pulling away with a load of passengers while Alpert says, "A ride on the charcoal bus costs five cents…" Incredible.

While the Vietnamese mind-set has shifted from a local to a more global orientation, the innate qualities of resilience, improvisation, drive, and entrepreneurship have remained steadfast. Maintaining the balance between short-term rewards and long-term value generation will be a challenge, but it may just be a matter of redirecting focus, efforts, and investments because an industrious work ethic is already largely present. It's this work ethic that led to the constant rebuilding of the Hồ Chí Minh Trail by 230,000 teenagers, many of them volunteers and more than half of them women,[17] with shovels and water buffaloes—often without the use of heavy machinery—after daily sorties during the Second Indochina War (Vietnam War).

It's this same kind of work ethic and drive that led *New York Times* columnist Nicholas Kristof to identify Nguyễn Thị Tây of Long An as the world's 2014 Graduate of the Year.[18]

Nguyễn, then twenty years old, was training to become an English teacher and was slated to become the first person from her village to graduate from college. In his profile of Nguyễn, Kristof explained how she fainted three times at college—because she was starving herself to afford her tuition. The eighth of nine children, she had overcome numerous other challenges growing up in the Mekong Delta, including her mother's demands that she drop out to become a live-in maid in Ho Chi Minh City. In fact, her mother was so adamant about Nguyễn dropping out that she burned Nguyễn's schoolbooks in an attempt to force her to drop out in eighth grade. Yet, Nguyễn persisted: she borrowed books and continued to perform well. Her parents burned her books again in the twelfth grade, and right before she had an exam (that she had secretly studied for), they told her that failure was the desirable outcome. Nguyễn still aced the exam.

Amazingly, Nguyễn persuaded her older brother to study as a mechanic after years of being a laborer. Then she persuaded her younger brother to follow in her footsteps and enroll in university. Nguyễn's parents, seeing that her income potential was now the highest in the family, eventually had a change of heart. As Kristof points out in another extraordinary profile[19] of a student, Abdisamad Adan from Somaliland, "Talent is universal, but opportunity is not."

More recently, Hanoian Trang Tuyết Ngà, cofounder and head of marketing, Medical Technology and Transfer Service, was recognized as one of the Schwab Foundation's Social Entrepreneurs of the Year 2017 and profiled by the WEF.[20] In an interview, Trang outlined her story:

> I'm just a regular girl, born and brought up in post-war Hanoi. My parents were running a small restaurant and things were not always easy for us. I always liked to study[,] but I was not able to go to the schools I wanted because my family could not afford them. It forced me to start working early, which I did in Hanoi's Old Quarter, where I mastered my English talking to tourists. English-speaking Vietnamese people were hard to find at that time.

Trang's comments highlight the typical thinking of some high achievers in Vietnam—this is the modesty that enables other, less-qualified individuals to be the loudest voices and to take advantage of voids that exist due to cultural aspects of humility.

The fruits of innovation are not always positive for all. A 2017 post[21] on *Medium* highlighted one Vietnamese scammer who was reportedly earning USD $80,000 per month via a virus-removal app scam, and Vietnamese IT researchers were among the first to fool the Apple iPhone X's face recognition security measures[22] using a "mask made with a 3D printer, silicone, and paper tape."

In this context, the irony is that the same driver of innovation—need—that is used to cheat is also used to find a workaround for a lack of resources or approval. It might sound strange that innovation can occur in a socialist republic ruled by a communist party—the de facto, sole political option. Yet innovating in pragmatic ways is exactly what the Vietnamese have been doing in order to survive—and to an extent, policy makers too, since 1986 with Đổi Mới.[23] As we'll see in the next section, foreign allies have helped along the way and will continue to contribute to Vietnam's success as the country seeks to move up the value chain.

LESSONS LEARNED

Many stakeholders—local and foreign—believe in Vietnam's potential. But the country still has a long way to go toward fully utilizing its natural and developed strengths—something we'll cover in chapter 8. However, with international cooperation and coordination, Vietnam's journey into the future can be supported and accelerated. Although the public sector often lags behind the private sector, it has the potential to develop policies for and with the people. By taking the best practices (not "copying and pasting" but "learning from other paths" or "borrowing") from Finland,

Japan, and even its former enemy, the United States, and customizing them for Vietnam's needs, a clearer path for Vietnam's full potential emerges.

But first, the Vietnamese need to thoroughly understand their needs in order to design appropriate mechanisms that will maximize benefits—and policy makers need to understand the people's future needs as well. This means identifying challenges in Vietnam now and in the future—notably the lack of trust and transparency—to fully develop the social and economic dimensions of Vietnamese society.

At one UNDP event held in The Hanoi Club Hotel in June 2016, the focus was on child labor and its effects on the community, the workplace, and the marketplace as part of the Sustainable Development Goals (SDG) promotion. At the event, participants were separated into three groups during breakout sessions and reconvened to share positive and negative examples of Vietnamese companies impacting the three realms.

Each group nominated a presenter, usually a younger Vietnamese female (a student or recent college graduate) who took mostly progressive stances when it came to environmental, social, and governmental issues. In a surprising role reversal, the young people at the front of the room were lecturing the older people in the audience about conservation, preserving the environment, and being socially responsible. It was a moment to be cherished as the younger generation temporarily "flexed its muscles," potentially revealing the new mind-set yet to envelop a future Vietnam.

Moments like this playing out across the nation will certainly influence the direction of Vietnam in the future. In the next ten to fifteen years, Vietnamese youth will play a critical role as the country grapples with its increasingly newfound confidence, going from a "poor and small country"[24] to "catching up with" other countries or even surpassing its own economic goals. Confidence (and more importantly, courage) is a key term, as Vietnamese people, especially those in the central region, are notoriously shy. If Vietnamese people can tap into the same streak of confidence that enables them to stand in front of a crowd and sing their hearts out, they will be able transform their anxieties into excitement and deepen their current repertoire of experiences as they "go beyond the village gates."

In today's Vietnam, the most forward-thinking leaders wish to inspire value creation, the boosting of entrepreneurial capabilities of young people, and the garnering of a stronger entrepreneurial spirit for the country. In part, success in these areas will require a mind-set shift, a way of not only thinking differently, but acting differently. Calling something innovative doesn't mean it is innovative. Thus, each community event is an opportunity for those on the front lines of building and shaping ecosystems to share ideas, failures, and successes with one another—and to build support for new initiatives. Overall, inclusive and collaborative events are good steps toward cohesively connecting key individuals and organizations, and they will hopefully lay down the groundwork for increased communication and cooperation across Vietnam's regions and in Southeast Asia in general.

Within the Vietnamese context,[25] at the center of the enterprise ecosystem lie the entrepreneurs, who need the infrastructure (telecommunications, talent pool, and other tools); followed by finance (or sales); an inclusive culture; and supporting elements such as coaches and mentors, with the foundational element being the marketplace itself. In this model, universities can be used as a catalyst to develop human resources—but improving productivity requires a holistic approach from stakeholders with beneficiaries in mind.

Thus, policy and infrastructure development should be a priority for ecosystem developers—by providing services and supporting enterprises, including finance in the form of grants and other soft support such as promoting ways of "thinking outside the box." All these efforts are to build trust and improve the current culture (organizational, business, market, etc.), which means focusing on changing mind-sets in order to build a sound national innovation ecosystem.

A nascent ecosystem such as Vietnam's needs both innovation and entrepreneurship education[26] in order to foster the creation of high-growth and innovative companies with a global outlook. Competition will increase regionally with freer movement of skilled labor within the ASEAN Economic Community and globally, with reduced barriers for foreign goods to enter the Vietnamese market via free-trade agreements. Thus, any Vietnamese company fully and fairly competing in the private sector that chooses to keep the status quo—whether formally or by inaction—will stagnate, or worse, die off. Copying existing models can be valuable, especially in order to initially master a skill or craft, but over the long term, it is not nearly as valuable as new ideas that lead to the creation of value for a large number of customers or stakeholders—and not at the expense of others (i.e., nondisruptive creation).[27] High-growth companies are innovative, and innovation requires changing from the status quo—there is no getting around this fact.

The collective output and secondary effects of such companies can transform an economy, as has been the case elsewhere in the region. Economies such as South Korea's or Japan's provide a road map for how a developing country can turn itself into a global leader in productivity and quality. In the 1950s, Japan's manufacturing and exporting structure was similar to Vietnam's current economic state. However, Japan developed into a high-income country and by the 1970s had become a leading industrialized country. Similarly, South Korea, Vietnam's largest foreign investor, went from being one of the world's poorest countries and war torn in the 1960s to the eleventh-largest economy in the world by 1995, despite having almost no natural resources and experiencing overpopulation. (South Korea consistently tops Bloomberg's Innovation Index,[28] which ranks the fifty most innovative countries in the world. Both South Korea and Vietnam have agreed to increase bilateral trade to USD $100 billion by 2020—a more than 50 percent increase from the 2017 total.)[29]

Sony, LG, Toyota, Hyundai, and Samsung are all prime examples of innovative companies that have emerged as a result of necessary investments in high technology, complementary skills, and making long-term choices. Vietnam can draw lessons from both other countries in the region and from those at the top of global rankings. For this strategy, there can be several approaches: pick an industry where Vietnam might become a top global player, or solve national issues—that is, not focusing on Global Innovation Index advancement, but instead tackling pollution. Everyone deserves clean and safe foods—a more relevant goal, in terms of priorities, than a key performance indicator (KPI) such as the number of patents filed per capita.

In order to further improve living standards in Vietnam and to attain higher KPIs, intellectual investments must be made in order to change mind-sets. One way to accomplish such change is to implement reforms in the primary schools (i.e., planting seeds for future generations)—again, taking the best from Western and Eastern approaches and localizing them. Vietnam's unique system requires the government to take a primary role in changing mind-sets, thereby changing an entire generation.

Vietnamese ministries that want to address gaps and shortcomings in Vietnam's human capital capacities should focus on proposals for education—that is, kindergarten or preschool—because Vietnam requires a change in culture and approach to innovation, changing how to think at the deepest level to address critical issues, ideally in the form of prevention. Especially in this realm, Vietnam can learn from the experiences of other countries as it tries new approaches.

Vietnam also needs to undertake new kinds of reforms, especially beyond the standard economic variety. This means prioritizing objectiveness, honesty, transparency, and integrity at all levels in order to ensure that Vietnamese society has good role models and education models enabled by excellent policies that are holistic—and not focused on personal benefits. Ultimately, Vietnam's competitiveness tomorrow is determined by the Vietnamese education system today.

Diving deeper into the research side, researchers' independence is critical, as is their competency (and the competency of human resources in general), which is why focusing on capacity building is important. This can take the form of executive training and the "training of trainers"—to build the people's capacity in order to ensure Vietnamese human resources are developed, thereby increasing productivity. Another area ripe for improvement is science and technology innovation results—there is a major disconnect between research output and commercialization here. Therefore, there needs to be a distinction between basic research and applied research; Vietnam has a lot of "thinkers," but it also needs many "doers." That means the Vietnamese need to experience more failures while seeking success; the challenges ahead present a variety of ways "to go forward" (and capture opportunities along the way), so to speak.

At Techfest Vietnam 2017, a government-sponsored ecosystem forum in Hanoi, Vietnamese American Uber Chief Technology Officer (CTO) Thuan Pham shared his approach to confronting failure: "There is nothing worse than a slow failure…if you are going to fail, fail pretty fast, learn very quickly, and then get back up and move forward and make other mistakes. Don't make the same mistakes, make other mistakes and eventually you will turn all that experience and battle scar that allow you to get better and better to move forward."

Pham wrapped up his remarks with "Be fearless…moving forward into the future." Great advice for anyone, but much easier said than done: going forward, the stakes are incredibly high and directly impact every facet of life in Vietnam. For example, within a given paradigm, the old ways (traditions and systems) and their benefits and limitations are better known and understood. Looking ahead, when including stakeholders and beneficiaries, no one really knows how proposed new ways (innovation and openness) will be implemented, and with what results or outputs. In other words, there is no guarantee that speed bumps and roadblocks won't appear along the way.

Therefore, everyone—or as many people as possible—must understand the vision and then collectively try to realize it. (There needs to be a vision in the first place, though.) One approach is to show the best practices—for example, importing success stories from Singapore or bringing Vietnamese people to places such as Finland to see what is possible and spur their imagination. Most importantly, people should be at the center of every policy and innovation—that is, treat people in society with dignity and respect, no matter their backgrounds. This attitude raises the question, How can stakeholders and policy makers maximize the national benefits for Vietnamese society?

Thus, policy makers must always consider national benefits for Vietnamese people—including asking, What are the benefits of Policy Y for the Vietnamese startup community? What is the expected outcome, and what is the output objective? Or what is the benefit of Policy X for the entrepreneurship and innovation community? This is why policy makers must consistently place national benefits at the highest priority within the Vietnamese legislative environment.

Ultimately, Vietnamese leaders will have to choose between boosting productivity and possibly reverting to protectionist policies in an attempt to prop up domestic industries. Specifically, policy makers in Vietnam's Ministry of Science and Technology (MOST) are facing two major challenges: (1) how to spur additional innovation based on technologies and innovative intellectual properties, and (2) how to better utilize university networks throughout the country.

Foremost, these policy makers' formal objectives are creating jobs through spinoffs, creating revenue for the state budget, and bringing value to society. But there is a disconnect—in other words, how can they transfer knowledge from the universities to industries? Granted, Vietnam is not the only nation that has commercialization difficulties in its higher education system, but any holistic approach should include ministries that touch the fringes of aligned efforts to promote a unified vision to mobilize and work together—that is, to line up ministries on one assignment. For example, the Ministry of Education and Training (MOET) is in charge of training in universities and education, whereas the MOST is in charge of research activities. Perhaps there should be a Ministry of Higher Education and Research to answer the underlying question, How do we encourage research and development in universities? (And what do we do with it afterward?[30])

For now, the established role of universities is training, research, and outreach to society—although not all universities in Vietnam realize their mission; some only focus on training. Thus, they need to bring research and development results into industry—some of which has been sponsored by foreign research grants—by commercializing it. Scientists, engineers, and technologists can collaborate toward these mutually beneficial efforts—even across borders, cultures, and fields—to accelerate achieving a prosperous Vietnam driven by sustainable, inclusive growth.

Above all, there's a lot that can be accomplished between countries that are seemingly different but share a common anchor, such as believing in Vietnam and the Vietnamese people. Friends can be supportive, but that support can be shown in different ways. Sometimes friends tell each other uncomfortable truths on the basis of trust, mutual respect, and effective communication. For example, this section is almost entirely the synthesis of conversations with Vietnamese government officials in Hanoi—not your author's directives.[31] Other times, the best thing a friend can do is to reassure. South Korean coach Park Hang-Seo, who led the Vietnamese football team[32] to historic victories in the AFC U23 Championship series before losing the final match in 2018, shared that his "main job is to make sure the Vietnamese players believe in themselves, because they are actually as good as big teams like Japan and South Korea."[33] Perhaps that's one of the most interesting lessons learned in Vietnam: the greatest struggle for progress, change, and achievement is internal, as we are constrained by our own perceived and self-imposed limitations, such as fear of failure.

Sometimes Vietnam's future path is hard to see clearly, especially when one is sorting through contradictions in trends and observations in Vietnam, juxtaposing innovation and tradition, contrasting macroeconomic trends with microeconomic opportunities, and looking forward to the promise of the future while remembering the legacy of its past. Life in Vietnam as an outsider entails squaring what you are told with what you see and what you eventually discover. What is clear, however, is that the Vietnamese people have a bright future ahead of them, especially if they are to be guided by an inspirational, aspirational, and multigenerational national vision fully embraced by all levels of the country's public sector. This should include a comprehensive and grand vision for Vietnam's future role on the global stage as the world becomes increasingly interconnected by technologies, relationships, and business. In the next chapter, we will look at how the oft-repeated African proverb in Vietnam, "If you want to go fast, go alone. If you want to go far, go together" applies to Vietnamese businesses on the front lines of "going global."

CHAPTER 5

CATALYZING GROWTH IN VIETNAM

ONE OF THE MANY FUNDAMENTAL QUESTIONS for a startup with initial success in Vietnam is, Should we fully focus on the local market or expand into the region and beyond? Within Southeast Asia, Vietnamese consumers are unique. As mentioned in chapter 3, the deeper you go into Vietnam, the harder it can be to go regional because of the breadth and differences in consumer preferences and behaviors across Vietnam. For example, Yamaha Motors Vietnam only launched its first dedicated model for Vietnam's female riders, the Nozza Grande, in 2014, even though it entered the market in early 1998,[1] because it took time to deeply understand Vietnamese consumers. After changing its website to a flat design the year before—an innovative approach to web design—the feedback from users was that the site was difficult to navigate, as Vietnamese users expected the entire site content on one page in an endless-scrolling fashion à la 1990s web design.

Thus, it can be challenging to design with Vietnamese users in mind when user expectations differ from global or regional norms, but this gap will decrease in the future as more Vietnamese consumers are exposed to more digital products and services—and when the resources to build great companies and access to mentors and experienced operators become more widely available.

Monk's Hill Ventures, a Southeast Asian venture capital firm based in Singapore, officially expanded into Vietnam in 2017 with its first local investment in OhmniLabs Robotics, a California-based startup with ties to Vietnam. This inaugural investment was followed up by the early 2018 announcement of a USD $3.2 million pre-A funding round led by Monk's Hill Ventures for English Language Speech Assistant (ELSA), an AI-powered English-accent improvement app cofounded by Vũ Văn in 2015.[2]

Justin Nguyen, Monk's Hill Ventures' operating adviser for Vietnam, who moved back to Vietnam in 2016, is specifically targeting companies with the potential to become valued at USD $1 billion or more as part of the firm's strategy for producing "Southeast Asia Globals," or companies that dominate their respective domestic markets. Nguyen explains what he sees in Vietnam in his own words:

> I came back to the country of my birth because I see the kind of vibrancy here that reminds me of my days in Silicon Valley. I believe Vietnam is ready to burst onto the international scene as the next technology hub—and so does Monk's Hill Ventures. Just look around. Vietnam has all [the] ingredients necessary to create international tech companies: youth, ambition, education, excellence, government support, a thriving expat community—and its secret sauce: a large Vietnamese diaspora returning to kickstart the tech revolution. It's mesmerizing. All you need to do is walk the streets and you'll see the same thing: a youthful, vibrant country filled with startups, meet ups, and entrepreneurs—locals, expats, returnees—cross-pollinating ideas, with ambitions of changing the world.

While the number of returning and foreign investors and entrepreneurs has increased in recent years, homegrown firms have long believed in and capitalized on Vietnam's economic growth. FPT, mentioned in the previous chapter, has also invested in building one version of a global future in Vietnam. In 2016, FPT teamed up with Dragon Capital, Hanwa Securities, and Bank for Investment and Development of Vietnam (BIDV) to form VIISA, or Vietnam Innovative Startup Accelerator, in Ho Chi Minh City. Led by Singaporean Adrian Tan (formerly of Joyful Frog Digital Incubator) for two years during three batches, and armed with a funding commitment of USD $6 million, the accelerator aims to produce global startups from Vietnam. According to Tan:

> With a fast-growing economy, talented technical talent and a returning [diaspora], we believe that Vietnam is poised to develop startup companies with [a] USD $100M market cap in the region. However, being [a] young country with [about half] under [35] years old, the tech ecosystem--startups, ideas, investors are still in a nascent stage, and need time to develop venture-fundable businesses.
>
> VIISA aims to plug the gap to be the catalyst for acceleration. As a tech accelerator and USD $6 [million] seed stage fund, we aim to invest in over 100 startups over the next five years. VIISA aims to run three batches of 10 startups each year. Each batch lasts four months. We do this with a USD $15,000 cash injection to each company. Should an investor commit to invest in our startup, we have the capacity to follow on and double down up to USD $200,000 each. VIISA also helps connect our startups with our extensive investor network.... Their experience investing in companies like Go-Jek will help [Vietnam–based startups] think about expansion from day one.

> Southeast Asia is an interesting market of more than 650 million people. However, it is also very fragmented, with different intricacies in each market. By taking a regional approach, VIISA will be able to help capitalize on social capital and economies of scale by helping each company expand rapidly across the region. For startups, it could mean finding the most efficient approach of extending runway for product-market fit. For example, startups could incorporate in Singapore, hire a development team in Saigon and business consultants in Kuala Lumpur for cost savings.

For foreign investors in Vietnam-based startups, one current way to mitigate risk is to require company incorporation in Singapore—usually where fellow coinvestors are based and a mere two-hour flight from Ho Chi Minh City, the universally recognized economic growth hub of the country. This arrangement allows a company's intellectual property to be "parked" in Singapore—which has a well-defined legal environment—while the company takes advantage of the lower cost of living in Vietnam for developers and other operational staff. However, this standard mode of investing in a startup in Vietnam raises the question, When does a Vietnamese startup cease to become a Vietnamese startup?

For now, Singapore-based investors seem to be leading the way in terms of a clear model for value creation and capture for Vietnamese founders executing startups. The relationship between Singaporean investors and Vietnamese startups is strong, with good reason—Singapore has largely driven the transformation of venture capital and high-growth entrepreneurship in Southeast Asia and has long held the affection of Vietnamese policy makers at the national and city levels. In turn, Singapore-based investors have been willing to reciprocate this interest and convert it into action in Vietnam.

In 2015, Douglas Abrams, CEO of Expara Ventures, visited Vietnam for the first time to attend Techfest, an event coorganized by the National

Agency for Technology, Entrepreneurship, and Commercialization Development (NATEC), a body of Vietnam's MOST.[3]

Expara Ventures, which was part of a group of Singaporean investors and incubators including Golden Gate Ventures, KK Fund, and JFDI, participated in the inaugural event held at Vietnam National University in Hanoi. The three-day event in May was the largest of its kind in Vietnam at the time and sought to bridge the gap between Vietnam and the region while providing a national platform to promote the best startups and entrepreneurs in Vietnam.

According to Abrams, an American-born investor who entered the Singaporean market in 2000 and Thailand in 2004, "Specifically in Vietnam, I see many promising young entrepreneurs, many with strong technology skills, active universities and research institutions, increasing use of internet, smart phones, social media and e-commerce, a relatively large domestic market and strong government support as factors which indicate a fast-growing market opportunity."

For the remainder of 2015, Abrams returned to Vietnam for four additional visits to create Expara Vietnam in Ho Chi Minh City, and launched the CLAS Expara Startup Accelerator with Microsoft Vietnam. In 2016, the accelerator expanded into Da Nang, where it ran a simultaneous batch with Ho Chi Minh City. Expara Ventures III (EV III)—a fund that focuses on Southeast Asia—invests USD $10,000 into each startup with up to USD $500,000 in additional follow-on funding. The Vietnamese startup ecosystem is still in its early days, but Vietnamese startups entering new markets in Southeast Asia are not unheard of—and may become the norm as the global mind-set shift, referenced in chapter 4, propagates.

One such startup aiming to go regional is OnOnPay,[4] a mobile top-up service. In 2015—the year it was founded by Hanoian Bùi Sỹ Phong—OnOnPay received six-figure funding from Captii Ventures, marking the fund's first deal in Vietnam; shortly thereafter, the startup started publicizing its plans to expand into Malaysia and Thailand. According to Bùi, "From OnOnPay's perspective, even the startup scene in Vietnam, especially in Hanoi is to be improved, in all three dimensions: founders' quality, community support, and funding, but it's already extremely helpful for us to have [the local community's] support since the beginning of OnOnPay; without that timely push, we cannot make it like today."

In 2016, OnOnPay raised USD $800,000 in Series A funding led by Gobi Partners. This was Gobi Partners's second deal in Vietnam, and according to Victor Chua, then vice president of the firm and now managing partner at Vynn Capital:

> Vietnam is an essential part of Southeast Asia and might eventually be the main engineering tech hub for the region. Being technically savvy means that Vietnam has its edge relative to other markets. As part of a fragmented region of 10 countries, Vietnam can help counterparts from China, Japan, Korea, and even the United States in building a platform that is localized enough for local consumption but also scalable enough to grow exponentially...It is very important for Vietnamese startups to learn about [the] cultures of other markets and communities if success is what they are looking for. Localization is as important as scalability.

Perhaps the best current example of a Vietnamese company that went beyond Vietnam is Topica Edtech Group,[5] which was founded in 2007 and now operates in five countries: the Philippines, Thailand, Indonesia, and Singapore (besides Vietnam). Topica provides online courses for higher education, English speech tutoring matching, and a platform for massive online open courses (MOOCs), and it has a partnership with Coursera, an online course platform based in Mountain View, California. However, before expanding to 1,400 full-time staff and 2,000 instructors, Topica had to overcome some initial challenges in Vietnam. At a 2015 event, Nguyễn Khôi, then a product director at the company,[6] noted that the first step for

Topica was to train people in Vietnam how to use computers, even before educating them to use their service.

In 2011, Topica deepened its entrepreneurial development offering and launched the TFI, which alternates its batches between Hanoi and Ho Chi Minh City. The Global Founder Institute Network, based in Silicon Valley, comprises over 150 chapters across more than sixty countries, trying to "globalize Silicon Valley" by helping entrepreneurs launch companies through its program. Through a combination of a fourteen-week curriculum, mentorship, and network building, participants accelerate the success of their nascent startups. By 2016, TFI had expanded into Bangkok from Vietnam and was considered a top-five accelerator in the region by technology media, having graduated sixty startups that raised USD $20 million in total, resulting in an aggregate valuation of USD $100 million.

As the perception of online education in Vietnam and Asia changes, Topica Edtech Group may be one of the first in a new wave of Vietnamese startups to expand beyond Southeast Asia as a result of positive interest in the vertical. At the same time, the organization will help seed the next generation of founders in Hanoi, Ho Chi Minh City, and Bangkok via its efforts with the TFI. However, education by itself is just theory—it requires practice in order to advance ideas, concepts, and solutions in the real world; relationships can help make the founder journey smoother. As we'll see in the next section, networks have played a major role in fostering innovation, action, and growth in Vietnam.

GLOBAL CONNECTIONS, GLOBAL OPPORTUNITIES

The ASEAN Economic Community (AEC), formed at the end of 2015, was a step toward the integration of the region. In 2018, all tariffs on goods bought from ASEAN countries were reduced to zero[7]—further cutting into state revenue—and specialized workers could freely move between the member states. Theoretically, engineers, accountants, dentists, tourism professionals, architects, surveyors, nurses, and doctors will be able to move and work more freely across ASEAN in a "highly integrated and cohesive economy"[8] by 2025. However, there aren't any obvious safeguards to prevent all the benefits of the AEC from going to countries such as Thailand, Indonesia, and Malaysia—that is, more developed economies. Possibly the only way that the AEC can reach harmony is through specialization, which requires communication among its members to determine what industries to invest in and develop. Thus, there are cooperation and competition elements to ASEAN as integration is realized.

One public-sector approach toward strengthening the region's business environment has been the ADB's Mekong Business Initiative (MBI), which covers Cambodia, Laos, Myanmar, and Vietnam (CLMV). The USD $10.5 million program, funded partly by Australia's Department of Foreign Affairs and Trade (DFAT), has been active in CLMV since 2015, with a head office in Hanoi. Currently, the MBI, in coordination with Destination Mekong and supported by DFAT, the ADB, and Mekong Tourism, operates Mekong Innovative Startups Tourism (MIST), which launched in 2016 and offers startup accelerator and market access program services in CLMV plus Thailand. In short, MIST has offerings for innovative startups in tourism and tech travel and SMEs interested in expanding in the region, which will continue into 2019.[9]

Among the MBI's aims is to incentivize business formalization, help small and medium-sized enterprises (SMEs) to grow and integrate into global supply chains, and to empower women-led businesses. Phan Vinh Quang, former deputy project director at the MBI, shares his personal views:

> Vietnam is on a high-growth path but the challenges are by no [means] insignificant. Vietnam is transforming and generating a lot of opportunities to tap into new markets, new production base, and tech talents. [While] policies remain a challenge, they have been improving and the leadership is committed to making [it] easier to do business in Vietnam. There [has] been a lot more dialogue and the society has become more open and [demands] more transparency…
>
> Changes and transformation are not easy especially when [these] kinds of changes may counter some of the old [beliefs]. The transformation and changes in [Vietnam during] the last three decades is good 'food for thought' for those who want to escape poverty and [central] planning to migrate to [a] market economy in a steady, gradual and peaceful way.

While Vietnam's prospects are bright (as the largest economy in the CLMV group), the reality is that CLMV are at different stages of development—and will experience different development arcs due to population variety (ranging from slightly less than seven million to almost one hundred million), different-sized economies (ranging from USD $12 billion to USD $238 billion), and different systems of government (ranging from a kingdom to a people's democratic republic). However, they are all lower-middle-income countries, and all receive generalized system of preference (GSP) benefits whereby exports are subject to zero duties or lesser duties. Although Vietnam has built up some of its domestic industries, notably textiles and apparel as well as electronic assembly, it is unclear what kinds of industries will develop in the CLM of CLMV as foreign investors continue to move into these economies. (The CLMV group was identified by the McKinsey Global Institute as "recent outperformers", that is, "growing at least 5.0 percent annually over the past 20 years."[10])

Another initiative targeting developing innovation ecosystems in the Mekong was Technology Innovation Generation and Entrepreneurship Resources (TIGERS@Mekong), a US State Department–funded public-private alliance that sought to create a forum for emerging enterprises from the Lower Mekong (CLMV + Thailand) and concluded in September 2017. Launched at the East Asia Summit (EAS) in 2012 under the Connect Mekong framework, TIGERS@Mekong created the Mekong Entrepreneurship Ecosystem Summit (MEES) for the first time in 2015, when it was held in Ho Chi Minh City. Over two days, entrepreneurs, ecosystem builders, and investors from the Lower Mekong descended upon Ho Chi Minh City to build and maintain connections. In 2016, MEES was held in Yangon, Myanmar, and rebranded into the Mekong Angel Investment Forum (MAIF), with 500 Startups as a cosponsor. In 2017, MAIF was converted into the Mekong Startup Ecosystem Summit 2.0 (MSES) and was held in Vientiane, Laos. These kinds of rotations are necessary to showcase the abilities and challenges of each city's community and national ecosystem. While Vietnam's population is ninety-six million, ASEAN's population is north of six hundred million—and much of it is fragmented across social, economic, and technological categories. Thus, bringing leaders from each ecosystem to collaborate and share solutions will only strengthen the human connections across the region—and globally.

For example, the Vietnam Climate Innovation Center (VCIC), a USD $4.18 million initiative funded by the World Bank (with support from the United Kingdom and Australia) and based in Hanoi, is one of seven Climate Innovation Centers (CIC) in the world—and the only one in Asia (though one is planned for Bangladesh). The other CIC are located in the Caribbean, Ethiopia, Ghana, Morocco, Kenya, and South Africa. The VCIC's mission is to tackle Vietnam's climate challenges head-on by attracting investment for renewable and green projects originating in Vietnam. Specifically, the VCIC "supports entrepreneurs and small enterprises to develop technological innovations and new business models offering commercially viable products and services that foster climate change adaptation & mitigation."

It has five priority areas for Vietnam: energy efficiency, sustainable agriculture, IT, water filtration and management, and renewable energy, and it now has a portfolio of eighteen startups and SMEs that it supports, one-third of which are owned or managed by women. The VCIC's services for startups culminated in a graduation in October 2018.

In September 2017, seven enterprises graduated from VCIC's incubation support program. During the ceremony in Hanoi, Australian diplomat Layton Pike recognized that "[the] group of entrepreneurs who are embracing innovation and who are driving change in Vietnam... [Innovation] is fundamental for increasing productivity and competitiveness, creating new jobs, and for driving economic growth. Difficult problems, like climate change, require new ideas and creative thinking—that is what will generate change."

During the same event, the then British ambassador to Vietnam, Giles Lever, expanded on the VCIC's mission: "In Vietnam, we've been proud to support [the] VCIC concept in the hope that it can develop into the key platform...generating transformational impacts at scale through the transfer of affordable...technologies, disseminating good practice, opening up new market opportunities, and driving commercial potential of Vietnamese businesses."

The overall goal for VCIC and similar efforts is that Vietnam may more easily meet its Paris Agreement commitments. However, the VCIC is not the only publicly funded initiative based in Vietnam; the UNICEF Innovation Lab is based in Ho Chi Minh City at Saigon Hi-Tech Park. Vietnam was chosen to host one of two initial UNICEF Innovation Labs in Southeast Asia after UNICEF's global innovation unit in New York City identified Vietnam as a regional leader with the potential to contribute to the emerging technology community worldwide. American entrepreneur Brian Cotter, who moved to Ho Chi Minh City in 2006 and is the

UNICEF Innovation Lab lead, says, "The velocity of change is increasing. Creativity in entrepreneurship is more and more obvious each year. In prior years, you'd see simple clones of businesses because there were so many greenfield opportunities. While these still exist, entrepreneurs in today's Vietnam must be more creative and be effective operators or they will quickly be out of business. Additionally, I believe that we are seeing a strong move toward greater trust in partnerships and transparency in [business-to-business (B2B)] partnerships."

But it's not just the public sector that is taking notice of Vietnam's potential for new kinds of success, whether by leveraging technology, talent, or time. In addition to public-private alliances, there is the Mekong Business Challenge, which has been active for over ten years in the region. Vietnam and its entrepreneurs do not operate in a vacuum, so it's good to bring together people from different sectors, countries, and industries to build, develop, and maintain regional and global relationships and facilitate knowledge and experience exchange.

In the past few years, Vietnamese entrepreneurs have begun tapping into global networks for mentorship, increased availability of funding, and soft-landing opportunities into other markets. South Korea, Morocco, Thailand, and Finland are some of the first countries Vietnamese entrepreneurs and startups have visited to participate in events, accelerators, or road shows—but local entrepreneurs and community builders are also setting up chapters of regional or global organizations catering to their needs.

Female entrepreneurship promotion has also seen a recent rise, as it was not visible on the local event circuit until 2016. SoGal, an early-stage venture capital (VC) firm focusing on female millennials, hosted a summit in Ho Chi Minh City via its local chapter, SoGal Vietnam. In early 2017, Woomentum,[11] a tech community based in Singapore, launched its inaugural event in Ho Chi Minh City: CrowdFundHer Live showcased several female-led startups in a variety of industries, with a spirit of female empowerment. (For female entrepreneurs starting out, there are also online resources available—offered for free in English—such as Thunderbird for Good's "DreamBuilder: The Women's Business Creator."[12])

In addition, Women's Entrepreneurial Centers of Resources, Education, Access, and Training for Economic Empowerment (WECREATE) was set up in late 2016 in Hanoi in coordination with the Vietnam Women's Entrepreneur Council (VWEC) of the Vietnam Chamber of Commerce and Industry (VCCI), the US State Department, Paz y Desarollo, and Griffin Worx via a public-private partnership. The center provides a space for women entrepreneurs and others to be mentored, develop the necessary skills to build a business, and get access to other resources.

The US embassy in Hanoi offers other support to Vietnamese entrepreneurs, including the Ambassador's Entrepreneurship Challenge (AEC), which focuses on the three major cities of Hanoi, Ho Chi Minh City, and Da Nang. Teams of two to five individuals, consisting of at least 50 percent Vietnamese nationals, submit a social entrepreneurship or startup idea—in English—for the chance to win seed funding and take their concepts to the next level.

Additionally, members of Vietnamese startups have traveled abroad to compete or participate in startup events such as the Global Entrepreneurship Summit (GES) in Morocco (2014), Startup Nations Summit in South Korea (2014), and TechCrunch's Disrupt in San Francisco.

Hanoian Phạm Thu Hà was the first Vietnamese woman to participate in the S Factory, a female-only accelerator part of Startup Chile. Phạm joined the program in 2016, receiving USD $15,000 in seed funding for her startup. Phạm shares more about her experience with the S Factory:

> The S Factory, powered by Start-Up Chile...was such a great experience that I was very honored to be a part of....I found this opportunity intriguing and...decided to move my life to Chile. I became the first and only Vietnamese woman, and one of the only two from Asia, to have joined this female-focused founders program.

> My startup idea was CICADA, the first online peer-to-peer ticket marketplace in Southeast Asia. CICADA helps users to reach out to each other directly without interruption to sell and resell tickets.…I learned a lot of firsthand experience in product design, product development, team management, etc. following the lean startup theory. Apart from that, living in South America was truly a once-in-a-lifetime opportunity. I met incredible, strong women in tech having different backgrounds coming from all over the world in my cohort.…I strongly encourage other Vietnamese women to join this program, because it will help you to learn about yourself, and grow the business with you.
>
> Being a woman seems to be challenging in a lot of different industries because we still have to face sexism in and out of the office. It is thrilling to witness the movement of #metoo or #timesup for all the progress it has made in exposing sexual harassment and abuse. We can't be—and should not be—silent. My real concern, however, is how to make this movement more systematized and effective. [It's the] same with female entrepreneurship in Vietnam: we will always need more support, but we should think thoroughly how to get support and grow the ecosystem in sustainable way[s]. Obviously, this is never [a] one-man job.

Besides Chile, Vietnamese entrepreneurs are also heading to the United States. In 2016, the GES was held at Stanford University, where eight Vietnamese entrepreneurs were in attendance. Among the participants was Đào Xuân Hoàng, founder of Monkey Junior (and Topica Founder Institute alum), an early-childhood education mobile application. In 2014, he left his corporate job to develop Monkey Junior, which teaches children to read at an early age. At the Global Innovation Through Science and Technology (GIST) Tech-I Competition, Đào won the first prize of USD $15,000, beating out over a thousand entrepreneurs and twenty-nine finalists representing 104 emerging markets. Today, Monkey Junior has been installed more than one million times in over a hundred countries.

For Vietnam-based startups keen to raise capital, the options in Southeast Asia are increasing. VC firms such as Singapore-based Golden Gate Ventures have turned their attention to startups in Vietnam, investing in companies such as Appota, a third-party app marketplace and distribution platform, and, more recently, Lozi, a food-ordering startup.

Jeffrey Paine, managing partner at Golden Gate Ventures, sees the unique strengths of Vietnamese startups being their "creativity, engineering, and ability to think out of the box to survive." However, Paine also believes that local government should support the startup community by providing "incentives for risk investors to make early investments into high-growth technology companies." Furthermore, it is important that there are "regulatory changes to make direct investment easier, [including] company and incorporation laws."

According to Paine, Vietnamese startups are ready to go global, "but they need more time and exposure if they are totally local. To shortcut the [process], enlist more mentors and friends who have 'been there, done that.'" When it comes to going abroad, he suggests that Vietnamese entrepreneurs "just be relaxed and make friends. Overall, try to improve your own English language skills, at least [on a] conversational [level]."

Despite clear and recognized technical talent, a lack of English literacy may delay the full development of aspiring Vietnamese coders. Googler Neil Fraser, creator of Blockly and whose wife is Vietnamese, visited Vietnam as a volunteer instructor. In 2013, Fraser's blog made headlines when he revealed how a group of eleventh-grade Vietnamese students could pass parts of Google's interview process without a problem. In fact, a colleague Fraser showed the problem to suggested that it would rank in the top one-third in terms of difficulty during a hypothetical interview process. In 2017, Fraser returned to Vietnam with his family to volunteer teach at a local high school in Da Nang. As he shared on his blog: "There was a notable correlation in the students between English skills and programming skills. The reason became apparent when they searched for documentation. A Google search for 'capitalize string Pascal' returns half a million results (including Pascal's official documentation and Stack Overflow), whereas searching for 'Pascal đổi sang chữ in hoa' reduces the pool to a handful of local blogs. Until machine translation can become completely transparent, English literacy remains an educational force-multiplier."[13]

As English comprehension levels continue to improve, we'll keep seeing additional talents displayed in and from Vietnam—or at least examples that are more easily consumed for non-Vietnamese speakers. The fact remains that English is the language of doing business around the world—but there are other networks to join and leverage as well. Notably, the French government created and promoted the brand La French Tech, which was launched in 2013. In 2016, the La French Tech brand was bestowed upon Vietnam's tech community by then-French prime minister Manuel Valls during a ceremony in Montréal, Canada.

Vietnam is now the first and only officially designated hub in Southeast Asia—La French Tech Viet. This demonstrates that Vietnam is recognized as a suitable location for French startups to develop because of a robust community of entrepreneurs, investors, coders, and leaders. Today, the French Tech network in Vietnam comprises 2,100 members, 120 companies, and five academic partners. It's important to note that the French Tech network is open to all nationalities—it's not just for French passport holders or francophones.

French national Marion Vigot, founder of Ma Belle Box—a lifestyle monthly subscription for Vietnamese women—and member of La French Tech Viet, shares two lessons from her experience in Vietnam:

> Number one is to not start a business again on my own…the reason why is because it's so much harder [being a solo-preneur] than having a partner and it's also lots of responsibility

on you—and only on you—because nobody will ever be taking as many responsibilities as you.

Number two is to not start a business in a country where I can't understand my customers…and that's something that I realized very late in the process. So the thing that happened is that at the beginning we were targeting Vietnamese women who could also speak English. So Vietnamese women who had more like an "international mind." The thing is that we quickly saw that people preferred to see everything in Vietnamese so we switched—slowly—to Vietnamese 100%. Even though some material is still in English and Vietnamese, most of it now is only in Vietnamese. And the fact that all my team is Vietnamese and to call customers and everything is easier to do in Vietnamese, even though I was still doing it in English at the beginning, like the first customers with problems…I was calling them in English, but later on it became someone else doing it in Vietnamese.

Actually, for a couple of…months I had no contact with customers because all of our customers are Vietnamese, and as we switched to a more Vietnamese population, most of them don't speak English or don't understand it well enough…If you don't master the language you're not going to be able to explain whatever you want. All of our communication is in Vietnamese as well, so there's no reason to speak another language…I felt that I missed something in my startup experience, I felt that I missed something which is very important, which is actually to directly be able to speak directly to your customers…and that's also one of the reasons why I'm not going to be in Vietnam anymore because most of the people here I can't understand and I've tried to learn Vietnamese…

> but you can never be a local. It's not like you go to England or in Australia where you can understand. Even if English is not my first language, I can understand everybody [there].

After three years, building up a team of over twenty women, and moving offices four times, Ma Belle Box was acquired in late 2017. Thus, Marion decided to start her next adventure: a road trip across Australia for 2018. As she traverses the Land Down Under, Marion could be a natural ambassador and connector for Australians or Vietnamese Australians curious about modern Vietnam—or she may find a new project to join in an unexpected place. After all, Ma Belle Box "came from the idea that launching the first beauty box in Vietnam would inspire Vietnamese women and help with their beauty routine."[14] No one knows what she'll encounter next on her journey as an entrepreneur, but it is clear is that Vigot is well positioned to connect foreign entrepreneurs and investors into Vietnam based on her experiences.

Overall, fostering the growth and development of global networks and connections enables the strengthening of Vietnam's brand visibility at strategic international events, such as SLUSH, TechCrunch Disrupt, or Web Summit. Attending these international startup events allows Vietnamese teams to see what's out there on the cutting-edge international market and perhaps even gain a serendipitous ally or deliver an off-the-cuff demo to a future stakeholder or potential investor.

So while Vietnamese startups continue to focus on growth and retention for their services and products, they might consider other kinds of network effects inside and outside of Vietnam. As we'll see in the next section, inflows and outflows of capital, talent, and technologies all play vital roles toward strengthening Vietnam's competitive profile in the region and world.

TWO-WAY STREETS

During the Cold War, Vietnam sent its youth to study in places such as then Czechoslovakia, the German Democratic Republic (GDR), and the Soviet Union. Sometimes, the outgoing waves of Vietnamese students had no control over what and where they studied. Some found love in a new country and stayed there to start a new family and life, while others returned to Vietnam and kept to their original plans. As the world changed, Vietnam never stopped sending students abroad—as mentioned in chapter 1, there are currently over 130,000 Vietnamese students studying outside Vietnam.

The graduates who return to Vietnam bring newfound understandings of market economies, new networks, and potential new products and services. Today, the students who return from overseas often experience reverse culture shock. Their colleagues—whether in the public or private sectors—simply do not have the same attitudes about what is possible and what is not.[15] For example, when someone is pitching a new idea, Vietnamese can be quick to point out that it wouldn't work, or someone else would have implemented it already. Moreover, how do you convince a potential customer of a solution if he or she does not acknowledge that a problem or pain point exists?

It's no secret that the best and brightest in a developing country often seek greener pastures, so brain drain is still a risk for Vietnam. However, it may be worthwhile for Vietnamese students to leave for a few years, gain international work experience, and then bring their robust networks back to Vietnam, reconnecting with the local economy.

Thus, the often-touted option of leave or stay is, in a way, a false dichotomy. If they can, Vietnamese innovators and entrepreneurs should leave Vietnam to get international experience in a world-class environment for a year or two in addition to their studies. Then they can return to Vietnam with new relationships from Singapore, Silicon Valley, Berlin, Sydney, or anywhere else. The returning students can take the best elements from

Vietnam and their adopted study or work home, mash them together, and create some magic—or serve as trusted advisers or cultural ambassadors. (Those who have already completed their formal education journeys should seek more travel experiences outside Vietnam, engaging with other cultures and nationalities.)

Until now, Vietnamese startups have entered new markets such as Singapore, Thailand, and Malaysia because of personal access, investor relationships, and media momentum. But Việt Kiều and foreigners can help increase the chances of Vietnamese success—and accelerate expansion plans by sharing knowledge, experience, and best practices honed at an international level.

When Swedish entrepreneur Anders Palm teamed up with his Vietnamese girlfriend, Vũ Uyên, to launch Eat.vn in 2011, they had to figure out how to sign up restaurants to their food delivery service. When the team met with local restaurant owners, Vũ would pitch the concept in Vietnamese while Palm would smile and nod. What finally got the restaurants on board was when they demonstrated the function of the mobile order printer while pitching Eat.vn as a "salesperson" the restaurants wouldn't have to pay. The team would place an order on a laptop at the restaurant. A few seconds later, it would print out on a mobile printer, allowing the restaurant owner to make the connection between a customer doing something on the internet and something of value happening in the physical world. In the first year, Palm and Vũ signed up more than a hundred restaurants. Palm reflected on the early days of Eat.vn:

> To be honest, it is sometimes hard for me to know what is part of our cultures and what are just personality traits, but the biggest difference between me and Uyên has always been that I look more at the long term and she [looks] more at the challenges and opportunities here and now. I do feel that the latter is often the case in Vietnam. We used this to our advantage (at least when not trying to kill each other) when

> Uyên used her drive and flexibility to run day to day operations while I focused on learning what our customers needed and building an e-commerce site with great conversion rates.

Today, Palm and Vũ live together in Gothenburg, Sweden, after selling Eat.vn to VC Corp in 2012 for USD $150,000. Eat.vn, still owned by VC Corp, operates in an intensely competitive space, as evidenced by the withdrawal of Rocket Internet's Food Panda from Vietnam in 2015.

Economically, setting up in Vietnam enables shared benefits for entrepreneurs and developers. Vietnamese American entrepreneur Alan Van Toai, cofounder of Crew Fire, a social media and brand ambassador platform, set up the company's technical team in Vietnam for a fraction of a comparable developer team's cost in the West. In 2016, he described the experience:

> Operating in Vietnam as a bootstrapped startup it gives us tremendous leverage. Our customers are all in the [United States], but because we bootstrapped we never really had the resources and capital of some of our venture-backed contemporaries. So we're able to hire people in Vietnam for a fraction of the cost. We pay our Vietnamese developers extremely competitive salaries for Vietnam—some of them are making up to twice as much as what some of their peers are making at similar Vietnamese companies in terms of monthly salary.

While it may be tricky due to the twelve-hour time-zone difference between the East Coast of the United States and Vietnam, it's manageable, even at scale. Toai suggests, "The best advice that I have for anybody looking to do it is…it really helps to be on the ground in Asia. We were able to meet all of our team members in person and we're going to look forward to doing that. All that in place, I consider us really blessed to have our team [in Vietnam] and we look forward to expanding our operations there."

One aspect of incoming Việt Kiều and foreigners that has often been overlooked is education and training, especially those with ties to the United States. According to an Open Doors report[16] issued by the Institute of International Education (IIE), out of more than 300,000 American students who studied abroad during the 2013–2014 academic year, exactly 1,000 Americans chose Vietnam for their studies, up from 683 the year before. In the 2014–2015 academic year, the number of American students studying in Vietnam dipped slightly to 922. In total, there were only about 2,000 foreigners studying in Vietnam in 2016, according to FPT University.[17]

While there are some university activities such as joint programs in Hanoi between the Paris Institute of Political Studies (Sciences Po) and Vietnam National University, Loyola University Chicago's Semester Abroad program in Ho Chi Minh City,[18] and the State University of New York (SUNY) Brockport Vietnam program in Da Nang,[19] more can and should be done to balance the lopsided flow of students between Vietnam and the world. Simply put, there is no substitute for on-the-ground and direct experience when learning about a country's and people's values, building relationships, and engaging in other cross-cultural experiences. The Vin University project between Vingroup, "a prestigious and reputable conglomerate located in Hanoi, Vietnam," and Cornell University, which "plans to open for the inaugural class of students in Fall 2020," may just be the kind of environment necessary to create these kinds of connections,[20] since there are few better ways than by learning alongside people with varied backgrounds and experiences in a new, unfamiliar environment. Already, one multicultural and multifaceted program in Hanoi is proving just that by getting its participants to tap into their "inner learner."

In 2013, Knowmads Hanoi launched with Team 1, comprising fifteen students from France, Vietnam, Bolivia, and the Netherlands. In September 2018, the program is on its tenth batch of future "change champions," training the 25 participants every Saturday and Sunday for nine weekends. The program is the product of a collaboration between the Center for Sustainable Development Studies Vietnam (CSDS) and Knowmads

Business School Amsterdam; it asks a sliding fee for local and international participants to join a team of approximately fifteen to twenty people.

The program's curriculum has an entrepreneurial focus, even while dispelling the notion that money should be the singular focus for success. Yet Knowmads Hanoi seeks people who can make an impact, specifically English speakers between the ages of twenty and thirty-five who are curious, creative, entrepreneurial, brave, involved, and ready to take action.[21]

In some developing parts of the world, the generation gap is widening (traditional versus modern lifestyles), so programs such as Knowmads Hanoi are essential to complementing the conventional education model (not just in Vietnam but worldwide, as Knowmads Hanoi had sister organizations in Berlin and Seville). Thus, the program helps participants tap into their inner entrepreneur and provides them a framework for making their ideas become reality.

Alumni of the program have shared that Knowmads Hanoi has been a transformative event in their lives; some made friendships that were as important as friendships from high school and/or university. The program builds confidence in its participants, inspires creative thinking, and promotes collaboration—all valuable skills for life in the twenty-first century.

Nederlander Guus Wink, trainer, facilitator, and founder of Knowmads Hanoi shared his thoughts on his experience in Vietnam:

> Young people in [Vietnam] have the keys in their pocket for a bright future. In my opinion it is all about "being able to respond," taking responsibility for yourself. Young people are challenged because of the fast-changing globalizing world they live in, while dealing with expectations from the generation above them. I feel they have to take the time to decide what they think about the world they live in. What are the choices they want to make in their lives? If they are able to take this responsibility, then I think they can build great companies and organizations.

After creating the space for almost sixty change makers to develop professionally and personally, Wink and the original founding team have moved on from Hanoi—but a new core team has taken shape since 2015, including former participants such as Taiwanese American Hailey Chang:

> I've always believed that human society can be built on trust. And I see that in Knowmads Hanoi, a community of learners who seek authenticity, non-judgment, support, mindfulness, and constant growth. From personal development to learning about the interconnectedness of things and how we can take action to create a better world, Knowmads provides a safe space for its participants to thrive and evolve. As Vietnam becomes more and more globally connected, I believe it's paramount for its citizens to be self-aware, to understand their impact on others and in the world, and to take leadership to create positive change on all scales.

Equally important and opportune is the introduction of more foreign college students—whether by exchange or jointly developed programs—to today's Vietnam in order to better prepare future global leaders in business, technology, and politics for tomorrow's ever-changing world, as well as to retire outdated perceptions of Vietnam, especially in the West. Such efforts would not only catalyze economic growth between Vietnam and other markets but personal growth between Vietnamese individuals and other nationalities as well.

Increased access to international resources and networks will help Vietnamese innovators and entrepreneurs to think of going global from day one, with eyes on a larger, reachable prize. Yet Vietnam is still building institutions and infrastructure, so while there has been development and progress, it will take time to see additional results.[22]

CHAPTER 6

THE BEGINNINGS OF A STARTUP NATION

In the twentieth century, whenever the two letters *V* and *C* were combined in that order, the acronym usually referred to the Việt Cộng—the Vietnamese communist political organization known for employing guerilla tactics in Vietnam's jungles and rice paddies. However, talk of VCs today in the streets of Ho Chi Minh City almost always refers to venture capitalists, who have flocked to (or set up in) Vietnam in recent years. According to the Vietnam Chamber of Commerce and Industry, there are more than 50 investment funds active in Vietnam.[1]

Even *Nhân Dân* (*The People*), the official newspaper of the Communist Party of Vietnam (CPV), joined the startup mood when it started 2016 by officially declaring it the Year of the Startup by the government of Vietnam, with an article on January 1, "Startup Spring,"[2] which covered startups and entrepreneurship and discussed improving institutional support to lessen the risk of attempting a startup in Vietnam. Vietnam's government is aiming to transform entrepreneurship in Vietnam via the country's education system, primarily targeting college students,[3] but it may be focusing too much on the "leaves" instead of the "roots" of the tree—that is, at the primary education level, as mentioned in chapter 4.

That doesn't mean that there hasn't been an effort from the public sector to improve the business environment overall—in 2017, more than five thousand administrative procedures were streamlined or cut by the government in an effort to reach the average level of ASEAN-4 countries (Malaysia, Thailand, Singapore, and the Philippines) for competitive capacity and labor productivity.[4] In early 2018, the government went even further when Prime Minister Nguyễn Xuân Phúc promulgated Decree No 08/2018/NĐ-CP, which eliminated 675 out of 1,216 business criteria, or 55 percent of the total business criteria managed by the Ministry of Industry and Trade.[5]

The nationwide Administrative Procedure Cost Index (APCI) 2018, a report by Vietnam's Government Office, revealed that 3,000 enterprises surveyed had to pay on average VNĐ 12.7 million (USD $550) to comply with start-up administrative costs, including customs, land, environment, taxes, investment, business licenses and work permits, and construction.[6] The Communist Party newspaper, *Nhân Dân* (*The People*), sums it up: "The APCI 2018 results are an indication that there remains a lot of room for further improvement in the execution of administrative procedures and the reduction of compliance costs for enterprises."[7] More reforms may be on the way, since in mid-2018 the Ministry of Finance proposed to cut 51.4 percent of total business investment conditions under the ministry's purview.[8]

As of early 2018, Vietnam had slightly fewer than 620,000 enterprises, which contribute to 40 percent of the nation's GDP.[9] Still, challenges remain for private-sector actors, evidenced by one European cofounder declaring to your author in late 2017, "Vietnam is a great place for startups unless you have to deal with the government."

Such publicly shared attitudes toward Vietnam's public sector may make it difficult to entice Việt Kiều or foreigners who are willing and able (i.e., qualified) to take risks by creating or building products or services in Vietnam. These attitudes also influence international perceptions of Vietnamese entrepreneurs looking to launch products and services abroad—that is, emerging from a place where one Indonesian functionary who joined the 132nd Inter-Parliamentary Union in Hanoi in 2015 jokingly described Vietnam's political environment as similar to "Indonesia prior to 1998." Domestically, there are also areas of misunderstanding and miscommunication at work that prevent standardized definitions from taking hold in Hanoi, Ho Chi Minh City, and Da Nang. Across the country, it will be increasingly important to distinguish details and to get the business, product, and customer service fundamentals down.

Glazing over differentiation points does a disservice to aspiring entrepreneurs and only muddles the dialogue. Defining terms matters, and getting everyone on the same page is the only way to move the dialogue forward. It doesn't help that local reporting sometimes gets it wrong. For example, local articles have been written about how Facebook's FB Start program directly invests in startups. Additionally, the term "startup" is commonly conflated with "enterprise."

These challenges are in addition to every other obstacle that entrepreneurs and startup founders face. More specifically, Đỗ Thị Thúy Hằng, former vice president of external affairs and business development at Seedcom, a venture builder in Ho Chi Minh City, sees the challenges that Vietnamese entrepreneurs face in a couple of ways:

> A big challenge for most enterprises is scalability, given the lack of infrastructure, capital, and human resources in the Vietnamese market context. Yet I also see mind-set of the entrepreneur a barrier to grow/scale, both for the company and for the entrepreneur him/herself. Specifically, his/her way to think about scale, system, processes, human resources… and think beyond a 6 to 12-month horizon.

> Another shortfall is marketability—the ability to articulate a company's mission, vision, and competitive offerings, as well as an understanding of the investor landscape, both domestic and regional, in order to gain access to capital.

For those looking to invest in early-stage companies in Vietnam, there is a whole set of other challenges. VIC Partners, formerly known as Vietnam Investment Club (VIC Impact), formed in 2016 to create a community of educated, vetted angel investors. Managing Director Trịnh Anh Đức outlines why it's important to have such organizations:

> The Vietnamese Government committed to launching detailed guidelines on the establishment of venture capital (VC) funds. This decree includes a legal framework for investment and requirements for individuals who want to become fund managers or angel investors. Since there isn't a standard requirement to be accredited angel investors yet [as of late 2017], a professional investment club like VIC Partners is very necessary because we act as a filter layer to qualify credible investors based on our private network. There are two big challenges that angel investors in Vietnam face: [the] first is limited access to good deal flow, and [the] second is investment know-how. Unlike other angel networks, VIC Partners adopts a club model; our priority is to help facilitating investment activities, not networking activities. We are committed to enriching Vietnamese angel investors by delivering superior investment services, deals origination strategy, and growth-fostering partnership.

While it's critical for Vietnamese entrepreneurs and startups to continue building bridges into other markets to gain the international experience and exposure needed to continuously improve, it's also important for the startup and entrepreneur communities in Vietnam to define and fully understand terms in order to facilitate effective cross-cultural communication outside Vietnam or with visiting foreigners. For starters, "startup" in Vietnam means any new business, ranging from a café to a clothing store. Of course, any interest in entrepreneurship should be encouraged, but the requirements to grow and sustain a café are different from what is needed to grow and sustain a software company. This sort of ambiguity limits conceptual dialogue from moving ahead in all segments of Vietnam's enterprise ecosystem—but the solution may lie in a neighbor's development story.

As mentioned in chapter 4, Japan went from a ravaged post–World War II economy to the world's second-largest economy in the 1990s.[10] What largely enabled Japan to be successful in its economic transformation was a stark shift in the workforce mind-set, which even facilitated new vocabulary to implement innovative solutions.

Before this paradigm shift in Japan, specific industry terms did not exist to describe small-batch, high-quality production to factory workers. The Japanese created their own processes with their own resources to drive economic growth in twenty years; Japanese engineers, managers, and leaders took innovative ideas and applied them to manufacturing and processes. The result was innovative products from brands such as Sony, Honda, and Toyota. Thus, the development of a new technical language was necessary, which involved a social level (individuals, units, company culture, and so on) of change in innovation and ultimately led to a change in the output of manufacturing (lean manufacturing).

Vietnam currently has a similar language challenge ahead of it; for example, the terms doanh nhân and doanh nghiệp can mean "entrepreneur" or "business," respectively, and are used interchangeably (and sometimes ambiguously) in Vietnamese. Along those lines, sáng tạo means "creation," while đổi mới means "renovation," so combining the two (đổi mới sáng tạo) is the closest meaning to "innovation" (literally "creative renovation") in Vietnamese.[11]

The language, which can be more easily used to describe "feelings" than scientific and technological terms due to somewhat open-ended definitions (and wide interpretations) despite the specific pronunciations of words (based on six tones), may have to evolve in certain industrial contexts in order to reflect the high technology standards, precision, and innovative thinking needed to maintain a competitive advantage in the global marketplace. Perhaps Vietnamese creators and innovators could start by inventing a wholly new and unique word for "innovation" in Vietnamese—in a *kaizen* fashion—which would be innovative in its own right.

Vietnam already has a strong bilateral relationship with Japan and wants Japan to be its top investor, especially in the area of high technology, according to Prime Minister Nguyễn Xuân Phúc's remarks reported by the *Japan Times*.[12] This clarion call is a natural advantage for Japanese investment firms. Principal Ryusuke Hirota of Spiral Ventures (formerly known as IMJ Investment Partners), a Japanese venture capital firm, shares his view on contemporary Vietnam after several years of activity in the market:

> If I would generalize from my experience, Vietnamese entrepreneurs are too focused on its domestic market and often lacking [in] vision to grow regionally due to, in my personal view, huge enough untapped domestic opportunity in a positive sense, and their introverted mindset as well as language barrier in a negative sense. However, I have seen that this is rapidly changing as significant number[s] of foreign-educated young Vietnamese and once exiled Overseas Vietnamese are coming back to their home and starting new business with local tech talents, which I would think one of the best in Asia, with [an] international business mindset. This trend won't [be] likely to stop by itself and therefore I believe in a bright future of Vietnamese startups that could bring a change not only into their home market, but also into the global markets.

But how exactly is such a bright future actualized? And, ultimately, whose vision is it? (In economic terms, this is easier than other dimensions such as social and political). In other words, Vietnam's economic growth rate should not be the only focus; increasingly, how it is achieved (and at what potentially long-term expense) is as important as the percentage of growth. As growth from the private sector increases in proportion to the total GDP growth, the voices emerging from the private sector will gain more weight in this dialogue.

Overall, the competitiveness of the domestic market economy is increasing, but competition is increasing from foreign firms, some regional and others from elsewhere. This is why it's essential to enable Vietnam's economy to develop and promote innovation—especially new business models—as well as apply technological progress to improving domestic firms' productivity and human resources capacity. Thus far, Vietnam's economy has largely developed in terms of quantity instead of quality: a foundation must be laid for more sustainable economic solutions to emerge and for worker productivity to increase. For example, how can future generations benefit from tourism if the environment is currently being exploited? These are some of the questions that need to be asked—and thoroughly answered—by Vietnam's people and its leaders (perhaps in reverse order).

Fundamentally, an early-stage ecosystem such as Vietnam's needs reinforcing themes, spirits, and cultures of entrepreneurship and innovation to foster the creation of high-growth, innovative companies with a global outlook or, at least, awareness. If a company chooses to keep the status quo, it will stagnate—or worse, die. Copying existing models can be valuable, yes, but it's not nearly as valuable as new ideas or ways of doing things that lead to the creation of value for a large number of customers or stakeholders. High-growth companies are innovative, and innovation requires change, whether folks like it or not.

New language can shape new segments of a culture, and creating new and/or dedicated Vietnamese words for entrepreneurship and innovation would allow the exchange of new ideas between people more efficiently. It would also help to facilitate a change in mind-set, as covered in chapter 4.

With the support of both the public and private sectors, as well as community support from the diaspora and other friendly parties, creative solutions will surely emerge that will enable more entrepreneurs, investors, and policy makers in Vietnam to get on the same page.

SUSTAINABILITY VERSUS SCALABILITY

Given the potentially high rewards, it should come as no surprise that startups are inherently risky propositions. Failure is often part of the startup experience; entrepreneurs sometimes need to experience disappointment for themselves in order to learn how to improve for the next time. Entrepreneurship is a long-term haul—not a short-term win. Some may prefer the stability of a conventional job, especially one provided by the state. However, this option may not be as viable in the future as it has been until now.

In a 2016 report[13] issued by United Nations Conference on Trade and Development (UNCTAD), two-thirds of all jobs (agriculture, industry, and services) could be eliminated in developing countries due to technology automation, which "risks eroding the traditional labor-cost advantage of developing countries." Furthermore, according to the McKinsey Global Institute (MGI),[14] the industries with the lowest digitization rates include agriculture and hunting, construction, and hospitality. Meanwhile, the percentage of time spent on activities that can be automated using currently demonstrated technologies (i.e., the technical feasibility of automating predictable physical work) is 78 percent, according to the MGI.[15] While these latter figures are for the United States, this kind of work includes food preparation, welding and soldering on an assembly line, or packaging objects—and it will only be a matter of time before the unit economics of automation make even more sense for Vietnam's economy and labor wages. Already, firms such as Foxconn[16] have begun automating large swaths of its workforce, making next-door China the largest, fastest-growing market for industrial robots in the world, according to the *Wall Street Journal*.[17]

At a 2016 event[18] held at Vietnam National University (VNU) in Hanoi, Vietnam's prime minister, Nguyễn Xuân Phúc, was asked by a Vietnam Youth Academy student, Phạm Đông Hiếu, "Prime Minister, how can political students start a business, because politics is not like the economic sector?" This sort of question may not be that unusual as the attractiveness of becoming a successful entrepreneur increases in Vietnam—but it may become a path more necessary for Vietnamese graduates in the future.

At the end of 2015, "about 114,000 bachelors and 135,000 associate's degree holders have to do menial jobs which require no certificate or diploma," according to the *Tuoi Tre News*.[19] In 2016, university graduates made up "as many as 192,500, or 15% of the country's unemployed," according to the *Nikkei Asian Review*.[20] Increasingly, college graduates are continuing with vocational training, and some high school graduates are opting to skip university altogether, according to the *ICEF Monitor*.[21] Thus, for some Vietnamese youth, the most promising option to invest their time in may be entrepreneurship. (Or it may be their only economic option to survive.)

Vietnamese entrepreneurs who take on risk by starting up encounter many pitfalls along their journeys. In 2016, more than 110,000 enterprises were incorporated in Vietnam, according to the Business Registration Agency at the Ministry of Planning and Investment.[22] Remarkably, during the first quarter of 2016, the number of troubled businesses and new businesses was almost on a parity: 22,000 businesses suspended or ceased operations, while 24,000 businesses were created, according to the *Vietnam Net Bridge*.[23] In the first quarter of 2017, a total of 23,900 enterprises suspended or ceased operations, or 265 per day, according to the *Vietnam Net Bridge*.[24] During this same period, there were 26,478 newly formed

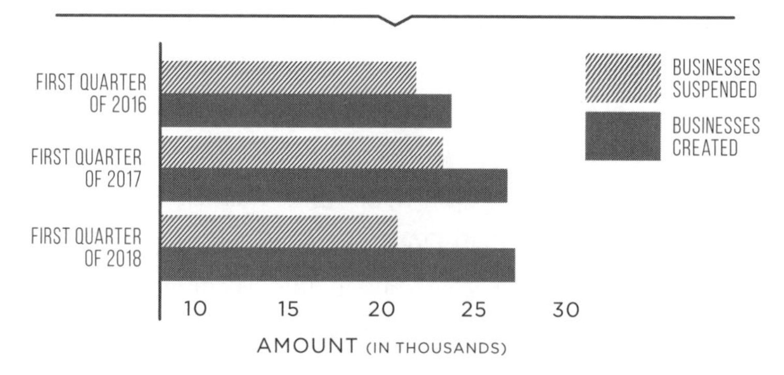

enterprises (294 per day), with a combined starting capital of USD $11.9 billion, resulting in a 11.4 percent increase in company registrations and a 45.8 percent increase in starting capital from one year ago, according to the Ministry of Planning and Investment's Enterprise Development Agency (EDA).[25]

During the first quarter of 2018, a seven-year record number of businesses were created: 26,800 or 297 per day.[26] Moreover, from January through July 2018, there were 75,793 newly established enterprises according to the *Hanoi Times*. Meanwhile, 59,910 firms temporarily suspended operations during this same time period.[27] For all of 2017, a total of 127,000 new businesses were established, according to the Vietnam Chamber of Commerce and Industry (VCCI)[28] and 38,869 firms temporarily ceased operations, according to the General Statistics Office.[29] However, more than 60 percent of all operating enterprises reported business losses, which could be due to either tax fraud or incompetence, according to Phan Đức Hiếu, deputy director of the Central Institute for Economic Research.[30]

Despite these operational challenges, the Vietnam Provincial Competitive Index 2016 (PCI)[31] report noted some "rising growth" trends: "The PCI 2016 survey continued to reveal signs of a positive business environment. Over the past year, 65% of private enterprises reported profits, the highest level in five years. Average capital size of enterprises has reached a new peak of 18.1 billion Vietnamese dong (USD $797,000), twice the [capital] size recorded in 2006. The percentage of firms that hired more workers also increased from 12% in 2015 to 13% in 2016."

Although antiglobalization rhetoric has increased in recent years, Vietnam has seen clear and substantial benefits from increased international trade: economic growth, increased opportunities, and increased access to quality goods. As outlined in the World Economic Forum's *Inclusive Growth and Development Report 2017*: "Between 2002 and 2004, the provinces in Vietnam that experienced the largest tariff cuts in the [United States] market also experienced the biggest declines in poverty. The reallocation of workers from the informal to the formal sector, induced by the agreement, played an important role in this outcome. Having joined the WTO in 2007, Vietnam has gone on to make great strides in its development, fueled in [a] large part by trade."[32]

However, increasing domestic production costs and competition from neighboring countries such as Thailand and China pose threats to Vietnamese enterprises. Failure in Vietnam's private sector affects the public sector in the form of reduced tax receipts, which in turn impacts the state budget. Thus, the public sector has a vested interest in developing the private sector into a robust, responsible, and resilient group of entrepreneurs and business leaders.

While the growing local interest in startups is positive, the reality is that the odds are against startup founders and employees in Vietnam—and globally. Between 2008 and 2017, CB Insights,[33] a big data and machine-learning research firm, followed more than one thousand companies in the United States from seed round onward and found that the odds of becoming a unicorn—a startup with a valuation of USD $1 billion or more—are less than 1 percent. In fact, 70 percent of the companies that raised their initial seed in 2008 through 2010 ended up failing or entered a self-sustaining pattern. Meanwhile, out of the startups that raised their initial seed funding in 2008 through 2010, 46 percent managed to raise a second round of funding. Despite these odds, Vietnam did, in fact, produce a unicorn.

In 2004, a company named Vinagame was started by five cofounders (including one foreigner) with a mission to deliver relevant software to Vietnamese gamers. Today, VNG (rebranded from Vinagame in 2010)[34] has an estimated valuation of at least USD $1 billion, making it Vietnam's only (and Southeast Asia's first) homegrown unicorn. In 2017, VNG announced its intention to launch an initial public offering (IPO) on the Nasdaq Stock Market in the United States, which would mark the first Vietnamese technology company to be listed on an American stock exchange.[35]

In an email sent out company-wide by CEO Lê Hồng Minh to mark the occasion, he shared that [translated from Vietnamese]:

> 1) This is just the first step on a long and difficult journey—to get there when VNG is actually listing shares at NASDAQ. Currently, considering the conditions for listing on the NASDAQ, VNG has met [them] almost fully, but in Vietnam there is no precedent for a company to list overseas, and when we are pioneers, the journey will not be easy.
>
> 2) So why do we choose to do this? Simply because VNG, if you want to truly become a leading technology company in Vietnam and the region, can compare with global technology companies, then we have to accept and participate in big games. Global—from fair competition to global products, direct access to the global market, access to capital and global investors, and the rigorous evaluation of the global stock market. In other words, this is the challenge that VNG embraces to step into the world.
>
> 3) The most important [part] of the whole process will be the pressure to change, to improve, and to continually

> grow—from people, cultures, systems, techniques, products and ultimately results, business. It means that our innermost ability is still the most important; external factors (such as today's events) are only the result or catalyst for the continued development of VNG. From the core (and old) business as the game is constantly refreshing itself by going global and regional markets, to the business core (but not as old) as Zing, Zalo must directly compete with the global giants, to new businesses like Payment [which] are striving to perfect the product and experience the user, to new tests like IoT, streaming—our opportunity and ability to change and innovate is zero. Limited, limited only to ourselves.
>
> Cheers to a new journey together,
>
> —MinhLH

While VNG focused mostly on the local market during its rise to success by offering Vietnamese consumers services such as Zalo (a chat app) and Zing (an online portal) in addition to its games portfolio, the next major Vietnamese success story reaching a similar level will most likely target regional or international consumers on the long road to becoming a unicorn.

The waves of nascent companies emerging from Vietnam and looking to scale need to be sustainable or have a strategy in place for becoming profitable. Today's efforts to foster entrepreneurship in Vietnam may be focusing too much on startups, and instead should focus on sustainable practices to keep SMEs operational. Of the SMEs that experience economic growth, a small portion will become startups—and an even tinier group will achieve anything close to unicorn status.

However, just because a company is valued at USD $1 billion or more doesn't mean that it will be a job creator. Instagram, which Facebook acquired in 2012 for USD $1 billion in equity and cash, had only twelve employees at the time. Most job creation in an economy comes from SMEs, so startups are only a small part of a country's economic growth model—but the successful ones have the potential to play a positive role in the long term. Still, for those aiming to create Vietnam's next top startup, policy makers might suggest that Vietnamese entrepreneurs use their local know-how and market insight to focus on the domestic market, while international investors might push for regional expansion as quickly as possible. Ultimately, founders should know what their vision is—whether for national, regional, or international dominance—and stick to it as conditions dictate. They know their companies best, after all.

The story of a wildly successful mobile game made in Vietnam illustrates the importance of sticking to one's vision as a creator. In early 2014, Flappy Bird, a simple side-scrolling mobile game, shot to the top of Apple's US App Store charts with over fifty million downloads and forty-seven thousand reviews. Created by Nguyễn Hà Đông, a software developer based in Hanoi, Flappy Bird was earning Nguyễn USD $50,000 per day in ad revenue, according to *The Verge*.[36] By late January, less than a year after Nguyễn created the game, he was fending off personal attacks on Twitter, and by February 1, his email inbox was full of feedback, interview requests, and investment offers. Interestingly, around that time he declared that "I am no businessman" and "I am not an entrepreneur :D" on Twitter,[37] perhaps because he wanted to retain his "indie game maker" title, as he alluded to in another tweet. By February 8, Nguyễn had decided that he had had enough of Flappy Bird and decided to shut the game down, effective February 9. The official reason Nguyễn gave for pulling the game was that it was "an addictive product," according to an interview with *Forbes*.[38]

However, by August, Flappy Bird was available again, exclusively for Amazon Fire TV in a different version: Flappy Birds Family. Since 2014, Nguyễn's game studio, dotGEARS, has released several other games, such as Swing Copters, Swing Copters 2, and Fabitalk. The success of Flappy Bird was a pivotal moment for Vietnam's digital community—it was proof that a Vietnamese product could compete with international developers on Apple's App Store and the Google Play Store and validation that Vietnamese game developers could make significant sums of money following their passions.

Thus, it's important for new entrepreneurs in Vietnam to understand the risks of any venture, especially given the local data on company formations and liquidations; Flappy Bird is among the best-case scenarios, but it's not a common outcome, given the fierce and increasing competition in Vietnam's marketplace. The good news is that the journey of an entrepreneur can be further de-risked with the increased availability of entrepreneur educational content, workshops, and market validation of a potential product or service as these activities increase in number in Vietnam.

Additionally, Vietnamese entrepreneurs usually have more than one side project going on—that is, they may have day jobs and work on projects at night. Thus, a Vietnamese entrepreneur may own or operate a café, a small e-commerce store, and perhaps a food shop. (There are a number of online retailers operating in Vietnam, including Shopee, Sendo, and Tiki.) This approach is fine for lifestyle businesses, but the needs and challenges of a coffee shop are very different from those of a software company. Also, as the saying goes, "you can do everything, just not very well."

Referenced data on company formation in Vietnam does not tell the entire story: the gray market plays a huge role in how commerce flows inside Vietnam. (In 2018, the "nonobserved economy" was proposed to be measured, which includes the underground economy, the illegal economy, and the informal household economy.[39]) Goods are regularly smuggled into Vietnam and then sold without official authorization from the brand's intellectual property owners. For example, in 2016, the *VnExpress*[40] reported that Vietnam loses over USD $300 million per year from its state budget due to tobacco smuggling. Even luxury brands aren't spared from smuggling, such as a case in 2012 when a smuggling ring transporting original Gucci and Dolce & Gabbana goods in Ho Chi

Minh City was busted—the ringleader was paying twenty times less than the full import taxes, according to *Tuoi Tre News*.[41]

Entering the formal economy requires complying with local taxes and regulations, some of which are arbitrarily enforced. One young Vietnamese entrepreneur bragged about not setting up a company because it was easier to cease operations "in case things don't work out." In the long term, this approach is not sustainable for entrepreneurs as they scale their enterprises, nor does it bode well for the state, which looks to fill gaps in the state budget in order to provide quality services for the people—now and in the future.

Currently, Vietnam has a mandated public debt ceiling of 65 percent of its GDP—in early 2016, Vietnam's public debt was equal to 64.5 percent of GDP,[42] according to the *VnExpress*.[43] The falling price of oil since 2015 has hit Vietnam's state budget hard; for every USD $1 decrease in the price of oil, the state budget experienced a deficit of approximately USD $45 million, since the state budget at the time was formed with a base price of USD $100 per barrel of oil.[44] The World Bank[45] and the Asian Development Bank[46] have both recommended that Vietnam improve its fiscal situation—and there are only two ways to do that: increase state revenue or decrease spending. (Although Vietnam's public debt was projected to fall to 61.4% of GDP in 2018, its public debt continues to increase at a rate of approximately USD $16 billion per year.)

While incentives to increase levels of entrepreneurial activity can be put into place, incentives for existing enterprises to invest in their workers in order to boost productivity levels may be more challenging to create. In 2013, Vietnam's productivity was ten times lower than South Korea's and fifteen times lower than Singapore's, according to the International Labor Organization (ILO).[47] While Vietnam's labor productivity has grown by nearly 24 percent from 2010 through 2015, according to the General Statistics Office,[48] it still has a long way to go to catch up to its neighbors Malaysia and Thailand.

Additionally, although manufacturing has transitioned from China to Vietnam in recent years, 29 percent of Vietnam's imports for 2015 originated from China.[49] Could this reliance on cheap Chinese imports stunt the growth of Vietnam's manufacturing base? And what are the incentives for business owners to invest in skills training for their employees? There are no easy answers to these questions, but considerations of sustainability and scalability should be at the forefront when deciding what to invest in—and where.

Thanks to the existing entrepreneurial spirit here, the ground is sweet in Vietnam, but this alone is not enough to guarantee sustainable growth. Throughout major cities in Vietnam, almost every home's ground floor is converted into a (formal or an informal) retail shop—a demonstration of an already strong and ubiquitous entrepreneurial spirit. However, more efforts need to be made in order to transition the innate passion for entrepreneurship (or default economic activity) into a formal vehicle that is sustainable—and, where appropriate, apply techniques to scale profitable business model(s). Only then can those successful entrepreneurs invest in the next generation of Vietnamese entrepreneurs and begin to foster a cycle of innovation and sustainable growth. As we'll see in the next section, pieces of this vision are coming into place.

AN INNOVATION HUB

If you are reading this in Silicon Valley, Vancouver, Berlin, London, or Melbourne and you want to build something that creates impact, solves real problems, or develops pipelines for new products and services, then you have to go where the frontier is and work with local communities to come up with local solutions. ASEAN is home to over 630 million individuals, of which more than 95 million live in Vietnam, making it the second-largest labor market in ASEAN with 55 million workers.[50] As noted in chapter 1, Vietnam has elements of the bottom billion (base of the pyramid) and the next billion to come online.

In a 2016 interview,[51] then US secretary of state John Kerry identified Ho Chi Minh City, the economic powerhouse of Vietnam, as one of four cities (all in Asia, with the exception of Guadalajara, México) that Silicon Valley should keep an eye on for innovation growth or investment opportunities. During the interview, Secretary Kerry described present-day Vietnam as "a place where that entrepreneurial energy and spirit is palpable on every street corner," in contrast to his experience as a civilian in the 1990s.

It's not just public-sector officials who are taking note of Vietnam's potential as a market for new products and services. When Google's CEO, Sundar Pichai, visited Hanoi in December 2015 he said,[52] "[Vietnam] will easily be in the top 10 countries for many companies and people who are building products. I think you're in the process of that transition. When I come here, see the energy, the optimism, the culture of entrepreneurs and the potential of the market, I think all the right ingredients are there."

Pichai wasn't the only senior-level executive from Silicon Valley to visit Vietnam's capital; Mike Cassidy, vice president at X (formerly Google X) also met with local and foreign entrepreneurs in late 2015, reaffirming the country's growing importance to Google, which considers it the most dynamic internet market in the world.[53]

In a 2015 TEDxLausanne talk (titled "Talent Is Everywhere"), Seedstars World cofounder Alisée De Tonnac stated, "I have met some of the most sophisticated companies in Vietnam that, if I hadn't told you the founder was from Vietnam, you would have accredited this company to Silicon Valley."[54]

The fact remains that Vietnam's private sector is still in a very early development stage; one Singapore-based American investor described today's Vietnam as "seed stage" in startup terms. This early starting point is both a challenge and an opportunity because Vietnam can leapfrog as it continues to develop. It can also make use of exponential technologies such as artificial intelligence and digital medicine (as they become available or localized) to overcome present and future challenges that aren't exclusive to Vietnam; we'll take a look at some of these in chapter 9.

Becoming an innovation hub requires coordination and specialization. As Vietnam develops a niche for itself in the region, individual cities across Vietnam will have to do the same. In a larger sense, major cities across North, Central, and South Vietnam, in particular Hanoi, Da Nang, and Ho Chi Minh City, will all need to support the rise of the startup economy in different ways, by leveraging their respective strengths and advantages. This does not mean solely establishing information technology parks, as has been a traditional method of attracting foreign enterprises. On the other hand, Vietnam had more than 2.7 million people working across 227 out of 328 industrial zones as of 2017.[55] (The role and acceptance of Special Economic Zones has not fully materialized in Vietnam as of 2018.)

For example, in Hanoi, engineering talent, the ability to form government and diplomatic community relationships, and proximity to Hải Phòng (the largest port city in Northern Vietnam) and China to the north for imports are all qualities that no other city in Vietnam can replicate.

Peter Petracca, founder of Chameleon.city, a service that helps expats settle into their new homes, says:

> When I launched my company, I chose Hanoi because I had already spent a significant amount of time there—nearly one year—building my network and getting comfortable with my new life in a very foreign place. That comfort is essential, as it allows you to focus on building your business while knowing the people who can help make it happen.
>
> Since expanding to Ho Chi Minh City, I've gotten a good read on how it compares to its northern counterpart. Ho Chi Minh City is more akin to my New York experience, with lots of driven, highly sociable people about (but you need to know where to find them). Networking events are aplenty, and happy

hour is everywhere. Hanoi, on the other hand, is a little sleepier—a Washington, D.C., if you will. Both locals and foreigners are more reserved, but in my experience, more genuine.

In Ho Chi Minh City, there is a natural gravitation toward a marketing orientation. The entrepreneurial spirit runs deep, and it's a two-hour flight to Singapore, where many regional corporate and investor offices are located. The city is the most cosmopolitan and international in Vietnam and has the largest consumer market. According to Shutta cofounder Bárbara Ximénez Bruidegom:

> We set up in Vietnam because we recognized the passion, ambition, and drive of a young, but highly educated tech workforce. We settled in Ho Chi Minh City over any other city, simply because the city produces more tech graduates than any other, and, in addition to that, there is a larger number of international tech firms based around this region. This means that it is ultimately easier to recruit mid-career tech talent in [Ho Chi Minh City] than elsewhere. Of course, the flip side of this is that we face stronger competition when we are recruiting, and, as a result, we need to be more competitive with the packages that we offer candidates, but this, to us, seems like a fair price to pay for access to such a large pool of resources.
>
> Saigon is becoming more cosmopolitan by the day, which is possibly leading to another distinct difference between Saigon and other regions [within Vietnam], as we find that the level of English tends to be higher. Hanoi is probably a better place to set up for companies that are focused primarily on the Vietnamese market, but as our outlook is global, the larger, more cosmopolitan workforce in Ho Chi Minh City means

> it makes more sense for us to be based here. I will admit that we are often tempted by the idea of a beautiful, large office right by the beach with plenty of fresh air, but this is not a realistic option for Shutta until the recruitment pool in Da Nang becomes larger and more experienced.

Da Nang, a coastal city, has beautiful beaches and terrain, a high quality of life, a low cost of living, accessible local government, and fresh air for performing outdoor activities—again, all unique qualities for a major city in Vietnam. It may be the only major city suitable for foreign families to live in—a statement the Asia Institute of City Management (AICM)[56] agrees with after a year-long study across Vietnam. The only ingredient missing is high-quality international education. Moreover, Shenzhen is one time zone and a two-hour flight away for foreign hardware startups, reducing lead times to hours instead of days.

For German Jan Zellmann and American Dr. Kasia Weina, cofounders of Evergreen Labs, a social enterprise builder, Da Nang was the natural choice in Vietnam for them. According to Zellmann, "While Ho Chi Minh City and Hanoi are relatively established and developed, Da Nang is just getting started. We came to Da Nang to be part of this transformation and contribute to positive change and mitigate the negative impacts that follow such growth (socially and environmentally)."

Dr. Weina expands on what specifically drew them to Da Nang:

> Da Nang is a place that has a very good infrastructure in terms of transportation (street network, international airport), utilities (water, electricity), internet and education (nine colleges within the University of Da Nang with 55,000 students) but still maintained its own character despite its rapid growth and development. While Hanoi or Ho Chi Minh City are working cities, Da Nang is a living city with a business-friendly city

government which attracts more and more expats and locals alike that are planning on starting their career in Vietnam.

In the coming years, it might prove necessary to develop specialization in Vietnamese cities or regions as the AEC becomes more interlinked. This convergence of regionalism provides the framework for a unified ASEAN market and the increase in competition that comes with reduced barriers to the flow of goods and workers across borders—for example, developing clusters of agtech in Cần Thơ; fintech in Ho Chi Minh City; edutech in Da Nang; or maybe nanotech, cleantech, or biotech in and around Hanoi in the future. Or, at the very least, reaching a point where domestic or international entrepreneurs and developers say to themselves, "I want to do *X*, so I will go to *Y* city in Vietnam."

For such specialization to occur, a broader, stable framework must be created for a healthy technology ecosystem in Vietnam. This has already begun: 500 Startups Vietnam, which set up in Vietnam in 2015 and has made thirty-five investments thus far as of September 2018, aims to accelerate the explosion of technology-based companies and interests in Vietnam due to its increasing potential in playing a major role in the Southeast Asian technology ecosystem. Venture Partner Binh Tran, a Vietnamese American investor, expands on the team's vision for Vietnam:

> We believe there's an opportunity of "Built in Vietnam for the Globe." With over four million Vietnamese living overseas and [the] returning diaspora, we see an increasing trend of founders migrating from Silicon Valley to Vietnam to have products built by talented and lower-cost Vietnamese engineers. Often these costs are 40–60% cheaper than their Japanese and Chinese counterparts.[57] Vietnam's tech talent can be attributed to over 15 years of Vietnamese companies providing tech outsourcing[58] and the strong educational emphasis on STEM [Science, Technology, Engineering, and Mathematics]. This

> educational component plays an important role in the future of tech in Vietnam as 15-year-olds in Vietnam rank 12th in the world in math and science.[59]

500 Startups isn't the only organization to advocate on behalf of a local development team in Vietnam. Misfit Wearables, founded by Vietnamese American Sonny Vu and acquired by Fossil for USD $260 million in 2015, was famous in Vietnam for hosting its technical team and other forms of talent locally. In a 2015 interview with *CNET*, Vu highlighted the reasons for operating in Vietnam:[60]

> We came to Vietnam with Misfit from the very beginning. We were founded both—in a sense—in San Francisco and Ho Chi Minh City. And it was really about going to places where we had the most competitive advantage in terms of recruiting. And so we've been able to find amazing talent here. And so it wasn't just about a cost difference, but also just about the level of talent. Talent, hunger, speed: that's why we're in Vietnam. Here in Vietnam, in Ho Chi Minh City…the roles really range from everything from supply chain, logistics, finance so business operations to customer service—we've got a great team here.

Vietnam's startup economy is clearly rising, and the Vietnamese market may develop more quickly than expected given the existing ecosystems in the region, as well as regional and international interest in Vietnam—along with Vietnam's middle-class growth. The ingredients for success are indeed here—the rest is up to the makers, designers, creators, entrepreneurs, investors, and other stakeholders in the community.

What makes Vietnam special for startups and entrepreneurship—and will continue to be an advantage for Vietnam's development—is the diversity and convergence of people, ideas, and subcultures across the three major cities: Hanoi, Ho Chi Minh City, and Da Nang. The art, music, and startup scenes across the nation are constantly evolving due to past policies, current trends, and new influences—including an increasing number of newcomers comprising designers, entrepreneurs, investors, and coders interested in modern Vietnam.

Looking to the future of Vietnam, while it can never fully replicate the factors that created Silicon Valley (no place can), it can create its own unique environment that leverages its people's strengths (including the global diaspora) to become a leader in innovation on its own terms in this century. For now, it's a great place to start something.

CHAPTER 7

CHALLENGES AND OPPORTUNITIES

ALTHOUGH IT IS NO LONGER strictly communist in its economic policies (e.g., land reform and collectivization), Vietnam remains a one-party state and is usually placed in the same category as countries such as China, Laos, North Korea, and Cuba. Despite efforts to liberalize its economy, Vietnam retains its communist moniker for the sole political party while embracing new and necessary initiatives to remain competitive regionally and globally, including the promotion of entrepreneurship, innovation, and startups at national and municipal levels.[1]

Considering this unique approach to governance in the twenty-first century, technologies—such as social media platforms—are changing the pace, tone, and direction[2] of provincial and national conversations. Today, the government of Vietnam's mass communication apparatus needs to encompass another medium beyond radio, television, and newspapers: the internet. In 1996 at Central Conference II, Vietnamese officials even considered the internet a threat to its national security, according to the *Vietnam Net Bridge*.[3] When social networks took off in the 2000s, Vietnam tried to create its own, called Go.vn,[4] which required users to use their real names and national identification numbers. It didn't pan out then, but that didn't stop new calls in 2017 from at least one Vietnamese official, Minister of Information and Communications Trương Minh Tuấn, for homegrown social networks to "replace and compete with Facebook in Vietnam," according to *VnExpress International*.[5]

While this isn't likely to happen, there are growing calls for Facebook and Google to localize Vietnamese user data in Vietnam, including a controversial cybersecurity bill that was passed in June 2018, taking effect January 1, 2019.[6] New requirements for technology companies include storing data on local servers, censoring users' posts, and opening local offices, according to the Lowy Institute (though not all requirements will come into effect in 2019).[7] Hanoi's interest in cybersecurity seems to be ramping up as the impact of "fake news" and "active measures" takes a toll on more open and transparent societies. On Christmas Day 2017, Vietnam's Cyberspace Operations Command was announced, and Force 47, a ten-thousand-strong cyberwarfare unit was unveiled as a result of increasing "wrong views" on social media, where "as many as 81 percent of Vietnamese [Pew Research] respondents aged 18–29 use social media daily to access news," according to the *VnExpress*.[8] Force 47 is meant to address critics on social media platforms such as Facebook,[9] one of the few places where Vietnamese have been able, until now, to consistently fully express themselves publicly.

Given the strong emphasis on political correctness in Vietnamese society, how can large swaths of Vietnamese society be fully and deeply innovative if Vietnam is to become a true "Startup Nation"? The country's leadership has publicly committed to transforming Vietnam into a "Startup Nation," in part by aiming to increase the number of enterprises to one million by 2020, up from approximately five hundred thousand in 2016. But is quantity enough?

Looking back ten years as of the time of writing in 2018, there was no Uber or Airbnb,[10] and the iPad and Bitcoin had not yet come into existence.

WhatsApp was a brand-new service, and Instagram wouldn't be created for another two years. (In March 2018, Amazon and Spotify announced plans to launch their services in Vietnam, and Uber was acquired by Grab, demonstrating how quickly market actors can change.) Legislating by prevention—as opposed to legislation by incentives to work toward a vision—has its limits; technologies proliferate and impact societies in new and unintended ways. Divergent political views aside, the fact remains that a fast, reliable, and open internet enables access to the markets and capital necessary for the private sector and the national economy to grow.[11] In an innovation-based economy, the best ideas rise to the top: many voices can build on a kernel of an idea, developing it into a fully fledged concept with eventual implementation that benefits all of society. (In early 2018, the government of Vietnam launched a "Digital Vietnamese Knowledge System," itrithuc.vn, a kind of *Wikipedia*-like service on cutting-edge technologies for Vietnamese youth.)

For those who wish to remain apolitical in Vietnam, there are other risks via compliance with local information and computer technology (ICT) laws. The Information Technology and Innovation Foundation (ITIF), an independent 501(c)(3) nonprofit, nonpartisan research, and educational institute, released a report in January 2017 that cited two Vietnamese policies as examples of "the Worst Innovation Mercantilist Policies of 2016" for forced data localization requirements and intellectual property disclosures. According to the ITIF, "By introducing data localization requirements, the Vietnamese government reduces the benefits that come from competition among foreign OTT services (such as WhatsApp, Viber, and Tango), local providers (such as Zalo, Mocha, and VietTalk), and traditional telecommunications service providers."

In an October 2016 letter[12] sent to the VCCI about Decree 72 (Management, Provision, Use of Internet Services and Information Content Online), the Asia Internet Coalition (AIC), formed by leading tech companies, stated, "The business conditions set forth in this draft Decree fail to reflect the development needs of an emerging ICT 'innovation hub' and the outward-looking ambition harbored by many Vietnamese SMEs to access foreign markets and integrate themselves within the global digital economy."

The other policy that led Vietnam to head ITIF's list of worst mercantilist policies relates to cryptographic key and source-code disclosures that could enable intellectual property theft. In effect, Vietnam is copying China via these types of legislation: "On July 1, 2016, the Law on Information Network Security (LONIS) came into effect. It opens the door to mandatory source-code and cryptographic-key disclosure, and applies onerous licensing and permitting requirements to millions of ICT products containing cryptographic capabilities."

It's unclear how many local or foreign firms are in compliance with these policies, but individual Vietnamese entrepreneurs have reported not fully disclosing their source code when filing a patent in local government offices—for fear of theft. On the other hand, the Ministry of Public Security considers user data to be national property, hence its push for proposed data localization requirements.

Even companies that are not directly impacted by data localization or intellectual property policies may still find their business disrupted in other ways. In March 2017, the local entities of Ford, Yamaha, and Unilever agreed to halt advertising on YouTube, Facebook, and other platforms that the Vietnamese government had deemed to be against it because of content hosted on those platforms. Vinamilk and Vietnam Airlines—two state-owned enterprises (SOEs) with plans to equitize—suspended ads on these platforms in February 2017, according to Reuters.[13]

It was an indirect approach by Vietnam's government since, according to the Ministry of Information and Communication, there were between 2,200[14] and 8,000 antigovernment videos on YouTube, although YouTube had blocked only 42, then 1,300, of these videos before finally removing 6,423 out of 7,140 videos, according to the *VnExpress*.[15] Thus, the government appealed to companies to pledge their support to Hanoi by not contributing advertising dollars that might support "toxic" antigovernment content. Whether or not this strategy will work in the long term for private firms remains to be seen, as compliance may carry additional hidden costs for operating in Vietnam.

For now, Facebook seems willing to comply with Hanoi's concerns as announced in April 2017, after a meeting between the company's head of global policy management and the minister of information and communication. "Facebook will set up a separate channel to directly coordinate with Vietnam's communication and information ministry to prioritize requests from the ministry and other competent authorities in the country," according to a government statement.[16] This news followed reports of popular and seemingly benign Facebook pages vanishing in Vietnam without any explanation, according to the *VnExpress International*.[17]

In late 2017, Deputy Prime Minister Vũ Đức Đam laid out the government's policy toward social media and compliance before the National Assembly: it "has to go hand in hand with political stability, and must not distort, defame, divide or disseminate content that goes against the policies of the Party and the State, or Vietnamese culture."[18] In short, balancing state cybersecurity needs with an increasingly innovation-based, expressive economy could be a stumbling block for Hanoi as younger generations of Vietnamese come online and seek new digital (and life) experiences.

Looking ahead to 2020 and beyond, Vietnam is facing mounting, complex challenges—undercutting potential solutions is a distinct lack of transparency, which enables the status quo to persist at the expense of accountability and unhampered progress in seemingly obvious areas. On a fundamental level, there seems to be a lack of consistent vision put forth by all bodies of the government of Vietnam regarding topics covered in this book, especially applicable to Vietnamese youth. These concerns can be distilled into two questions:

1. HOW DOES VIETNAM WISH TO BE PERCEIVED BY THE INTERNATIONAL COMMUNITY IN THE TWENTY-FIRST CENTURY?

Vietnam enthusiastically welcomes foreign direct investment (FDI)—but not all FDI is equal. In addition to the sustainability described in the last chapter, there's another aspect of sustainability—sustainable development that is commonly described as "development that meets the needs of the present without compromising the ability of future generations to meet their own needs."[19]

Today, many companies in Vietnam would refer to sustainable development as corporate social responsibility (CSR), which seems to be increasing in popularity in recent years. Do the enterprises and entrepreneurs operating in Vietnam have a responsibility to consider environmental, social, and governance (ESG) issues? Furthermore, do foreign enterprises and entrepreneurs have a greater responsibility to consider ESG impacts, especially if they are benefiting from Vietnam's people or the nation's resources? Or should Vietnamese communities be leading the way? For example, according to the *VnExpress*, "Out of 50 major toxic waste scandals recorded in 2016 by the Ministry of Natural Resources and Environment, 60 percent were caused by foreign invested firms, including the notorious mass fish deaths that made international headlines."[20]

As Elliott Harris, assistant-secretary general for economic development, chief economist said at the United Nations President of the General Assembly's High-Level Sustainable Development Goals event on climate change (at the time he was with the United Nations Environmental Programme) in 2017, "Sustainability is not just good business, it's good for business." Developing a sustainable economic growth model will not be enough; it will also have to be inclusive in order to tap into the full potential of Vietnam and its people. The public sector needs to set the environment for the private sector to operate in; if policies and goals are clear from policy makers, then it can foster a cycle of discovery, innovation, investment, and growth to get Vietnam's economy to the next level.

Cross-sector collaboration requires elements of confidence, credibility, and clarity. If the legal environment, the playing field, and information on developing regulations is not clear, it confuses domestic and foreign entrepreneurs and investors.

As a follow-up question, do foreigners—as guests and stakeholders in Vietnam—have a responsibility to support the development of an equitable and just society?

The second question is also tied to the future of Vietnam and its youth, but it seeks to direct their energies and efforts during a time of spectacular transition. Before, life was as simple as an agricultural society and living in villages. Today, life moves at a breakneck pace, and there are many temptations, distractions, and novel challenges for young people.

In their leisure time, young people in Vietnam can interact with different cultures, building and developing cross-cultural relationships more easily than ever before as they embrace modernity while balancing traditional values. However, at home and in school, things are different, as young people have very little control over their lives. In a traditional setting, young people in Vietnam are told what to do, how to do it, and when to do it by their parents. And when they enter the learning environment, they are told what to think, how to think it, and when to think it by their teachers and professors, who hold esteemed positions in society.

Too often, people in Vietnam seem to fall back on "not knowing" or self-censorship in order to avoid any risk to their personal reputation, or worse, of being charged with "abusing democratic freedoms" or other similar charges with limited media coverage and few, if any, international observers.[21] Often, writers on sensitive issues of contemporary Vietnam have relied on euphemisms and other literary mechanisms to allow readers to read between the lines.

Given these realities on the ground, how can innovation—that is, thinking about existing concepts in a new way—truly occur? In such an environment, how can the best ideas be put forth, challenged, and adopted if people are uncomfortable expressing themselves fully and openly?

That leaves the government of Vietnam to determine the future course of the country, or, in other words:

2. WHAT VISION CAN BE CREATED TO MOBILIZE YOUNG VIETNAMESE PEOPLE TO BUILD A BETTER FUTURE FOR THE NATION?

Many young people in Vietnam seem to have adopted consumerism as a de facto raison d'être. As a follow-up, what is the best way to instill a foundation for a sustainable system of values, morals, and ethics to take hold for the next generation of Vietnamese experiencing these rapid changes?

As Vietnam continues to grapple with current and novel challenges, it will have to confront various issues of sustainability and sovereignty as more foreigners and foreign-owned entities move into the marketplace. At the same time, the perception of Vietnam largely hasn't changed from the Western perspective. Many Westerners perhaps think of war first when they hear "Vietnam." Vietnamese students who study abroad are sometimes asked if they are communists or what "part of China" Vietnam is located in by fellow students. These issues relate to the current and future branding (and perception) of Vietnam (the term, country, people, etc.). If the rest of the world sees Vietnam through an outdated lens, what then are the expectations of the global community for a changing Vietnamese society—especially if it is investing in elements of its development? Or will Vietnam be resigned to forever being "war torn and recovering" in the minds of foreigners near and abroad?

Vietnam—not the war—but the country, the people, and the experience today are what should define how to engage with the nation's political leaders, who hold very different worldviews and values from the West, especially values such as freedom of speech and human rights.

The good news is that some of these challenges—at least the practical economic issues—are getting much-deserved attention. At the first-ever

Vietnam Private Sector Forum in 2016, representatives from the public and private sectors came together to engage in dialogue around seven industries and three fields:

1. Digital Economy: Solutions to promote the development of the digital economy?
2. Agriculture: How to encourage the participation of the private sector in agriculture?
3. Education and Vocational training: Revolution in vocational colleges for the benefit of businesses?
4. Logistics and Distribution: Which route for Vietnam to become a logistics center of the region?
5. Capital market and Fund raising: How does M&A become businesses' new funding resources?
6. Industry and Auxiliary industry: How to support auxiliary enterprises connecting to the supply chain?
7. Clean energy and Energy saving: How to promote investment in clean energy?
8. Integration and Globalization: How to best benefit from globalization?
9. Startup and Innovation: How to support startups and innovative companies?
10. Industrial clusters: How to create a value supply chain? [22]

Sustainability was also a major theme of the 2018 Vietnam Economic Forum hosted by the Central Economic Commission of the Communist Party of Vietnam. In addition to systemic risks, at *The Economist's* Vietnam Summit 2016, a number of macroeconomic challenges were outlined for Vietnam, including 1.5 million new jobs needed annually to keep up with population growth. These targets arrive during a phase when automation technologies will begin to impact Vietnam and SOEs are undergoing equitization (what privatization is called in Vietnam) processes, thereby reducing their large workforces. In 2018, about eleven million people are on the state's payroll,[23] including 265,100 civil servants.[24]

At the other end of the employment spectrum, up to 70 percent of low-wage jobs could potentially be automated in Vietnam, according to the World Bank. Even worse, although traditionally a strength sector, agriculture in Vietnam is threatened by climate change, drought, and saltwater intrusion into the Mekong Delta.

Other unforeseen hurdles will surely materialize on Vietnam's path toward a firmly middle-income country and "comprehensive development." There is no playbook to confront some of these challenges—novel solutions will have to be designed and implemented during dynamic social and economic change. Thus, a guiding star—not beholden solely to ideology—will have to keep Vietnam and its citizens oriented, even when national efforts may seem unclear or in doubt. Ultimately, the two questions posed in this section will have to be addressed by policy makers and leaders if Vietnam is to optimize its plentiful resources and fully tap into its strengths to seize current and future opportunities for sustainable and inclusive prosperity.

VAST OPPORTUNITIES

In 2012, the lotus was voted as Vietnam's national flower during a nationwide contest held by the Ministry of Culture, Sport, and Tourism (MCST). The lotus, widely adored by Vietnamese, is found only in muddy waters and has unique origins. A lotus begins its life at the bottom of a turbid body of water and slowly rises toward the surface before punching through and blossoming into a beautiful flower. Within murky waters lies something as beautiful as the lotus flower: similarly, within Vietnam's grand challenges, lie opportunities.

As Deputy Prime Minister and Foreign Minister Phạm Bình Minh said at *The Economist's* Vietnam Summit 2016, the "driver for [economic] growth is approaching its limits, so it requires a new growth model." That new growth model—and its powers—is slowly taking shape as Vietnam tries to chart a new course away from low-wage manufacturing. In early 2016, then outgoing prime minister Nguyễn Tấn Dũng[25] announced a change to Vietnam's energy policy. At the time, more than twelve gigawatts of thermal plants (coal-powered) was under construction, and Vietnam had outlined a plan to bring an additional sixty gigawatts of coal-generated power online by 2030, largely expected to use imported coal, according to the US Energy Information Administration.[26] According to Electricity of Vietnam (EVN),[27] an SOE that reports directly to Vietnam's prime minister, at the end of 2015, Vietnam's total installed capacity was thirty-nine gigawatts. Additionally, in 2015, Vietnam became a net importer of coal for the first time, according to the Asia Business Council.[28]

Much of Vietnam's economic growth has been fueled by coal. Electrification rates in the nation were at 98 percent in 2013, up from 2.3 percent in 1975, according to the World Bank.[29] In 2014, the World Bank recognized Vietnam as the developing country with the highest rural electrification ratio in the world. However, it has come at a price: Vietnam's per capita carbon emissions grew—at a rate of five times—from 1990 to 2013.[30] However, this trend is being supplanted at global scale: humanity's contribution to climate change is being replaced by humanity taking climate action and building climate resiliency.

In 2015, the world came together in Paris at the twenty-first Convention of Parties to the United Nations Framework Convention on Climate Change (COP21) to make a historic commitment. A total of 196 signatories pledged to "pursue efforts to limit the temperature increase to 1.5 degrees C above pre-industrial levels, recognizing that this would significantly reduce the risks and impacts of climate change."[31]

To help developing nations such as Vietnam transition from fossil fuels to greener sources of energy, developed countries will provide USD $100 billion per year in the form of the Green Climate Fund (GCF) and other finance vehicles, although the details are still being worked out. During COP21, Vietnam also pledged USD $1 million to the GCF, for the period of 2016 through 2020, while continuing to "implement the national strategy, program, and plans in response to climate change in various areas with concrete measures."[32] Vietnam's Intended Nationally Determined Contribution (INDC) calls for an 8 percent reduction in greenhouse gas emissions by 2030 compared to business-as-usual (BAU) projections, and with international support, up to 25 percent.

Although renewables (hydropower, wind, solar, and biomass) will account for 21 percent of Vietnam's total installed capacity in 2030, Vietnam's Power Master Plan VII Revised[33] calls for coal generating 53 percent of Vietnam's electricity during the same time frame, according to the Green Innovation and Development Center (GreenID),[34] a Vietnamese nongovernmental organization (NGO). (In April 2018, Ngụy Thị Khanh, GreenID's executive director, and founder, won the Goldman Prize, a first for Vietnam.)

Vietnam's growing energy needs are an opportunity to invest in green technologies—and to use new technologies to mitigate the risk of current renewable energy sources, such as hydropower's[35] effects during the rainy season, including landslides[36] or floods.[37] As the United States looks inward on a streak of economic nationalism, China seems to have taken the lead on green energy. Simply put, if the United States doesn't lead in clean energy and renewables, then other nations will. Is Vietnam going to be among them?

In 2015, Vietnam had 16,882 megawatts of renewable electricity-generating capacity, according to the International Renewable Energy Agency (IRENA),[38] and it produced 66,489 gigawatt hours of renewable electricity in 2014, primarily in the form of hydropower. However, in early 2017, Vietnam's prime minister, Nguyễn Xuân Phúc, approved Decision No. 11/2017/QĐ-TTg, the first solar law that supported the development of solar power projects in Vietnam, thus enabling a new stage of renewable energy investments in Vietnam.

The impact of climate change on Vietnam is complementary to Vietnam's energy challenges. According to the UNDP Human Development Report 2007–2008,[39] twenty-two million Vietnamese could be at risk of being temporarily or permanently displaced if global temperatures rise three to four degrees centigrade. As global temperatures increase, so does the sea level, producing stronger, more frequent storms. The Mekong Delta, where 20 percent of Vietnam's population resides and 50 percent of the country's rice is produced, is at risk of going under as sea levels rise and saltwater penetrates farther inland. (The Red River Delta, where Hanoi is situated, has also experienced saltwater intrusion.[40])

Cần Thơ, the largest city in the Mekong Delta and the fourth-largest city in Vietnam with a population of 1.1 million, is 0.8 meters above sea level, situated sixty-five kilometers (about forty miles) from the ocean. A one-meter sea-level rise could displace up to seven million people, according to a study by the UN Refugee Agency (UNHCR), the Columbia University Center for International[41] Earth Science Information Network,[42] and other groups. A two-meter sea-level rise could double the number of internally displaced persons (IDP).

Indeed, Vietnam is among the most threatened countries in the world when it comes to climate change—that's why it's vital for Vietnam to lead the charge for climate action. Radical challenges, such as Hanoi enjoying only twenty-eight days of clean air in 2017, according to Green Innovation and Development Center, need radical solutions; Vietnam should embrace technologies that will enable it to meet its obligations under the Paris Climate Agreement. Coal power will do the exact opposite and make it increasingly difficult for Vietnam to fulfill its responsibility. According to the World Resources Institute,[43] "Vietnam set a target to achieve 25% renewables in its energy mix by 2030 and 45% by 2050."

On renewable sources of energy, according to the *Vietnam Net Bridge*,[44] "the Vietnamese government's targets, solar power is expected to become the main new renewable energy source in the future, with an installed capacity to be increased from around 6–7 MW by the end of 2017 to 850

MW by 2020 (equivalent to 1.6% of the country's power generation) and 12,000 MW by 2030 (equivalent to 3.3% of the country's power generation)."

However, the Solutions Project, based at Stanford University, has already mapped out how to transition Vietnam to 100 percent wind, water, and solar (WWS) energy for all purposes (electricity, transportation, heating/cooling industry) by 2050. It's a good start, but Vietnam can and should be even more aggressive in achieving and implementing its green energy plan.

In *Before the Flood*, produced by actor and United Nations Messenger of Peace Leonardo DiCaprio, there is a scene at Tesla's Gigafactory in Storey County, Nevada, with DiCaprio and Elon Musk, Tesla founder and CEO. The two are walking through the factory space, which produces batteries and, when completed, will be the largest building in the world. At one point, DiCaprio asks, "How is [the Gigafactory] going to help developing nations that have massive populations that need to have power?"

Musk responds, "So the advantage of solar and batteries is that you can avoid building electricity plants at all. So you could be a remote village and have solar panels that charge a battery pack that then supplies power to the whole village without ever having to run thousands of miles of high-voltage cable all over the place. It's like what happened with landline phones versus cellular phones."

Musk goes on to explain to DiCaprio that with a hundred Gigafactories, all of the earth's energy needs would be met. DiCaprio misunderstands him, thinking Musk meant the United States, and Musk reemphasizes that with a hundred Gigafactories, we would be able to meet the earth's total energy needs. So, could a Gigafactory be in Vietnam's future? Tesla's Gigafactory is estimated to cost USD $5 billion and is expected to produce USD $100 billion in economic impact for Nevada over the next twenty years. Remittances account for USD $12 billion of capital flowing into Vietnam, FDI stands at USD $21-plus billion (in 2017, according to the Ministry of Planning and Investment's Foreign Investment Agency), and then there is the GCF, which is designed to help developing countries transition to renewable resources. Could some remittances be diverted to investment vehicles—literally investing in the future of the country by becoming a stakeholder in a greener, cleaner, healthier Vietnam?

While solar energy isn't viable throughout Vietnam and its electrification rate is among the highest, infrastructure is already in place to leverage new green technologies and offset the dangerous, dirty effects of coal-generated electricity via Tesla Powerwalls and other renewable sources of energy.

For 2017, Vietnam received a score of 78 by Regulatory Indicators for Sustainable Energy (RISE),[45] which examines a country's regulations and policies in the energy sector. This score placed Vietnam in the top thirty countries in the world and as the top country in Southeast Asia. While Vietnam performed well in the areas of energy access and energy efficiency, there was room to improve in terms of renewable energy.

Additionally, in the Happy Planet Index (HPI),[46] Vietnam ranked fifth in the world and first in Asia-Pacific with a score of 40.3 based on well-being, life expectancy, inequality of outcomes, and ecological footprint. The HPI noted that Vietnam's ecological footprint was smaller than it should be, given the size of its economy. The HPI also pointed out that Vietnam has some important choices ahead as its economic growth projection continues to increase. If it follows a standard development path, then its ecological footprint will increase, driving the country's HPI down. This will be a continual challenge for Vietnam as more people move to urban areas and consume more products and services.

According to the United Nations,[47] by 2050, two-thirds of humanity will live in cities, the majority of which will be in Asia. Already, 60 percent of the world's 7.3 billion people live in Asia. By 2050, the global population will be 9.7 billion, with two billion elderly—1.3 billion of which will be in Asia-Pacific, according to the World Economic Forum.[48] Vietnam is in both groups: in 2009, 10 percent of Vietnam's population was sixty or older, but by 2034 there will be one elderly person for every child in Vietnam. In other words, in fifteen to twenty years, the elderly will make up more than one-third of Vietnam's population.[49] Around 2047, there will be more elderly than children in Vietnam, according to the 2014 Vietnam Intercensal Population and Housing Survey: Population Sex-Age Structure and Related Socioeconomic Issues in Vietnam,[50] produced by the General Statistics Office (GSO) and United Nations Populations Fund (UNPF). This increase in an elderly population means that Vietnam's urban designers and architects will need to think quite differently about mobility challenges in the future.

Today, Vietnam is home to the sixth-largest urban population in East Asia, with twenty-three million city dwellers. Ho Chi Minh City has already become Vietnam's first megacity—that is, a city with a population over ten million. Hanoi isn't far behind—if both cities' current growth rates are maintained at 4.0 percent and 3.8 percent respectively, in 2020 they will both be officially twice as large as they officially were in 2000. The urban expansion of these two metros is greater than any other area in the region, except for China. Already, in Hanoi's densest areas, such as Hoàn Kiếm District, population density exceeded forty thousand per square kilometer in 2010, according to the World Bank.[51]

The infrastructure investments made today will remain in place for twenty or thirty years. If Vietnam invests in coal, then it will come at a cheap price today but with large direct and indirect costs in the future. However, if Vietnam invests in solar, wind, hydro, and so on, then it will lead the way in transitioning from fossil fuels, literally saving the lives of its own citizens in the process. The good news is that by 2020, the cost of renewable energies such as wind and solar will be less than that of fossil fuels, according to the International Renewable Energy Agency.[52]

The public sector has a role to play in promoting a more mindful approach to environmental and social considerations as well; Vietnam's policy makers are noticing the potential for social impact and purpose from the private sector. In 2015, Decree 96 (No. 96/2015/NĐ-CP) was issued,[53] which stated in Article 2, "The State shall encourage and create conditions for organizations and individuals to establish social enterprises to operate for the purpose of solving social and environmental issues in the interest of the community."

However, the Vietnam Enterprise Law 2014 (Law No. 68/2014/QH13) outlines the obligations of a social enterprise (with an objective to resolve social or environmental problems, or to serve public interests) in Article 10, section C, which maintains that "at least 51% of annual profit is used for reinvestment in order to serve the social, environmental purposes as registered."[54]

This definition of a social enterprise may prove too narrow, but overall, it's refreshing to see that there are increasing options for those who want to focus on social entrepreneurship in Southeast Asia, notably in Indonesia, the Philippines, and Vietnam. For now, social enterprises are clustered in major cities in Vietnam, according to *The Landscape for Impact Investing in Southeast Asia* report by the Global Impact Investing Network (GIIN) and Intellecap Advisory Services.[55] However, doing good is no longer limited to charities and NGOs—and grassroots campaigns can directly address the most vital needs and concerns. (In January, 2018 Laurence D. Fink, founder and CEO of BlackRock, with USD $6 trillion in investments under management, wrote to business leaders, "Society is demanding that companies, both public and private, serve a social purpose," and stipulated that businesses would need to contribute to society in order to receive the firm's support.[56])

In November 2016, Vietnam's government canceled plans[57] for its first nuclear power plants due to environmental and financial concerns, a sign that it is aware of growing citizen engagement in the area of environmental safety, especially after the Formosa crisis in central Vietnam wreaked havoc on the livelihoods of fishermen, resulting in a USD $500 million fine for the Taiwanese firm. (To date, no information on how the fine was disbursed nor victim compensation data has been publicized.) However, the country's "twenty-first-century energy plan"[58] is still developing. A brighter future awaits, powered by clean and renewable energy; the timing is ripe to commit[59] and dispel renewable energy myths[60] in

Vietnam. Hopefully, Vietnam's contribution to ocean pollution will be addressed concurrently. Out of the eight million metric tons of plastic that are dumped into the oceans each year, five countries contribute up to 60 percent of this pollution, including Vietnam, according to a 2015 study[61] published in *Science*.

Startups may not be the answer for some of these challenges, but the startup mind-set and a different approach from "business as usual" can contribute to a culture of materializing cross-sector efforts spearheaded by innovative models with an engaged populace. That would be the biggest opportunity of all in Vietnam: a chance to save and improve lives.

REQUEST FOR VIETNAM STARTUPS

In 2015, Vietnam celebrated its seventieth anniversary of independence to much fanfare across the country. In Hanoi, the capital of Vietnam, a massive parade effectively brought the city to a standstill on September 2 as Vietnamese citizens lined more than forty streets across several districts in the then 1,005-year-old city. In early 2016, the Twelfth National Congress of the Communist Party of Vietnam (Đại hội Đảng XII) set the agenda for the nation's short- and long-term future as its leadership was renewed.

Since the trade embargo ended in 1994, Vietnam has reached several major economic milestones, such as becoming a full member of ASEAN in 1995, joining APEC in 1998, and accession into the WTO in 2007. At the end of 2015, the AEC took shape, creating a single unified market across ASEAN member states. As Vietnam continues to liberalize its economy, additional foreign investment will follow, leading foreign companies to hire greater numbers of skilled Vietnamese workers (with an increase in wages) and contributing to the rise of Vietnam's middle class (though this will not be the only factor). Future consumers with increased purchasing power will soon have improved access to a variety of new goods via Vietnam's participation in an assortment of free-trade agreements (FTAs). But in the near future, we won't just see capital and goods flow into Vietnam—we will also see startups, technology, and innovation emerge from Vietnam, such as Money Lover, a fintech mobile application.

There has been a lot of discussion about *Kinh tế khởi nghiệp*, or the startup economy in Vietnam. Taking stock of the current pipeline of growing interest in startups (and inspired by Y Combinator's Request for Startups), the following is a Request for Vietnam Startups (RFVS)—created in collaboration with several investors and stakeholders across the country by asking them where they saw opportunities in Vietnam and what areas they believed Vietnam-based startups should focus on—along several lines:

1. Guidelines for developing agtech, fintech, and products/services for rural Vietnamese consumers (i.e., ~65 percent of the country);
2. Looking at demographics and trends; both short- and long-term (e.g., approximately one million babies born annually, climate change affecting the Mekong Region);
3. Leveraging relative and absolute advantages of Vietnam / Vietnamese talent (e.g., low cost of labor, long coastline, renewable sources of energy in Ho Chi Minh City versus Hanoi);
4. Exploring critical issues (e.g., pollution, traffic, low standards in public education, corruption, and so on); and
5. A passion for wild cards/moon shots.

When it comes to startups, the selected definition is any project that is sustainable (able to generate revenue) and is designed to scale very quickly—perhaps even designed to scale out of Vietnam. (This is different from a small business or a franchise.)

This RFVS isn't all-encompassing—it's not meant to be final, but, rather, it's part of the foundation for the community to disseminate and discuss:

it's a starting point. Not everyone will agree with this version, but that's to be expected. Nonetheless, an inclusive approach was utilized in putting this RFVS together: Patamar Capital, 500 Startups Vietnam, 8 Bit Rockstars (.NFQ Asia), the US embassy in Hanoi, and the UNICEF Innovation Lab were asked for their feedback, comments, and input.

AGRICULTURE

Vietnam is the world's largest producer of pepper, the second-largest exporter of coffee, and the third-largest exporter of rice, making it an ideal prototyping arena for new farming techniques and technologies. Thus, agtech developed in Vietnam has the potential to be exported across other markets. For starters, how can crop yields be efficiently increased without overfarming existing land?

BRAND

Vietnam has a lot of potential to develop its international brand: it already has a strong reputation for IT outsourcing. Furthermore, the Vietnamese conical hat (known as nón lá) has near-instant brand recognition. What's the most effective way of enhancing Vietnam's perception abroad?

CHALLENGES

Counterfeit goods, collusion (pricing), traffic congestion and pollution, endangered species trade, climate change effects in the Mekong Delta, water treatment and management, gender inequality, lack of transparency, cybersecurity, and so on. Pick an area—how can it be addressed?

COMMUNITY

Most of Vietnam's major cities are made up of locals, foreigners, and Việt Kiều, but sometimes there isn't much overlap among the English-teaching, business, diplomatic, freelancing, arts, and other communities. One idea: how do we tap into these diverse groups and make it easier for people who want to move and contribute to Vietnam (or any country) to do so? On the other hand, what about solutions for marginalized members of their communities, such as (global) sex trafficking victims?[62]

COLLABORATION

There are almost two million Vietnamese in the United States, with approximately one million in California alone. Surprisingly (to some), Vietnamese is the third-most spoken language in Texas. Furthermore, there are Overseas Vietnamese communities in France, Germany, Poland, Russia, and Australia. A steadily-growing portion of Vietnamese already study abroad, and second-generation Vietnamese have returned to Vietnam to work, study, or live. Linking the diaspora back to Vietnam means benefits at home and abroad. How can these links be strengthened and deepened?

CONSTRUCTION

There are a number of high-rises under development in Ho Chi Minh City, and buildings are constantly being razed to make way for new ones in Hanoi. Vietnam's builders have focused on high-end accommodations, but there is also a need is for middle- to lower-income housing. Approximately three million workers need accommodations by 2020, while in 2017 1.2 million workers needed accommodations, according to provincial and city reports.[63] The pace of construction will only accelerate in the future, but construction sites are often hazardous, with lax safety measures, waste, delays, and overages. Not to mention some "badly designed" features to begin with—which begets the question, Can the industry begin to innovate en masse?

COPIES

Vietnamese entrepreneurs, developers, and product managers might consider trying to copy more: best practices, successful models, and building up expertise to a point where they have mastered a skill, product, form, and so on. Taking a proven business model in the region and localizing it for Vietnamese tastes and styles isn't necessarily a bad idea: it lowers risk especially when taking a "study, copy, then innovate" approach. What else could or should Vietnam copy?

DATA

Getting accurate data in Vietnam can sometimes be difficult, but "data is the new oil" in terms of value. Collecting data and making decisions with it is a competitive advantage, given the right data. Depending on industry context, what kind of data should be collected to make the right decisions?

DEMOGRAPHICS

There are approximately one million babies born annually in Vietnam, while people from rural areas continue to move into major cities. Moreover, people are living longer—what will the family unit[64] in the future look like? What kind of services and care will they need that don't exist yet?

DIGITAL

Paper is inefficient to store, whether it's triplicate invoices or money. Finding a way of getting medical and other records into digital databases could be the beginning of a digital transformation in Vietnam. As a starting point, what can be stored digitally today?

EDUCATION

Vietnam needs to revamp its higher education system; more banking and finance majors in Vietnamese universities is not viable in the long term. Vietnamese youth need to develop more critical thinking skills, creative abilities, and confidence in asking questions and executing tasks in order compete internationally. How can these skills be developed within and outside of the school system?

ENERGY

Vietnam's largest source of electricity-generating capacity is coal, and this trend will continue well into this century. When might we see the emergence and mass adoption of renewable energies such as solar and wind, as well as the development of "smart" homes, buildings, and cities en masse?

FINANCE

Fintech is on the rise (especially access to peer-to-peer lending beyond informal loans), but credit card adoption rates are still low in Vietnam, and access to loans for SMEs can be improved—perhaps via crowdfunding combined with better investment management tools. How can Vietnamese consumers adopt e-payments more quickly?

GAMING

Vietnamese love to play games of all kinds: mobile, arcade, board, casino, and video. Could the concept of gamification be utilized to educate, raise awareness, and drive action for societal issues, driving change that otherwise would not occur?

GOVERNANCE

Vietnam is a top-down country. However, within the country's political system, the government is experimenting with e-governance, including mobile applications, in places such as Da Nang and Ho Chi Minh City, in an effort to improve public services—that is, standardizing and optimizing legal processes.[65] In August 2018, a national committee on e-governance was established by Vietnam's prime minister. Along this theme, how can citizens positively engage the government so that everyone benefits?

HEALTH

Digital health, animal health, and biotech. More specifically, cardiology, oncology, women's health, ophthalmology, radiology, intervention, supplements, anticounterfeit measures, general awareness, prevention, and treatments that are developed in Vietnam for a (presumably) lower cost than they would be in the developed world have the potential to outcompete similar solutions in other markets (e.g., clinical trials). Not to mention growing diabetes, asthma, and chronic illnesses in Vietnam's youth and elders as the population ages. Air and water pollution, concerns about food safety, and divorce are all on the rise as well. Getting ahead of the curve: what will be the biggest health concern in five to ten years in Vietnam—and do solutions exist for it yet?

INFRASTRUCTURE

With metro projects coming online in both Ho Chi Minh City and Hanoi, both cities may see an alleviation of traffic congestion. On the other hand, obtaining a car is the new Vietnamese dream, and rush hour is already near gridlock in major Vietnamese cities. How can Vietnam design and execute smart urban design and planning?

LOGISTICS

Last-mile distribution is still a huge challenge—distribution channels and supply chains that have not yet been streamlined affect almost every sector. In its current state, what is the best way to aggregate demand, capture data, and process payments within the logistics and shipping infrastructure?

REAL ESTATE

Renting in Vietnam can be a mixed experience, but it is sometimes not economical to buy a home. More and more inventory is coming online—is there a way to optimize underutilized (entirely bare) real estate units until they are sold?

SMEs

SMEs are the backbone of the economy and will continue to be as SOE reforms and equitization efforts are accelerated in order to give space to private sector growth.[66] New digital tools are a start, but how can SMEs better compete, go abroad (products or services) more easily, and reduce the risk of doing so?

SUSTAINABLE DEVELOPMENT GOALS

The pillars of the 2030 Agenda:[67]

- ☐ Goal 1. End poverty in all its forms everywhere.
- ☐ Goal 2. End hunger, achieve food security and improved nutrition, and promote sustainable agriculture.
- ☐ Goal 3. Ensure healthy lives and promote well-being for all at all ages.
- ☐ Goal 4. Ensure inclusive and equitable quality education and promote lifelong learning opportunities for all.
- ☐ Goal 5. Achieve gender equality and empower all women and girls.
- ☐ Goal 6. Ensure availability and sustainable management of water and sanitation for all.
- ☐ Goal 7. Ensure access to affordable, reliable, sustainable, and modern energy for all.
- ☐ Goal 8. Promote sustained, inclusive, and sustainable economic growth, full and productive employment, and decent work for all.
- ☐ Goal 9. Build resilient infrastructure, promote inclusive and sustainable industrialization, and foster innovation.
- ☐ Goal 10. Reduce inequality within and among countries.
- ☐ Goal 11. Make cities and human settlements inclusive, safe, resilient, and sustainable.
- ☐ Goal 12. Ensure sustainable consumption and production patterns.
- ☐ Goal 13. Take urgent action to combat climate change and its impacts.*
- ☐ Goal 14. Conserve and sustainably use the oceans, seas, and marine resources for sustainable development.

- ☐ Goal 15. Protect, restore, and promote sustainable use of terrestrial ecosystems; sustainably manage forests; combat desertification; halt and reverse land degradation; and halt biodiversity loss.
- ☐ Goal 16. Promote peaceful and inclusive societies for sustainable development, provide access to justice for all, and build effective, accountable, and inclusive institutions at all levels.
- ☐ Goal 17. Strengthen the means of implementation and revitalize the Global Partnership for Sustainable Development.

**Acknowledging that the United Nations Framework Convention on climate change is the primary international, intergovernmental forum for negotiating the global response to climate change.*

TECHNOLOGY

This means doing more (or the same) with less—that is, finding international products and producing them for 30 percent of the current cost and with 65 percent of the feature set, so that technology sharing across Vietnam and around the (developing) world can flourish. Which product to start with?

TOURISM

Approximately ten million people visit Vietnam every year; this industry has room to grow, especially in customer service—it can be improved, particularly in northern Vietnam. Training, language skills, and anticipating customers' needs are all in short supply. How can three-star hotels in Vietnam deliver international three-star experiences?

TRADE

Vietnam's export turnover reached USD $214 billion in 2017. A 2018 *Quartz* article titled "Vietnam is the most globalized populous country in modern history" noted "In 2017, Vietnam's trade as a percentage of GDP reached over 200%. This is the highest level for any country with over 50 million people in the World Bank's data, which goes back to 1960. Of the world's twenty most populous countries, it blows away number two Thailand at 122%."[68] The revamped Trans-Pacific Partnership (CPTPP), formation of the AEC, the EU-Vietnam FTA, Eurasian Economic Union (EEU), the ASEAN-Australia-New Zealand FTA (AANZFTA), and Vietnam party to 16 total FTAs—how can Vietnam (and first-time importers/exporters) maximize these opportunities, expand into new markets, and move up the value chain?

WILD CARDS

Artificial intelligence, machine learning, natural language processing, neural networks, quantum and cognitive computing, robotics (Vietnamese teams won first place at the International Robothon Competition 2017 and the Asia-Pacific Broadcasting Union Asia-Pacific Robot Contest 2017), moonshots, and so on. What is Vietnam in a position to develop, via the sheer will of researchers?

Y COMBINATOR'S REQUEST FOR STARTUPS

1. AI
2. Bio
3. Brick and Mortar 2.0
4. Carbon Removal Technologies
5. Cellular Agriculture and Clean Meat

6. Cleaner Commodities
7. Computer Security
8. Diversity
9. Education
10. Energy
11. Enterprise Software
12. Financial Services
13. Future of Work
14. Healthcare
15. Improving Memory
16. Longevity and Anti-aging
17. One Million Jobs
18. Programming Tools
19. Robotics
20. Safeguards Against Fake Video
21. Supporting Creators
22. Transportation and Housing
23. Underserved Communities
24. Voice Apps
25. VR and AR

Visit https://www.ycombinator.com/rfs/ for more information.

YOUR IDEAS

No one has a monopoly on good ideas. What are yours and how can you start implementing them today?

YOUTH

The future of Vietnam can sometimes be in flux between traditional parenting forces and the desire for modernity—at times, not solely from the youth. However, developing content based on topics that youth can relate to, such as careers, life lessons, relationships, and etiquette advice across social media and applications could help to ease the transition to adulthood in a globally connected Vietnam.

More importantly, what are their hopes and dreams for Vietnam in this century?

SECTION III

REQUIREMENTS FOR SUCCESS

CHAPTER 8

BUILDING A SOLID FOUNDATION

In early 2016, the Ministry of Planning and Investment (MPI), along with the World Bank, released a report titled *Vietnam 2035: Toward Prosperity, Creativity, Equity, and Democracy*. Almost two years in the making, the report took a frank look at the aspirations of and expectations from Vietnam in order to actualize "a modern and industrialized nation moving toward becoming a prosperous, creative, equitable, and democratic society" by 2035. These ambitions, outlined in the *Vietnam 2035* report, are not so different from what is set forth in Vietnam's constitution: "The State shall guarantee and promote the People's right to mastery; to recognize, respect, protect, and guarantee human rights and citizens' rights; and to pursue the goal of a prosperous people and a strong, democratic, equitable, and civilized country, in which all people enjoy an abundant, free, and happy life and are given conditions for their comprehensive development."

The year 2035 will mark ninety years since Vietnam's Declaration of Independence and sixty years since reunification, and it will be just short of fifty years from the launch of Đổi Mới in 1986. The investments made today—or lack thereof—in smart urban design and planning, in developing homegrown or adapted innovative technologies, and in education will pay dividends—or increase costs—in a future that will only become more globalized, competitive, and unpredictable. Progress does not exist in a vacuum; as the *Vietnam 2035* report outlines, the foundation for Vietnam's continued success depends on "balancing economic prosperity with environmental sustainability, promoting equity and social inclusion, and bolstering the state's capacity and accountability."

Vietnam's economic growth model since the start of Đổi Mới has come at a high environmental price, as covered in chapter 7. However, there is another blueprint that Vietnam can follow: the United Nations' SDG, which came online in 2015. This was not the first time that Vietnam adopted a global framework for achieving national economic, social, and health goals.

The Millennium Development Goals (MDG), established in 2000, were the precursor to the SDG, with a target year of 2015. From 2001 through 2015, Vietnam aimed to implement the eight MDG, which were to:

1. eradicate extreme hunger and poverty;
2. achieve universal primary education;
3. promote gender equality and empower women;
4. reduce child mortality;
5. improve maternal health;
6. combat HIV/AIDS, malaria, and other diseases;
7. ensure environmental stability; and
8. develop a global partnership for development.

The good news is that when it came to the MDG, Vietnam was one of the best-performing nations on poverty reduction, achieving MDG 1 ahead of the 2015 target.[1] Overall, Vietnam made good progress on realizing the MDG, in particular MDG 1–3. But there were shortfalls on MDG 4–8 despite remarkable efforts and/or progress in these areas.[2]

In 2015, the world came together again to establish the SDG, which build upon the MDG. The SDG are seventeen specific goals across economic, social, and ecological domains. Between the seventeen goals, there are 169 indicators to measure progress. The public sector alone cannot achieve the goals, so the private sector can apply the SDG framework to its activities to achieve social impact while achieving profit. Thus, Vietnam's business community, including startups, can leverage the best elements from the private sector and have the government scale them.

The seventeen Sustainable Development Goals (SDG)[3] of the 2030 Agenda are relevant and applicable to Vietnam. In 2015, the then president of Vietnam, Trương Tấn Sang, pledged[4] the government's support to accomplish these goals: "Vietnam wholeheartedly supports the 2030 Agenda and pledges to do our level best to ensure its successful implementation. We will mobilize all necessary resources. We will engage all ministries, sectors, localities, organizations and communities. And we will place the people in the center of this major endeavor." With that spirit in mind, in 2017 Vietnam created the 115 Viet Nam SDG (VSDG) targets in its "National Action Plan for Implementation of Agenda 2030 for Sustainable Development"[5] under the purview of the Ministry of Planning and Investment with support from the German Federal Ministry of Economic Cooperation and Development (GIZ).[6] So far, Vietnam has made some progress in these areas, according to the 2018 Voluntary National Review of the High-Level Political Forum on Sustainable Development's key messages: "To date, Viet Nam is proud to have achieved a number of SDG-related results, including:

1. A substantial reduction in the national multi-dimensional poverty rate from 9.9 per cent in 2015 to less than 7 per cent in 2017;
2. Health insurance coverage reaching 86.4 per cent in 2017;
3. A primary net enrolment rate of 99.0 per cent;

4. Women's representation in the National Assembly in the 2016-2021 term reaching 26.7 per cent;
5. The proportion of households having access to safe water reaching 93.4 per cent in 2016;
6. Access to electricity by more than 99 per cent of Vietnamese households in 2016;
7. Internet use reaching 54.2 per cent;
8. Annual GDP growth rates at 6.7, 6.2, and 6.8 per cent for 2015, 2016, and 2017 respectively;
9. Improvements in the protection and management of the environment and natural resources and an increase in forest cover to 41.5 per cent in 2017; and
10. A reduction in inequality and an improvement in the promotion of access to justice and information."

Elements of the private sector have also adopted the SDG framework to drive social entrepreneurs and technologists to be mindful of the 2030 Agenda. For example, in 2017, HATCH!,[7] a Hanoi–based startup incubator, partnered with Viet Youth Entrepreneurs (VYE), a Ho Chi Minh City–based business organization, combining resources into the HATCH<>VYE Acceleration Program 2017, a strategic partnership targeting teams with early-stage products or services in one of two tracks: IT and science, or social impact based on the SDG.

American Aaron Everhart, cofounder of HATCH!, has been working and living in Hanoi for over ten years. He shared his personal views on how entrepreneurs can become more socially engaged:

> I think internet-connected millennials are in tune with the major issues, so more and more impact-oriented firms will come to life as time goes by. The generation before was oriented toward personal survival, often harming society and the environment. From what I've learned (and by no means am

> I an expert), this was out of necessity more than ignorance. I think humans often know when they are doing something bad, but sometimes doing the long-term wrong thing is perceived to be the right thing in the short term, resulting in what we're all facing today, especially with the environment. For example, when a forest is systematically removed, the resulting erosion is no surprise to anyone.
>
> So what can we do? Since I am a communications expert, it's what I will prescribe. I think governments should invest more into mass communication, to continuously remind all people of the issues. In the US, where I come from, we have state-sponsored PSAs (public service announcements), and this is very effective. Over time, behavior change happens faster if we have the right communication approach taking place at the right time: mass communication is most relevant during the initial steps of change...Later, we can depend on strong social support for the big issues leveraging tactics that would stir peer-to-peer communication. But always first, leaders need to initiate big, challenging discussions on these topics, in the news media, and interrupt our beloved TV shows, movies, and songs with PSAs.

HATCH! and VYE are among two of the oldest entrepreneur networks in Vietnam geared toward young people and startups. Founded in 2012, HATCH! has built a community-led event series, HATCH! Fair, which has increased in size and scope every year since the inaugural HATCH! Fair in 2012.

VYE, founded in 2011, is the first and only student-run organization for entrepreneurship in Vietnam, with strong ties to Stanford University lecturer Thomas Kosnik. In a 2017 interview with *Vietcetera*,[8] Nguyễn

Thái Đông Hương, cofounder of VYE, described how she saw herself operating in Vietnam:

> I'm part of a new wave of entrepreneurs. We're challenging the incumbents in the industry, while also working alongside them. Most, if not all, are open to working with me. It takes some time, but I am successfully managing to build relationships with older-generation business leaders, some of whom don't speak English. We can and do find middle ground when conducting business within a more traditional framework. It probably helps that I'm Vietnamese at heart. I'm able to communicate our shared values.

In a way, Nguyễn's view is a microcosm of Vietnam's balance of relationships in the region. As the Fourth Industrial Revolution picks up steam, Vietnam will have to compete and collaborate with its neighbors in the region: for example, Thailand, which has its own 4.0 initiative; Malaysia, which is looking to be a launchpad into the region; and the Philippines, which has the advantage of a strong English base and IT outsourcing. (Not to mention Alibaba and Ant Financial coming into the region from mainland China.)[9] What will be Vietnam's role in the region?

In the last century, Vietnam's role—guided by Hồ Chí Minh's vision[10] for his people and country—was to give hope to colonized peoples around the world through the military victories achieved by General Võ Nguyên Giáp. In other words, independence. Without a doubt, every country has a right to self-determination. But this is a new century: what will Vietnam's role in the world be in this century?

Yes, Vietnam does have its 2020,[11] 2025,[12] and 2035 initiatives, but these largely fail to personally and impactfully connect with the youth in Vietnam. ICT development alone is not going to motivate young people to put down the trà đá (iced tea) and build a better future for Vietnam. Nor does it give youth a foundation of values or an orientation for their moral compasses, or lend purpose to their lives—or instill high self-esteem. Vietnam's challenges are not just economic—they are political, environmental, and social. These kinds of challenges are not confined to Vietnam, either; they encompass its diaspora and are shared by its neighbors in the region in terms of input and impact.

For example, urbanization will strain existing city services as population density increases, so it is critical to prevent and reduce destitution, deprivation, and discrimination and to promote development, dignity, and dialogue across Vietnam.

Crowd sourcing can help do this while boosting community engagement rates. Who better than the people to share their environmental, health, and safety concerns? Crowd sourcing would also help to promote local sustainable development practices and enable local representatives engaging with citizens to develop local solutions for local challenges. It's not out of the question that the impact of such an initiative would be measurable and quantifiable.

In fact, Vietnam already has the Public Administration Performance Index (PAPI), which, in 2016,[13] sourced the experience and views of 14,063 Vietnamese citizens across the country who were eighteen years or older. At the "Vietnam Provincial Governance and Public Administration Performance Index (PAPI) in 2016: Measuring Citizens' Experiences" launch in Hanoi in early 2017, the SDG figured prominently in the distributed materials, especially SDG 16, which is to "promote peaceful and inclusive societies for sustainable development, provide access to justice for all and build effective, accountable and inclusive institutions at all levels"—the most sensitive SDG in Vietnam's political context.

The PAPI[14] is the largest annual survey in Vietnam on "public opinion on governance, election quality, satisfaction, corruption, environmental quality." Beginning in 2009, PAPI has covered 103,059 randomly selected citizen interviews, resulting in fifty-one provinces issuing action plans, provincial official letters, or resolutions since 2010 and sixty-one (out of sixty-three) provinces convening or hosting PAPI diagnostic workshops since 2009.

For 2016, the issues of greatest concern were environmental and poverty related, while the emerging issues included electoral participation, gender equality, and land-use rights. In addition, there were some changes made to the questions in 2016, including new questions about citizen perspectives and experiences with environmental issues; new questions about citizen support for the then Trans-Pacific Partnership (TPP); new questions about citizen engagement with candidates and elected officials; new questions about citizen perspectives on inequality; and streamlined questions about the quality of public administrative services. In 2017, 14,097 respondents answered the 2017 PAPI survey. Almost one-third of respondents believed that "poverty/hunger" was the "most important issue the government should address." Despite being technically savvy, only 9.3 percent of Vietnamese surveyed were aware of the Law on Access to Information, and 12 percent had ever used e-government portals, mostly for construction permits. Overall, while land seizures had decreased compared to the 2016 PAPI, compensation for the land had not increased, and there was more gender equity in land use registration.[15]

Effectively, the PAPI provides a snapshot of how citizens perceive critical issues, what their concerns are, and how they are impacted by services that government provides. More importantly, it shows where there are gaps in the citizen experience via extensive data collected nationwide since 2011.[16] Using PAPI data can lead to scale—and to creating sustainable and scalable value within a given framework such as the SDG, so that efforts can be focused and fine-tuned to improve Vietnam's future.

Regarding the effectiveness of the PAPI or similar efforts, a 2017 article in the *International Journal of Development Issues*[17] found that

> monitoring appears to improve a wide range of governance aspects, including local participation in village decisions, transparency of local decision-making, accountability, administrative procedures and public service delivery.

> [Specifically]...governance quality reported in later years by citizens in the surveyed provinces and districts of the 2010 PAPI survey was significantly higher than the quality reported by citizens in locations that were not surveyed in 2010.

Another example of the growing influence that citizens have on high-level decision making is the USD $10.6 billion steel plant that was halted in 2017 by Prime Minister Nguyễn Xuân Phúc, who cited not wanting a repeat of a "Formosa incident," according to the *New York Times*.[18]

In addition to continuing efforts to improve governance quality that are supported by data and evidence, Vietnam should take greater care to preserve and promote some of its deep and rich cultural heritage and traditions such as crafts and other artisanal products. One Ho Chi Minh City–based startup that attempted to do just that was Efaisto (the name relates to Hephaestus, the mythological Greek god of craftsmen), which aimed to create a global maker's network—starting with Vietnam. Cofounded by a Belgian-French duo, Bernard Seys and Lou-Adrien Fabre, Efaisto was an e-commerce marketplace where anyone could order made-on-demand and personalized clothing, accessories, and eventually furniture from artisans around the world, but especially from Vietnam.

Although it was not successful in its original vision, this kind of convergence of technology, innovation, and tradition is one hope for keeping the crafts industry alive[19] and well in Vietnam—by efficiently and ethically connecting more local artisans to international markets. Consumers outside Vietnam have shown that they are willing to spend upward of USD $1,000 for hand-carved dragon wedge shoes, so they will have high expectations for other products at similar price points. However, there are major challenges along the way for these new kinds of startups to consistently deliver quality products to customers—something the Efaisto team found out firsthand.

Today, there are approximately 1,500 handicraft villages in Vietnam, specializing in products such as pottery, silk, and lacquerware. Vietnam is a popular destination for tourists looking to buy inexpensive tailored clothes while traveling in places such as Hội An, a central coastal town (and a UNESCO World Heritage Site). Perhaps we will witness the emergence and clustering of more startups like Efaisto in Vietnam: imagine experiencing a slice of preserved ancient Vietnamese culture without ever having set foot in the country. It could be the starting point for someone to discover her or his Vietnamese love affair. Ultimately, everyone can benefit when the best elements, qualities, and attributes of Vietnam—and its people—are shared with the world.

LEVERAGING STRENGTHS

In a 2012 Reuters Breaking Views feature,[20] journalist Rob Cox described Vietnam in the following way: "The nation boasts a large youthful population, a very high literacy rate, abundant natural resources, agricultural self-sufficiency, a stretch of coastline to rival California's or Thailand's, and a strategic position amid the trade routes of the Pacific."

So, what can Vietnam offer the world in the future as it changes its development orientation? One way to answer this question—purely in economic terms—is to think about the challenges that Vietnam will face in the future (and that other countries will have as well). If Vietnamese companies continue to or start working on solutions for those problems, they can be ahead of the curve. After all, there are innovative people here—as shown in chapter 5, many Vietnamese are "professional improvisers" in their daily lives and are quick and resilient learners, as history has proven.

Furthermore, Vietnam's public sector seems to support the exchange of knowledge and resources within the national context. In the aforementioned key messages from the 2018 Voluntary National Review of the High-Level Political Forum on Sustainable Development, Hanoi recognized the opportunity to contribute to the ongoing global dialogue: "Increasingly integrated into the world economy, Viet Nam is therefore more vulnerable to its fluctuations. As such, to successfully achieve all 17 SDGs, Viet Nam requires technical and human resources, financial support, as well as strengthened cooperation and exchange of knowledge with the international community. At the same time, Viet Nam is eager to share its own experiences and innovative approaches with other countries."[21]

In the future, Vietnam won't be the only country that has a rising national power consumption (and therefore rising demand for coal if alternative sources don't emerge), it won't be the only country with more cars on the road (and therefore more air pollution), and, when sea levels rise, it won't just affect a single city such as Cần Thơ[22] in the Mekong Delta—it'll affect hundreds of cities and displace millions of people. The point here is that the challenges of the future will originate or appear early in Vietnam without being exclusively Vietnamese, while Vietnamese solutions can help overcome the challenges of the future (if those problems are solved in Vietnam first, then at least the knowledge can be shared abroad). However, it takes a long-term mind-set to tackle the transnational issues of our time in addition to investments in education, human capital, and research and development—that is, taking current challenges and reframing them into future opportunities.

In the short term, IT outsourcing will increase in Vietnam, and the shift to using Vietnam as a place to develop minimum viable products (MVPs) and prototyping in general will also attract the interest of local and regional operators as well as entrepreneurs from the West (who can't compete with local wages or local market knowledge but can build MVPs for their markets back home—perhaps even more efficiently than doing it in their home markets since the dollar/pound/euro goes further in Asia).

Companies with more established local presences, such as Gear Studios,[23] CoFounder Venture Partners, and .NFQ Asia, all have slightly different approaches when it comes to IT outsourcing, software development, and venture building, respectively, but the net effect is that risk for building products is lower across the board (at least initially) when companies utilize a version of these models—and it will largely be Vietnamese engineers who will build and integrate new technologies to be launched in Vietnam, the region, or in a market on the other side of the world.

German entrepreneur Lars Jankowfsky, founder of .NFQ Asia, shares his Vietnam experience thus far:

> Vietnam has long been known as a great tech outsourcing destination: that's part of the reason why I came here when we first set off on our NFQ Asia journey. Vietnam offers us great resources of talented developers with decent English and experience working for offshore clients and with offshore team cultures.
>
> In addition, Vietnamese are young (approximately 40% of Vietnamese are less than 25 years old), hungry for success, and extremely hardworking. They share the same mind-set you find in Silicon Valley (optimistic about the future, innovative, and flexible with change) yet very regionally unique (respectful, and they have a great sense of community). It's very common here for things to get done 10 times faster compared to Western counterparts. It is because people here are very willing to go the extra mile, learning on daily basis, and they never accept "no" for an answer.
>
> From day one in 2015 with three people in an office less than 100 square meters, we've now become a great team of over 150 awesome techies in a fully-occupied 1,500-square-meter office within a short span of 36 months, all thanks to the wonderful people here that I had the great honor to work with. Our people never cease to amaze me with their work ethic, their gratitude, and their commitment to delivering great work.

Today, the "low-hanging" innovation hub potential in Vietnam is for foreign teams to try to take advantage of the low cost of living, high technical talent, and ideal working conditions insofar as a team can fully focus on product development. However, Vietnam has the potential to tap into growing waves of startup interest globally; it has the resources to help entrepreneurs build their prototypes: a low cost of living, ample skilled technical talent, and access to regional and global investor networks.

There's another advantage that Vietnam has: a network of Vietnamese around the world. While some members of the diaspora might be more engaged than others, there are formal institutions driving dialogue about Vietnam's sustainability, such as the University of California, with Davis's New Viet Nam Studies Initiative (NVNSI).

Asian American Studies professor and director of the NVNSI Kiều-Linh Valverde expands on why the timing is right for such an initiative:

> Viet Nam's dramatic growth is happening at a dynamic time. There are many more opportunities for paradigm shifts with new unexpected trade partners, and less reliance on old models of development supported by major economic powers. With this dynamism, it is important to have a good grip on what it can possibly mean for Viet Nam in the long term. The interest, understanding, and expertise in Viet Nam's economy spans the globe, as it logically should in our technological era; thus making the presence of something like the New Viet Nam Studies Initiative at the University of California Davis, all the more necessary.
>
> The New Viet Nam Studies Initiative brings together scholars, industry experts, government officials, activists, and artists to lend their knowledge of the many dimensions that comprise contemporary Vietnam. New Viet Nam Studies, or the study of the economic reconstruction and cultural renewal of

Vietnam, can potentially help move this country beyond the major conflicts of its recent history to chart its own course into the future. Those with vested interest in Viet Nam, and the power to move it toward the best direction for sustainable growth, would do well to consider international and cross-disciplinary approaches to ensure this future remains bright.

Furthermore, members (twenty-five students) of the Vietnam Global Insight Expedition (GIX) at Tuck Business School, Dartmouth College, traveled to Vietnam in 2015 in their efforts to "study Vietnam's business environment given several post-war decades of rapid social and economic change, evolving capital and investment flows, political balancing of communist ideology with capitalist growth, and the country's increased integration in international trade and labor regimes."[24]

Similarly, seven MBA students from the Kelley School of Business, Indiana University, visited Ho Chi Minh City in 2015 to "[work] on a project with a Vietnamese startup company for the past three months now. Currently, we are in Vietnam and working to align the company's future goals with potential investors. The client is a three-year-old company which is doing extremely well, but has been unable to reach its maximum impact or potential. The client is looking for a strategic investment which can assist the company both financially as well as technologically. We were in Ho Chi Minh City this whole past week working with the client on-site."

UC Davis's, Dartmouth College's, and Indiana University's current and future students with similar profiles and interests would all be interested in helping Vietnam chart its own course into the future.

Further out, it will be Vietnamese-led innovation and ingenuity[25] (partially in the form of venture building or developer skills gained from it) that will propel the local economy forward as Vietnam becomes more integrated into the global economy and in turn faces more direct regional and global competition in the form of ASEAN integration and upcoming FTAs. For now, Vietnam-based outsourcing companies are in the position to build business process outsourcing (BPO) automation technologies and experiment with venture-building models themselves, since they are currently at the forefront of the global IT outsourcing industry (and have the experience, talent, and entrepreneurial mind-set to do so). Whether they capitalize on these transformational opportunities or not remains to be seen.

A 2017 World Bank report,[26] *Vietnam at a Crossroads: Engaging in the Next Generation of Global Value Chains*, sums up Vietnam's current position:

> As successful as Vietnam has been, within the context of [Global Value Chains], its specialization has been in low value-added, end-production activities. Its challenge is to move up the value chain into higher value-added functions. Even more ambitious would be to grasp the opportunity to become an originator of products by nurturing a nascent set of domestic firms that have the potential to carve out an 'invented in Vietnam' niche in local, regional, and global markets. In short, Vietnam is at a crossroads. It can continue to specialize in low value-added assembly functions, with industrialization occurring in enclaves with little connection to the broader economy or society; or it can leverage the current wave of growth to diversify and move up the chain into higher value-added functions. Success will require Vietnam's policy makers to view the processes of development differently and to take new realities of the global economy more fully into account.

While Vietnam has a growing number of technically skilled workers (in IT and high-tech manufacturing) with low salaries (in addition to domestic migrant workers), these forms of human capital are not sustainable competitive advantages in the long run, as local wages increase over time and FDI runs the risk of shifting to places with even lower wages (the rest of Indochina and other parts of Southeast Asia). So Vietnamese

IT outsourcing firms with excess capacity have the opportunity to use their underutilized resources to develop MVPs internally or with external local or international partners. Alternately, these companies can become investors themselves in order to attract global founders with suitable ideas—that is, "If you dream it, then we will build it."

The window for Vietnam to move up the value chain is closing; inexpensive labor won't last forever, nor will Vietnam's "Golden Population Structure" (more than half of its population of working age)[27] remain intact. Just as foreign investment has flowed into Vietnam away from China, so too will investment flow into a location with less expensive labor costs—perhaps to another regional neighbor. Looking ahead, what product or service might Vietnam have in the future that will give it an advantage in the global marketplace?

Whatever it is, a brand must be created around it in order to improve the startup/enterprise/innovation ecosystems and establish a unique selling proposition (USP) to differentiate it from other landscapes. Members of the community can start by figuring out what's unique in Vietnam—or build a brand or identity around something new and create it.

At the 2017 Global Entrepreneurship Community Summit in Kuala Lumpur, Malaysia, Steve Hoffman, "Captain Hoff" of Founder Space, outlined his philosophy:

> The biggest problem in countries like Malaysia [and Vietnam] is that many of your angel investors, they have lots of money, there's lots of rich people here—some very wealthy people—but they tend to be conservative with their money. And they also didn't get rich building tech startups so they don't really understand it and even if they give you some money, they don't know how to be a great mentor to you. So you need to take it into your own hands to be that mentor. There is a lot of knowledge and a lot of great mentors online; they put out videos, they put out information, there are great books.

> You need to work a little harder to tap those resources. In Silicon Valley, you can literally walk—step out your door and you meet all these successful entrepreneurs who have done tech startups who can help you. We have that advantage. But [here], we [Silicon Valley folks] aren't going build a product for Southeast Asia, right—we don't understand your market. It's hard for us to execute here—we will focus on the US. You have to look at your strengths; your position, where you're located, what markets you have access, what knowledge you have that we wouldn't have.
>
> The other big advantage you have here is sometimes you can look into the future because things that are taking off now in Silicon Valley will come to Malaysia [and Vietnam]. But they aren't here yet so you have a chance to actually see the future—which we don't—and say, "wow, this is working in one of the major tech centers, I'm going to bring it to Malaysia [or Vietnam] and I'm going to be the first to build this huge business in Southeast Asia."

Today, many people are quick to identify what's wrong with Vietnam—and it can be quite easy sometimes (but that won't always be the case). Even ministry officials will admit the numerous challenges ahead, especially for those who are less educated, resulting from lack of opportunities. Fewer people talk about what's right in Vietnam: a young and energized workforce, a love for all things technological, and a solid work ethic. Without a doubt, there are many hard workers, but they don't usually focus on things that scale—for example, fruit or other mobile vendors (carrying quang gánh*)*. The dialogue has to start somewhere—to transition, at some point in the future, to an equilibrium based on sustainable, inclusive growth, fully leveraging the country's strengths.

In fact, Vietnam's youth could be its biggest strength of all. Ambassador Nguyễn Phương Nga, former permanent representative of the Socialist Republic of Viet Nam to the United Nations, elaborates:

> People, especially the young people, are Vietnam's biggest advantage. Vietnam ranks number 14 in the list of countries by population with over 90 million people, of which the median age is over 30 years.
>
> Industriousness, resilience, eagerness to learn, and [the] ability to adapt to new tendencies are the well-known virtues of the Vietnamese people. Vietnamese young people are very intelligent, dynamic, and creative. Providing the young people with good education is a tradition of the Vietnamese society and it is now a priority of not only the state and government, but also [of] each Vietnamese family. At present, Vietnam has more than 21,000 students studying in the [United States].
>
> Investing in the young people, trusting them, empowering them and creating favorable condition for them to innovate will bring Vietnam to success and sustainable development.

Additionally, the Vietnamese outside Vietnam (the diaspora) offer an opportunity to connect with new markets—and Vietnam offers the diaspora the opportunity to reconnect with the homeland. If Vietnamese entrepreneurs are missing know-how, they can find someone who has it; there is a huge Vietnamese community overseas. In August 2018, the Vietnamese government launched the Vietnam Innovation Network, which will enable Vietnamese expatriates in the fields of science and technology to assist in the technology transfer back to Vietnam.[28] But the diaspora long has been adding a different kind of value to Vietnam's economy.

In 2015, remittances to Vietnam topped USD $12.24 billion, up from USD $6.18 billion in 2007 (the year Vietnam joined the World Trade Organization), according to the World Bank. These incoming funds—about half of which came from the United States—contributed to 6.4 percent of Vietnam's GDP and solidified the country's status as the eleventh-biggest remittance recipient worldwide.

In early 2017, the Ho Chi Minh City Department of Planning and Investment released a report that showed the impact the Vietnamese diaspora had in the city: Overseas Vietnamese had invested USD $1.8 billion in more than nine hundred businesses in Ho Chi Minh City in 2016, according to *Dan Tri News*.[29] About half of the incoming remittances to Vietnam go to Ho Chi Minh City, so the diaspora plays a significant role in Vietnam's economic health.

Mapping out and executing a high-level vision with the diaspora's input would be an opportunity for Vietnamese entrepreneurs and companies to more easily rise to the challenge of international standards by making the capital and training investments, as well as the education and long-term commitments necessary to create innovative company cultures and individual mind-sets. In terms of reaching the latter two, only then will Vietnamese enterprises be in a position to fully reap the benefits of a burgeoning, increasingly globally connected economy.

Vietnam also has the advantage of learning from the mistakes of countries that have already undergone part of the economic transformational journey. For example, Egyptian American Mohamed El-Erian, chief economic adviser at Allianz, shared in a 2017 post,[30] "Rather than investing in genuine drivers of economic growth and human productivity—from education to infrastructure and from well-operating labor markets to non-distortionary tax regimes—the West fell in love with financial engineering as the way to deliver prosperity."

At the 2017 World Economic Forum Annual Meeting,[31] Chinese entrepreneur Jack Ma, founder and chairman of Alibaba, homed in on where he specifically believed the United States' strategy went astray: "American international companies made millions and millions of dollars from globalization...The past 30 years, companies like IBM, Cisco and Microsoft made tons of money...The question is: where did that money go? It was wasted...What if they had spent part of that money on building up their infrastructure, helping white-collar and blue-collar workers...You're supposed to spend money on your own people."

Vietnamese policy makers and business leaders would be wise to avoid the missteps currently plaguing other countries further along the path toward economic development goals, instead focusing on the nation's nascent brand beyond five-year timeframes. Perhaps most saliently, Peter Drucker, the twentieth century's greatest management thinker, advised to "keep [your] noses to the grindstone while lifting [your] eyes to the hills."[32]

In other words, focus on your long-term strategy, but take advantage of the short-term opportunities in the meantime—that's how any future brand in Vietnam will be forged, and that's how Vietnam—the brand—can begin to take on a new shape as well.

MAKING A COMMITMENT

While segments of the private sector and the youth in Vietnam seem to have fully embraced the country's future potential, it may be necessary to change the mind-set of conventional policy makers before engaging in national efforts to try altering the international perception of Vietnam or promoting Vietnamese innovation and startups abroad. The private sector can't develop Vietnam's enterprise ecosystem alone—the public sector plays a critical role in developing a foundation for the private sector to build upon. In other words, how can Vietnamese policy makers empower, incentivize, and attract (social) entrepreneurs? What will be the balance for preparing the youth—not just training for the vocational jobs of today, but also to prepare their mind-sets for jobs that don't exist yet and will emerge in ten, fifteen, or twenty years?

These are critical years for Vietnam's policy makers to develop and promote national legislation, frameworks, and incentives to foster local and foreign entrepreneurship in Vietnam, to incentivize continued investments in Vietnam–based startups, and to enable technology and innovation to drive the Vietnamese economy forward. Hanoi's Project 844, a cross-sector steering committee launched in 2016 and described as "Supporting the National Innovation Startup Ecosystem by 2025," is a good start; additional meaningful, committed, and sustained initiatives (incentives, calls, challenges, etc.) would send a clear signal to foreign entrepreneurs, investors, and developers that Vietnam is indeed open for business and serious about entrepreneurship at the startup level—in addition to a track record of courting multinational corporation (MNC) interest.

In 2015, the Vietnam Chamber of Commerce and Industry (VCCI), along with the American Chamber of Commerce (AmCham) and the US Chamber of Commerce, hosted an event in Hanoi, Building Vietnam's Innovation Economy: Discussion on Digital Trends and Cross-Border Data Flows. At this event, the now-converted TPP seemed to be on everyone's mind. According to Bloomberg,[33] Vietnam might have been the biggest winner from the trade agreement, due to expected increased trade activity. One of the key takeaways was that digital tools are not just for IT but for all potential sectors of the economy—that is, all successful businesses use the internet. Cross-border data flows are not just important to ICT access but necessary for the best technologies. A major point driven by more than one speaker during the event was that the "digital economy" is actually the economy, and any attempts to restrict the flow of data would impede trade as well. (Domestically, Hanoi aims to collect 80 percent of tax payments in provinces and cities via banks by 2020, with all state treasuries having cashless payment devices by then. Cashless payments and e-commerce in Vietnam have been on the rise as more companies offer mobile payment options—including public utilities—via applications and QR codes.)

While the TPP has transformed into the CPTPP—the Comprehensive and Progressive Trans-Pacific Partnership—it still could accelerate much-needed domestic reforms and boost Vietnam's economy.

"'Even under conservative assumptions, the [2018 World Bank] report estimates that CPTPP would increase Vietnam's GDP by 1.1 percent by 2030. Assuming a modest boost to productivity, the estimated increase of GDP would amount to 3.5 percent from CPTPP,' according to Ousmane Dione, World Bank Country Director for Vietnam."[34]

Overall, technology allows better customer service—whether it's e-commerce or payment facilitation—and Vietnamese companies need to be able to "talk to the world" in order to verify payments, especially as the numbers of Vietnamese tourists abroad increase; digital products and services help facilitate free trade across borders. With FTAs, the biggest opportunities of growth and jobs are for Vietnamese SMEs. However, they can't compete unless they have access to the world.

Additionally, a 2013 report[35] by Harvard Kennedy School's Thao Nguyen, now head of strategic partnerships, Asia-Pacific, at Airbnb, concluded that "Vietnam should consider an Internet governance strategy that prioritizes transparent regulatory practices that enable growth in the area of user-generated content (UGC) platforms, rather than simply building up hard infrastructure. Such a shift in strategy is required for Vietnam to remain competitive with its regional neighbors."

The ITIF goes even further to suggest, "If Vietnam wants a vibrant, competitive, and world-class digital economy…it should not be prescribing how users access and use digital services and how these digital services operate, as this limits both consumer choice and engagement as well as business innovation."

Again, this doesn't mean that Vietnam hasn't made any efforts or progress to address the challenges for the private sector. Decree 60,[36] which lifted the foreign ownership ratio ceiling; Decree 118,[37] which streamlined and clarified foreign investment requirements; Circular 155,[38] which outlined disclosure requirements for securities markets; Resolution 19,[39] which improved the business and investment environment; and Resolution 35,[40] which created favorable business conditions via the public-sector apparatus, are all positive signs. Still, Vietnamese American Eddie Thai, venture partner at 500 Startups Vietnam, says that entrepreneurs in Vietnam are succeeding despite the government—not because of it. "While the government is taking the right steps, they are not moving fast enough," said Thai at *The Economist's* Vietnam Summit 2016 in Ho Chi Minh City. Thai expands upon his remarks at the event:

> What is the final ingredient needed to help Vietnam jump the digital divide and achieve its full tech potential? Courage from the older generations. Courage to invest in technology, courage to embrace new technology, and especially courage to level the playing field. We youth, we know that the older generations have courage. You showed the courage to fight the French—my ancestors lost their heads doing so. You showed the courage to fight over competing visions for the future of a unified Vietnam. You showed the courage to emerge from 20 years of poverty and develop what we see around us today. We ask you to show your courage to fight one more time: break down the barriers of regulation and corruption so that founders can start to be successful because of the market conditions, not despite them.

Creating optimal conditions for business in Vietnam will be increasingly important and should not be overlooked.[41] As of 2015, there were more than sixteen thousand foreign companies operating in Vietnam—this number will increase as the number of FTAs, enterprises, and startups increases and the middle class grows. Additionally, more can be done from the public sector to even the playing field for foreign businesses and entrepreneurs in Vietnam and, more importantly, to prepare the youth for Industry 4.0 impacts.

As the Asia Society Policy Institute (ASPI)[42] outlined in its *Charting a Course for Trade and Economic Integration in the Asia-Pacific* report, issued in 2017, "trade has been one of the strongest drivers behind global growth and stability, particularly in Asia." ASPI's Independent Commission on Trade Policy Commission Members

1. Advocate that countries collaboratively intensify multifaceted capacity-building efforts to help developing countries raise standards, to be included in their trade agreements;
2. Urge multilateral trade fora to focus their work on emerging trade issues such as digital trade, state-owned enterprises, and [Global Value Chains], noting that Asia-Pacific Economic Cooperation (APEC) is particularly well positioned to do so; and
3. Recommend countries that are interested in pursuing regional trade agreements consider establishing a stand-alone [Small and Medium-sized Enterprises] agreement, based largely on the relevant provision in the TPP.

In its follow-up 2018 report, *Shifting Trade Winds: US Bilateralism and Asia-Pacific Economic Integration*, the ASPI recommended that

- Regional actors should consider pursuing the negotiation of a stand-alone regional agreement on an issue-specific basis, such as digital trade.
- The digital sector and related regulatory frameworks are still evolving, providing a unique opportunity to policy makers to establish a flexible regulatory framework for regional digital commerce that encourages trade, growth, and innovation while protecting privacy and security.
- Digital technologies play an increasingly vital role in enabling broader trade in manufactured and agricultural goods, as well as services. By significantly lowering barriers to entry, they

make it easier for SMEs in particular to participate in, and benefit from, regional commerce.
- The Asia-Pacific region has a unique opportunity to play a leading role in setting standards and norms for global digital trade.[43]

Ultimately, through collaboration, local and international partners in Vietnam can help to form an ecosystem where all can flourish: an ecosystem full of promising, fast-growing companies participating fully in the digital economy. That journey is already underway via recent cross-sector efforts, and it seems that trade, investment, and enterprise creation will continue in the short term.

Taking a long-term view, to better position itself for the coming future, a new model for schooling in Vietnam will have to emerge by combining learning with experiences in and out of the classroom—that is, learning by doing and by sharing with others. Students cannot afford to be mere bystanders or observers of history because the classroom of today will be the workplace of tomorrow in terms of diversity, culture, and foundations of excellence. Successful students will be able to communicate effectively, engage with different and relatively unknown cultures, think critically, ask thoughtful questions, reflect upon their experiences, and work together with anyone to succeed.

In Vietnam, the best international schools realize that we all live in a new world: the Information Age. They seek to prepare students for a rapidly changing and volatile world by enabling them to craft and assemble the tools to understand and overcome the complex global challenges that they will encounter. This task is critical because one day in the near future, students will have to answer a vital question: What do these grand challenges mean for me?

If Vietnam can address the concerns in chapter 7, it will enable concentrated efforts, attention, and focus on economic issues—and opportunities for Vietnam. However, addressing international concerns does not mean propping up Vietnamese versions of Facebook, Google, and Twitter à la China's model—the market size does not support this strategy. More likely, it means having Vietnam's leaders—at all levels—commit to SDG implementation[44] to achieve the 2030 Agenda—and a deep revamp of the country's primary and secondary education systems for "where the hockey puck is going" so to speak. New business models based on new technologies are emerging in the global marketplace from new and unexpected places; for example, Tencent's WeChat provides a glimpse into a digital future for payments. Workers will need to develop new skills and ways of problem solving. Where clients once paid for delivery, they are now paying for services via a subscription—and will pay for impact in the future, according to John Hagel of Deloitte's Center for the Edge.

In a 2017 article published[45] by the World Economic Forum, Hagel laid out his views for the systemic transformations ahead:

> The notion here is that, while you can't control a system, you can shape its direction and evolution over time and accelerate learning within the system, so that the system becomes more and more effective in terms of addressing the challenges and opportunities. Platforms can play a significant role in accelerating learning through things like providing more real-time feedback loops, where system participants can see what results their current actions are producing and reflect and adjust and refine based on real-time feedback.

Across the various components of Vietnam's system, there are already many challenges for existing business models and fulfillment: low consumer credit card adoption rates, the logistics of transporting goods to irregularly numbered addresses, consumers' skeptical perception of so-called quality products, cash on delivery (COD) policies and expectations, and a potentially uphill battle in educating consumers about a new business model. (Sometimes, one can't reliably project how consumers will react—or even if commuters will pay attention to traffic signals.) Where and when such new platforms and feedback loops emerge will be up to service providers and consumer advocates—though it's unclear which group will lead the way. Of particular concern will be the role of cybersecurity and how it will impact the way Vietnam adopts digital technologies while maintaining privacy standards around increasing amounts of consumer and user data.

Vietnam is already amassing vast amounts of IT outsourcing knowledge as it continues to build up its low-tech manufacturing capabilities—and now multinationals are training the nation's workforce on how to assemble high-tech components. For some Vietnamese, it may only be a matter of time before the opportunity cost to start their own company becomes too great to ignore. In the not-too-distant future, attempts at a "Vietnamese Samsung," a "Vietnamese Xiaomi," or a "Vietnamese Nintendo" may emerge to challenge established high-tech players. (Already, there is VinFast, Vietnam's first domestic car firm, a subsidiary of Vingroup, one of Vietnam's most powerful corporations.)

Despite the coming challenges, education and innovation are the two pillars that will support Vietnam's future development path. The "startup wave" combined with the decoupling of SOEs from the economy is a once-in-a-lifetime opportunity for the country, for it will require remarkable engineering and courage from the leadership in Vietnam to abandon some of its past practices and use the momentum to keep the country's economy growing.

In general, the people who are in power today—that is, the members of the Politburo and the Central Committee of the Communist Party—were—at the upper limits—between twenty and thirty-two years old when the country was reunified in 1975. (In fact, former president Trương Tấn Sang spent time in a Phú Quốc prison during the First Indochina War.) By the Fourteenth National Party Congress (in 2025), and surely by the Sixteenth National Party Congress—in just short of twenty years[46]—there will be few, if any, members in the Politburo who were alive during the

Second Indochina War (also known as the Vietnam War and known in Vietnam as the American War).[47] As new waves of Vietnam's leadership are further removed from the direct impacts of war, poverty, and famine, the national—and individual leadership's—orientation to these horrors may change in unforeseen ways.[48]

For those who aren't in a position to exercise political capital, innovation can even be championed by individuals in smaller—though still impactful—ways. In a 2016 interview with Sam Altman of Y Combinator, Elon Musk, Tesla founder and CEO and SpaceX cofounder and CEO, explained how to figure out how to be most useful: "Whatever the thing is you're trying to create, [ask] what would be the utility delta compared to the current state of the art, times how many people it would affect? So that's why I think something that makes a big difference, but affects a small to moderate number of people is great, as is something that makes a small difference but affects a vast number of people. The area under the curve would be roughly similar for those two things. So it's really about trying to be useful."[49]

Similarly, Reid Hoffman, cofounder of LinkedIn and partner at Greylock Ventures, came up[50] with a formula for prioritizing time spent on activities that matter:

Hoffman also advocates for volunteerism in subjects that one is an expert in—that is, sharing what you have developed as a specialization. Thomas Friedman, *New York Times* columnist, goes even further in describing what kind of formula a society should embrace to navigate through a "transition moment." In early 2017, Friedman responded to an audience member's question on advice for promoting resilience during economic structural changes during an event[51] at the University of Chicago, where he was speaking:

> In a period of rapid change, you actually want to be radically open. I want [Trans-Pacific Partnership] everywhere, actually. Because the most open society is going to get the signals first and is going attract the most high-IQ risk-takers to start new jobs. You want to be radically open, you want to educate everybody as much as you can, and you want to strengthen your safety nets because it will be too fast…for a lot of people. If you close off…you will be doing the most dangerous thing you could be doing…
>
> All I know is generally, what I would do in a moment of transition like this is be radically open and trust human creativity.

While Friedman's comments were generally about the United States, he is no stranger to Vietnam, having visited[52] the Diplomatic Academy of Vietnam (DAV)[53] in 2014 to discuss topics such as green technologies, political and global forces, historical lessons learned, and challenges and opportunities for Vietnam.

A more Vietnam-centric take (after fifteen-plus years of research) would be the following, according to Finn Tarp, director of the United Nations University World Institute for Development Economics Research (UNU-Wider):

1. Stay on target—continue investing in physical, human, and social capital;
2. Maintain increase in agricultural productivity and innovation;
3. Ensure job opportunities created outside agriculture;

4. Pay attention to gender balance and minorities; and
5. Support people in adapting to new circumstances.[54]

For those who may want to cling to institutions of the past, incoming technological and social changes will only accelerate in Vietnam, in part due to a rising middle class who will want to show—and even flaunt—their newfound wealth and express themselves in ways previously unavailable. (Note: this could be in the form of purchasing habits, hobbies, or social media expression.) Ensuring that these changes are largely positive will require a commitment from the public and private sectors to make innovative educational and economic opportunities available, accessible, affordable, and sustainable—especially for those who have not benefited from Vietnam's economic growth until now.

CHAPTER 9

LOCALIZING GLOBAL SOLUTIONS

NONE OF VIETNAM'S TOP THIRTY companies disclosed sufficient transparent information in 2016, according to a 2017 report by Toward Transparency, a local consultancy that operates as the national contact for Transparency International. The report portrayed a fairly dismal state of affairs as of November 30, 2016, according to the *VnExpress*:[1] four of the top thirty companies had no functional website, and none displayed transparent information on company structure and ownership, anticorruption measures—or detailed reports for multinational corporations with activities in other markets. Foreign-owned subsidiaries also lacked transparent information, including corporate structures for Unilever, Canon, and Microsoft Mobile.

However, these firms may be missing out on an opportunity to tap into and lead a trend likely to strengthen in the future. According to the 2015 Corporate Sustainability Report by Nielsen,[2] Vietnamese consumers are the most socially conscious in Asia-Pacific. Up to 86 percent of Vietnamese consumers are willing to pay a premium "for products and services that come from companies who are committed to positive social and environmental impacts, compared to 76% of consumers in Asia Pacific."[3]

Thus, the Vietnamese business community can create, as well as import, frameworks, best practices, and techniques from abroad, but not all frameworks or targets—at face value—are suitable for Vietnam, at least for the short term. In general, the headlines coming out of Silicon Valley—or China—highlighting massive rounds of funding are not realistic data points for Vietnamese startups, or even most Southeast Asian startups.

While increased focus on environmental impacts, such as carbon footprints, is well intentioned, this is also not a realistic priority for the Vietnamese business community at present. In 2017, the Bank of Åland unveiled the world's first bank index that assesses the environmental impact of every individual credit card transaction. In an "Executive Perspective"[4] feature by Thomson Reuters, the Åland Index was described in the following way:

> The application is quantifying consumers' carbon footprint and the social cost of carbon by using Environmental Social Governance (ESG) data. First, revenues and CO_2 data was analyzed and matched by KPMG with the top 50 merchant category codes (MCC) from MasterCard. Then we could calculate the average carbon footprint per category for every Euro spent. The Åland Index matches the footprint with the individual spending and computes the cost by using the price of carbon from the World Bank. With leading Environmental, Social, and Governance (ESG) data, merchant category codes and a fixed price, the Åland Index is scalable to fit any other bank.

In the Vietnamese context, the only bank that might be able to incorporate the Åland Index today is Timo Bank, Vietnam's first "digital lifestyle bank," which launched in 2016 in Ho Chi Minh City and Hanoi. The bank has a total of three physical locations (including a Hangout in

Da Nang)—mainly to fulfill banking regulations. However, Timo customers have access to over fifteen thousand ATMs in Vietnam thanks to Timo's partnership with Vietnam Prosperity Bank (VP Bank), which provides back-end services for Timo. For now, Timo has plans to offer additional products beyond the four currently available, as well as to continue expanding geographically.

However, what is applicable to all businesses in Vietnam is the *CEO Guide to the Sustainable Development Goals*, issued by the World Business Council for Sustainable Development.[5] The guide is currently being translated into a variety of languages, so perhaps it will be in Vietnamese soon enough[6]—or elements of Vietnam's community can take the lead and turn it into a crowd-sourcing project (or sponsor it).

Ceres is another organization that provides resources for firms looking to become sustainable. As the organization's website states,

> The Ceres Roadmap for Sustainability is a resource to help companies re-engineer themselves for success in a world beset with unprecedented environmental and social challenges that threaten the economy and local communities. It is designed to guide companies toward corporate sustainability leadership, and ultimately support an accelerated transition toward a more sustainable global economy. The Ceres Roadmap contains 20 specific expectations for corporate sustainability leadership, broadly divided into four areas of activity—governance, stakeholder engagement, disclosure and performance.

Additionally, CDP, a not-for-profit charity, formerly the Carbon Disclosure Project, enables companies and cities to measure and understand their environmental impact. Ban Ki Moon, former secretary general of the United Nations, had this to say about CDP, according to the CDP website:[7] "The work of CDP is crucial to the success of global business in the 21st century...helping persuade companies throughout the world to measure, manage, disclose and ultimately reduce their greenhouse gas emissions. No other organization is gathering this type of corporate climate change data and providing it to the marketplace."

As of early 2018, no Vietnamese entities could be found on CDP's data portal. The EDGE certification is another international framework that can help to achieve the SDG in the area of gender equality (SDG 5) in Vietnam. EDGE helps close the corporate gender gap, primarily in three areas, according to its website:[8] (1) the underrepresentation of women in senior areas, (2) the pay gap between men and women, and (3) different advancement and career opportunities. Research has shown that women in businesses—whether managing money[9] or in the boardroom[10]—create higher returns for investors (and diversity in general leads to better profits). As of 2017, there was at least one "Global Development Institution" undergoing the EDGE certification process in Vietnam.

Ellevate, a global professional women's network, helps women by connecting them to one another, by providing knowledge via digital and in-person events, and by investment through Pax Ellevate Global Women's Index Fund.[11] As a Certified B Corporation, Ellevate partners with companies who invest in their women. As of publication, there is not an Ellevate chapter in Vietnam.

Remarkably, Vietnam has Southeast Asia's only female billionaire,[12] Nguyễn Thị Phương Thảo, founder of Vietjet Airlines, whose net worth was estimated to be USD $1.7 billion.[13] Furthermore, in 2016, Nguyễn Thị Kim Ngân was the first woman to become the National Assembly chairperson, paving the way for a female prime minister in the future. Similarly, Đặng Thị Ngọc Thịnh became the first female president of Vietnam in 2018, taking on the role of Acting State President after President Trần Đại Quang passed away.

The Vietnamese economy has benefited from the pioneering role of women in the labor force relative to other economies. As the IMF noted in a 2018 Finance and Development article: "Vietnam's performance is particularly noteworthy. Its high female labor force participation rate outstrips the best performers among advanced Western economies. And it has also succeeded in maintaining female labor force participation of some 70 percent for more than two decades—a feat unsurpassed even among advanced economies."[14]

In a 2018 Mastercard report, Vietnam ranked sixth out of fifty-three countries with highest women business ownership. Almost one-third of businesses in Vietnam are owned by women, reflecting the nation's eighteenth worldwide ranking in the Mastercard Index of Women Entrepreneurs (MIWE). In the MIWE, Vietnam scored 65.5 points based on supporting entrepreneurial conditions, women's advancement outcomes, and knowledge assets and financial access.[15]

Similarly, in the 2017/2018 Global Entrepreneurship Monitor (GEM) Global Report, Vietnam was one of just three economies where women reported equal or higher rates of entrepreneurship compared to men.[16] Overall, Vietnam ranked 15th (tied with Estonia and Guatemala) out of 54 countries in the Entrepreneurial Spirit Index, which is based on "Total early-stage entrepreneurial activity (TEA), the proportion of established businesses (EB) among the respondents and entrepreneurial employee activity (EEA)."

Vietnam was recognized in BCG's 2017 *Moving Toward Gender Diversity in Southeast Asia*[17] report for having one of the highest shares of women in top positions—with 25 percent of 500 female respondents in Vietnam reporting that they held CEO or board level positions—and acknowledged in Deloitte Global's *Women in the Boardroom: A Global Perspective*[18] study for leading gender equality in Asia—with women holding 17.6 percent of board seats. However, there is more work to be done. A 2018 *Financial Times* (*FT*) article highlighted long-standing gender inequality issues: "Vietnam is likely to suffer the most from gender inequality if no action is taken. [The December 2017 FT Confidential Research] survey showed Vietnam has the lowest female-to-male ratio in top management, with one woman to every eight men, compared with 5.6 men in Malaysia and 2.8 men in the Philippines."[19]

The *FT* article continued:

> As in many south-east Asian countries, women in Vietnam still suffer from gender-based discrimination at work. According to a 2015 report by the International Labor Organization (ILO), Vietnamese women have less access than men to productive resources, education, and skills development, and fewer job opportunities. The [(ILO)] says that gender discrimination in Vietnam is the product of a society that still thinks women have a lower status than men. Women are expected to take on unpaid care work and engage in subsistence agriculture, particularly in the central-north and Central Highlands regions. In [the] ASEAN-5 survey, Vietnam had the largest proportion of respondents who said that "women have fewer opportunities than men."
>
> Notably, the 25-to-35 age group was most likely to agree to this statement. These are well-educated millennials with several years of working experience and good promotion prospects, but women in this age bracket are also pressured by society to marry and have children. Our survey suggests that even in urban Vietnam, women feel their careers are being held back. A 2017 report from the United Nations Entity for Gender Equality and the Empowerment of Women also highlights discrimination in the Vietnamese workplace. The report says that while there are new job opportunities in Vietnam's growing manufacturing sector, women still receive less training than men and are not as likely to be promoted.

A 2017 BSR[20] report titled *Women's Empowerment in Global Value Chains* made similar observations about the lack of gender equality in Vietnam's blue-collar workforce: "Women represent around 80% of

Vietnam's 700,000 light manufacturing workers, but they tend to be in lower-paid positions as seamstresses and helpers, while men are in higher-paid occupations such as cutters and mechanics."

For those who doubt some of the frameworks being applicable, it's already happening in Vietnam with the Higg Index by the Sustainable Apparel Coalition.[21] Furthermore, the IIX Foundation,[22] based in Singapore, works with at least one Vietnamese startup, Hamona, to track its coconut products from farm to table. Moreover, the UNICEF Innovation Lab in Vietnam imported[23] the UPSHIFT program, which was pioneered in Kosovo.

Currently, social entrepreneurs can choose Impact Reporting and Investment Standards (IRIS) or Global Impact Investing Rating System (GIIRS) for measuring the impact of their efforts. New or incoming investors looking to incorporate social elements into their activities can look to the United Nations Principles for Responsible Investment (UNPRI),[24] which outline six principles and ways to implement them. Considering the amount of infrastructure investment needed in Vietnam, new roles and responsibilities for development banks[25] might also be piloted.[26] In the future, lessons learned from infrastructure investment can be shared with entities such as the Global Guidelines Project, which seeks "ecological and environmental guidelines on all aspects of road planning, design, construction and maintenance from around the world" in order to be made freely available on its website.[27]

However, Vietnamese organizations and innovators can also create their own frameworks or institutions, such as the LOTUS rating (in lieu of LEED), a product of the Vietnam Green Building Council (VGBC), or the Vietnam Sustainable Energy Alliance,[28] composed of five core members in 2012. Another Vietnamese creation is the *Provincial Competitiveness Index Report*, which has been annually produced since 2005 by the VCCI with assistance from the US Agency for International Development (USAID). The report—"from 12,000 enterprises, including more than 10,200 domestic private enterprises from 63 cities and provinces and nearly 1,800 foreign invested enterprises in 21 provinces in Vietnam"—is used to assess the "ease of doing business, economic governance, and administrative reform efforts by the provincial and city governments in Vietnam in order to promote the development of the private sector," according to the 2017 Provincial Competitiveness Index Report Launch.[29]

On the topic of good governance, the Vietnam Institute of Directors (VIOD) "promotes corporate governance standards and best practices in the Vietnamese corporate sector." Launched in April 2018 with support from the IFC and Switzerland's State Secretariat for Economic Affairs (SECO), the VIOD board of directors is comprised of a diverse group of local and foreign business leaders, of which two out of seven are women.[30] As corporate governance increases in importance and moves to the forefront of Vietnamese business priorities, sharing best practices and promoting transparency and business ethics will become more vital for instilling additional investor confidence.

New markets may also be designed by entrepreneurs pioneering novel business models—which can be a daunting task. In order to overcome these challenges, startup teams and Vietnamese entrepreneurs should seek as much international exposure (to standards, mind-set, language, etc.) as possible—for example, participating in regional and global events such as competitions; visiting technology and innovation hubs (to build up networks and pipelines) in places such as Singapore, Europe, and the United States; and mastering the English language. In terms of the latter, building soft and pitching skills should be a priority for all teams seeking investment and opportunities abroad, especially since this could be an untapped area. (Note: this does not mean supplanting elements of Vietnamese culture or identity.)

Echoing Green, a social innovation fund, received 2,879 applications for its 2017 Fellowship class. Just 3 percent of applicants were from East Asia and Pacific (EAP), higher only than the 1 percent applying from Middle East and Africa, according to the firm.[31] That means that eighty-six people from EAP applied to this fellowship opportunity. Yet there is at least one active former Echoing Green fellow in Vietnam—so why isn't there more interest in the fellowship? One possible explanation may lie in cultural orientations toward creation.

A 2017 report[32] published by the Martin Prosperity Institute at the University of Toronto's Rotman School of Management, called *The Rise of the Urban Creative Class in Southeast Asia*, examined "the intersection of urbanization and the rise of the new creative or middle class in Southeast Asia." Vietnam and Thailand fell into a third tier of creative class, with about 10 percent of their populations comprising members of the creative class. Globally, both countries rank in the second half of all nations for the Global Creativity Index and for their shares of creative workers, at number eighty-one and number eighty-two, respectively.

In terms of economic output per person, Vietnam and Thailand (Vietnam's largest trading partner in ASEAN) fell into a fourth tier, with USD $8,700 and approximately USD $10,000, respectively.[33] Ho Chi Minh City's economic output per person is almost six times higher than the national economic output per person, with the city's total economic output reaching USD $71 billion. In 2016, Ho Chi Minh City's GDP growth rate was 8.05 percent,[34] with the services sector expected to comprise 60 percent of the city's GDP by 2020.[35]

The study, which assessed innovation rankings based on the number of patent applications per million people, ranked Vietnam sixty-fourth, with forty-two patent applications per million people in Vietnam. However, this framework may not recognize all of Vietnam's innovations. In a 2016 report[36] produced by the Vietnam National Office of Intellectual Property (NOIP), a major concern identified was that Vietnamese firms were not registering trademarks at foreign intellectual property agencies for protection.

Additionally, the NOIP received thirty thousand registration applications for trademark protection from Vietnamese firms and seven thousand applications from foreign companies in 2015. Vietnamese enterprises may not see the value in filing for patents or trademarks; there are plentiful examples of foreign and domestic intellectual property violations across Vietnam, with seemingly little repercussion.

The Martin Prosperity report goes on to state, "In emerging countries like those of Southeast Asia, entrepreneurship can help generate economic development and the development of a broader middle class." However, there are also new challenges to capturing the economic benefits of urbanization, such as getting the timing right between a shrinking manufacturing base and a growing class of creativity workers. As the report concludes, "It is harder today to develop a middle class based on blue-collar manufacturing. The urban middle class is either developing slowly or failing to develop in some Southeast Asian nations and cities. This will continue to be a critical challenge for the region, its nations, and cities for the future."

Effectively, a vote in the form of FDI into one country removes that possibility (and its benefits) for other countries in Southeast Asia and around the world. Thus, it would be advantageous for Vietnam to encourage more foreign and diaspora entrepreneurs and product developers to come to Vietnam and team up with local talent—in the form of, but not limited to, coders—to create products and services. In this scenario, a Vietnamese development team could possibly leverage newfound skills, experience, and network to develop its own products and services.

While FDI is critical to growth, the most impactful activity in Vietnam today might be fostering additional collaboration between various actors on the ground. In this realm, one answer might be Village Capital's peer-selection review framework, which strongly encourages cooperation among community members in order to accurately rate one another and determines the best-qualified startup to receive an investment. Village Capital is unique in that it focuses on high-growth entrepreneurs outside the usual locations of California, New York, and Massachusetts—where half of all venture capital funding goes.[37] Given Vietnam's three distinct ecosystems, a variation of this activity could be deployed locally, with the winners moving on to national or regional competitions. However, Village Capital, based in Washington, DC, does not have a dedicated Southeast

Asia presence, although it has conducted programs in China and, more recently, Indonesia. Another organization, also based on the East Coast of the United States, albeit in New York City, is Endeavor Global, a community of entrepreneurs, mentors, and investors. According to its website,[38] "as of November 2017, Endeavor has supported 1,563 entrepreneurs leading 978 companies in 30 markets around the world. Supported and mentored by our growing network of 4,000+ local and global business leaders, these entrepreneurs have created over 600,000 high-value jobs and generate more than USD $10+ billion in annual revenues."

In 2018, the Endeavor Vietnam chapter was announced via a call for a managing director position on the organization's website. The global organization, which utilizes an independent chapter model of thirty worldwide, will be based in Ho Chi Minh City and cover the entire country. Given its overall track record, Endeavor Vietnam could turbocharge innovation and entrepreneurship actors locally.

In the near future, a six-month startup or entrepreneur visa (without excessive strings) could incentivize foreign developers, project managers, and others to be based in Vietnam, taking advantage of the low cost of living and adding value to the local ecosystem by sharing experiences and know-how with local colleagues. Such a scheme could accelerate a mindset shift from "Made in Vietnam" to "Created (or Invented) in Vietnam" and enable a clearer path for the country to move up the value chain for digital products and services.

RELATIONSHIPS VERSUS KNOWLEDGE

At a 2016 informal dinner among foreign investors and members of the public sector in Hanoi, a vice minister was asked, during a Q&A session, "In what industry can Vietnamese be number one or number two in the world?" The vice minister responded to the question by stating that before, Vietnamese entrepreneurs relied on knowledge of relationships, but the shift these days is toward knowledge of information as an advantage, and that Vietnamese talent can shine in ICT.

Since joining the WTO in 2007, Vietnam has progressively become more integrated with global markets more than ever before, party to sixteen FTAs as of 2018, and a rising middle class. Increased trade has driven relationships between Vietnam and the world, and, increasingly, Vietnamese startups desire to go abroad. This interest is not one sided; there is reciprocal foreign investor and mentor interest in the country for entrepreneurs to benefit from.

Since the startup scene is at such an early stage of development, the basics and fundamentals of business have yet to be mastered in Vietnam (for startups), as some entrepreneurs struggle with collecting and interpreting customer/user feedback. For many entrepreneurs, it is equal parts exciting, frustrating, rewarding, and challenging to bring a product or service to market in Vietnam.

According to some estimates, there are at least a thousand and perhaps more than three thousand active startups in Vietnam, depending on whom you ask. In the long run, it's more important for founders (and the supporting community) to focus on sustainability, scalability, and defensibility of their business models (and, of course, value creation) rather than purely on quantities. More fundamentally, if you don't have sales, then you don't have a business.

In discourse about Vietnam's startup scene, most think of Ho Chi Minh City and for good reasons: it's the largest city in Vietnam, it has a robust

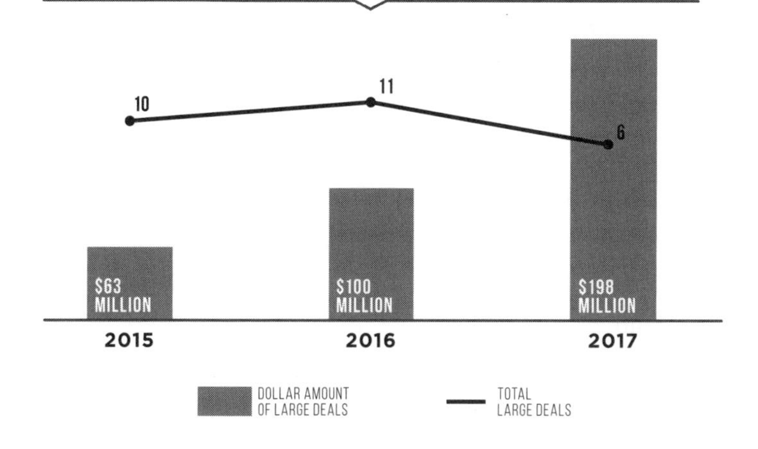

expat community, and it's the economic center of the country. However, this is an oversimplification of Vietnam's startup potential: there are other ecosystems within Vietnam, including Hanoi (Vietnam's capital) as well as Da Nang, a central coastal city with a population of over one million people. It's particularly encouraging that many people—who are staples of their respective communities—are willing to meet newcomers and make introductions.

Too often, local startups complain that there is not enough available funding, while some active investors in Vietnam cite lack of sufficient deal flow. Despite these criticisms, there has been a lot of increased interest from regional and foreign investors, especially in the past two to three years as the number of deals has increased, on average, from twenty deals annually from 2011 through 2013 to forty-eight annually from 2014 through 2016, based on data aggregated by TFI.[39] Of note in 2016, seed and Series A deals made up 70 percent of the fifty documented deals, according to TFI.[40] Additionally, the number of large deals (greater than USD $5 million) remained relatively unchanged (ten in 2015 and eleven in 2016), but their collective value grew 60 percent (USD $63 million compared to

USD $100 million). Furthermore, in terms of deal value, foreign funds outperformed local funds.

In 2017, there were ninety-two deals, valued at USD $291 million—up from fifty in 2016 (then a total startup deal value of USD $205 million)—with eight acquisitions totaling USD $128 million,[41] according to TFI.[42] The year 2017 also marked the first time that local angel and institutional investors bypassed foreign entities, but with a smaller aggregate deal value.

The good news is that foreigners seem interested in investing in Vietnam and in Vietnamese startups. What is less clear is whether there is enough follow-on funding available for startups emerging from the growing number of incubators and accelerators in Vietnam. Teams applying to any structured program need to ask what value—beyond capital—these programs and other investors are offering them and take a hard look at the opportunity costs when reading the fine print to avoid potentially unfavorable terms, especially for young and inexperienced operators.

Vietnamese entrepreneurs will have to learn more quickly and build a more diverse network to utilize strategic connections. Future success will require both relationships and knowledge to develop local solutions for local challenges—solutions that can then be exported via trusted global networks. Many choices need to be made between protectionism and preparation—will Vietnamese entrepreneurs and companies fully participate in the Digital Economy/Industry 4.0, or will they fall back on traditional relationships as an advantage? More importantly, how can young Vietnamese effectively engage with other young people around the world? And how can sister city relationships be better leveraged? For example, Ho Chi Minh City and San Francisco are sister cities, as are Oakland and Da Nang; Seattle and Hải Phòng; and Cần Thơ and Riverside respectively—but what are the short- and long-term (optimal) benefits of such arrangements?[43]

It is also prudent to be aware of the relationships between global institutions and how Vietnam fits into their respective visions—and how it helps reshape those visions if they don't reflect conditions on the ground.

ASEAN, which Vietnam joined in 1995, turned fifty years old in 2017. At the World Economic Forum's summit on ASEAN in 2017, the theme was "Youth, Technology and Growth: Securing ASEAN's Demographic and Digital Dividends." According to the World Economic Forum,[44] "At the start of 2016, the 10 economies of ASEAN were collectively the seventh largest economy in the world. By the start of 2017, that rank had improved to sixth, and by 2020 it will be fifth."

Thus, relations between Vietnam and other ASEAN countries will be critical, especially in avoiding overreliance on any single trade agreement or partnership.[45] However, ASEAN is not the only influential institution in the region. The Asian Infrastructure Investment Bank (AIIB), which China launched in 2016, is expected to lend USD $10–15 billion per year for the first few years, according to Reuters.[46] In its first year, the AIIB reached its funding target of USD $1.2 billion in projects by committing USD $1.73 billion to nine projects, according to the *Nikkei Asian Review*.[47]

China is also promoting its One Belt, One Road (OBOR) initiative, which promises over USD $1 trillion in infrastructure investment across sixty countries, its most ambitious megaproject yet.

Vietnam is expected to receive over USD $10 billion in investment from China from 2017 through 2021 as part of this initiative, according to the *New York Times*.[48] However, as the Asia Maritime Transparency Initiative (AMTI) pointed out in a 2017 post,[49] "Though China's statements about [the 'Belt and Road Initiative'] align with ASEAN financial aspirations, these infrastructure systems hold a very different strategic weight for Beijing than they do for ASEAN. If strategists in Southeast Asia do not take this into account, the new infrastructural connections—which would tie Southeast Asian nations individually to China, rather than connecting China with ASEAN as a whole—would pose a threat to ASEAN connectivity, a key principle in the strength of the organization."

Even collaboration has its own set of challenges for Vietnam, but going it alone would only reap so many benefits, stunted by the lack of cooperation with regional and international partners.

Some of the most important relationships with Vietnam are currently being forged in the form of people-to-people ties, such as the Australia–Vietnam Young Leadership Dialogue (AVYLD), which was held for the first time in 2017. The AVLD is described on its website as "an independent non-profit initiative that was established to nurture relationships, promote engagement, and incubate collaboration between Australian and Vietnamese young leaders from a broad spectrum of society. Through people to people links, we believe the bilateral relationship between Australia and Vietnam can be strengthened to contribute to the development of each respective nation."

Chinese Australian Shuyin Tang, partner at Patamar Capital (formerly Unitus Impact), an impact investment firm based in San Francisco, joined the AVLD in 2017. Tang lived in Hanoi for three years before moving to Ho Chi Minh City in early 2017. According to Tang,

> Though impact investing is nascent in Vietnam, we feel like we're here at the right time. Vietnam is certainly an integral part of the ASEAN growth story, with fast GDP growth, increasing foreign investment, and attractive demographic trends. At the same time, though, the majority of the population is still low-to-lower-middle income, and GDP per capita is still only 60% and 70% of neighbors Indonesia and [the] Philippines respectively. This means there is tremendous opportunity to build businesses which improve the livelihoods of the working poor, are highly scalable, and can achieve attractive financial returns.

Impact investing has increased in popularity in recent years, despite its relative difficulty (compared to conventional investing). After all, the requirements of a suitable investment need to be met—and then the business needs to have a quantifiable social impact element in its product or service as well. Yet impact investors have a role to play in Vietnam. The lines between civil society and the private sector are becoming ever more blurred; it's increasingly difficult to identify a social enterprise from a sustainable NGO. (Though there are important differences and priorities, such as revenue model and mission.)

Furthermore, civil society has a greater role in implementation and accountability—as stakeholders and as the link between governments and communities. Drawing out the best in and from Vietnam requires knowledge about Vietnam and having the relationships in place to act as a trusted adviser.

Strategic and innovative partnerships are vital to achieve this, and they will provide the foundation for flexibility and strength to overcome current and future cross-cultural challenges. Considering that Vietnam is the only country in Southeast Asia to recognize the concept of a social enterprise via a regulatory framework (as of late 2017), it follows that there will be additional local interest in this space.

For those who are not ready to commit to being on the ground long term in Vietnam due to mismatched risk profiles—a very real challenge—there are other options for establishing contact or relationships, such as a social sabbatical. In early 2017, twelve employees of SAP, the enterprise software application provider, completed a month-long trip to Vietnam, where they worked with a nonprofit organization, two social enterprises, and a registered charity to overcome operational challenges and implement their respective organizational missions.

According to SAP,[50] the twelve employees hailed from different geographical and functional backgrounds and worked as independent consultants with their partner organizations in Vietnam. The social sabbatical activities were part of SAP's global CSR program, which aims to promote and leverage skills-based volunteering, considered to be the most effective form of volunteering.

In 2017, Freight Farms, a provider of urban agricultural solutions, partnered with Everlane, a San Francisco–based retailer, to deliver three Leafy Green Machines (LGMs—container-based farm units) to an Everlane supplier factory in Ho Chi Minh City so that Vietnamese workers could enjoy pesticides-free vegetables as a result of Everlane's annual Black Friday Fund, "an annual initiative that uses their Black Friday sales to improve the lives of factory workers at their factories."[51]

While these programs are corporate examples, there is nothing to prevent freelancers or even remote workers from conducting similar trips to Vietnam. Remote Year, a year-long structured program for fifty to eighty remote workers, has visited Vietnam twice as of 2017, with Hanoi and Ho Chi Minh City in its 2018 itineraries. Some remote workers, or location-independent professionals, are at the cutting edge of their respective industries, be it digital marketing, Amazon reselling, or web design—so they can offer training or workshops to update standard practices, or even stay in Vietnam for a while to join a project.

Overall, each interaction between a Vietnamese person and a foreigner is an opportunity for another data point to better understand each other. It affords vested parties the ability to build confidence—taking smart risks to enhance creativity via collaboration and to develop critical thinking skills by asking the right questions. These are the vital interpersonal skills[52]—also known as soft skills—required to be successful in the twenty-first century and to foster a growth mind-set.

EXPONENTIAL TECHNOLOGIES

Today, more than four billion people, mostly in developing countries, don't have access to the internet. Digital regulations in these countries have not caught up to the times or are punitively designed instead of incentivizing positive engagement. Ultimately, the full potential of a country's citizens cannot be unleashed if they are censored or self-censoring. In an era when solutions can come from anywhere in the world, an open web is integral to achieving equality and prosperity for all.

The major societal benefit of a global user base means that even with regulation holding back the advancement of an industry in one country, breakthroughs will be made in others. Organic and engineered "innovation hubs" will continue to spring up in unlikely places as nations seek to have products not just made in their countries, but designed and created there as well.

However, this "opportunistic proliferation" of concepts into workable solutions also poses risks to heavily regulated established markets, such as medicine in the United States. Thus, as commodity capitalism continues to shift to forms of intellectual capitalism, we will witness the complete transformations of whole industries.

As the world seeks to implement sustainable and inclusive economic growth models, entire industries will be disrupted—and governments will be tested. The unique challenges faced by developing nations must also be considered when envisioning a future where emerging technologies will play critical roles in the lives of everyday citizens. By 2050, two-thirds of humanity will live in cities; the social, economic, and governance implications—buoyed by technology—of this migration are profound.

Consider open source: This business model draws on globally engaged users (they choose to be involved, after all) from diverse and creative backgrounds who seek to change the world in (largely) positive ways, whether by promoting open-source information or adding their expertise or experiences to a discussion on someone else's idea—or even taking an existing idea and executing it for the benefit of all. Alternately, take a look at crowd sourcing: It's already promoting collaboration on an unprecedented global level, as anyone can add or build upon the current discourse about a particular challenge, concept, or idea.[53] In early 2017, Hanoi's Department of Transportation offered a USD $200,000 prize to members of the public who could offer a viable solution to the city's growing traffic problem. According to a *VnExpress* article,[54] "statistics show that Hanoi has more than 5.5 million personal vehicles (nearly 500,000 cars and more than five million motorcycles), and an average of over 19,000 new vehicles are registered each month. The numbers are expected to increase to more than 7.3 million motorbikes and 1.3 million cars by 2025."

On the topic of innovation in transportation, Grab cofounder Tan Hooi Ling shared the following at the 2018 Rise Conference in Hong Kong:[55]

> EV [electric vehicles] is already here today, AV [autonomous vehicles] will likely happen in Singapore, but for other countries, for those of you who have been to Vietnam, I don't think that's going to happen anytime soon... because when you cross the road, you don't see traffic moving in one directions or two directions or three directions, it's like 360 [degrees]. Intersections have bikes crossing endlessly and they don't care about you, by the way.

A crowd-sourced and solution-based approach certainly seems more sound than other proposals put forth, including banning motorbikes. Still, this crowd-sourcing problem can and should be applied to other pressing problems within Vietnam (such as the fifty-five thousand coal stoves used by Hanoians)[56]—and the region. However, it's not just open source or crowd sourcing that is changing the way people around the world innovate—including places such as Vietnam: new ways of manufacturing will continue emerging into the mainstream as well.

For example, this century will see the rise of 3-D printing or "additive manufacturing" as opposed to "subtractive manufacturing." 3-D printing will use less materials to create the same products and will be remarkably faster than traditional manufacturing methods. Already, villas are being built using 3-D printing technology—in less than a day—in some parts of the world.

On a smaller scale, Fab Labs have been popping up around the world as "prototyping platforms for local entrepreneurship," although the cost to set up a proper Fab Lab (as recognized by the Fab Foundation) is more than USD $100,000—a sum that is largely unaffordable in the developing world. However, USD $250–$500 3-D printers are affordable and can also be used for prototyping (even though "a 3D printer is not a Fab Lab," according to the Fab Foundation).

In true startup spirit, Fab Labs in Vietnam have sprung up in Ho Chi Minh City, Hanoi, and Da Nang in the span of one year. In 2014, Vietnam's Fab Lab Saigon was set up in Ho Chi Minh City in March. Fab Lab Hanoi had its first meet up in 2015, and Fab Lab Da Nang was set up in 2015. (In 2017, a Maker Innovation Space was launched at the University of Da Nang via a partnership between Fab Lab Da Nang, Arizona State University [ASU], and USAID.)

These kinds of maker spaces serve as a converging point for the startup community, youth, and schools, expanding traditional networks and forming connections across society to create things. Researcher Ryo Seo-Zindy, affiliated with the Center for Development Informatics, Global Development Institute at the University of Manchester, shared this perspective after several trips to Vietnam and Southeast Asia:[57]

> Besides being a place for sharing tools and resources, makerspaces and Fablabs have now started to foster, support and facilitate programmes for entrepreneurship and STEAM (Science, Technology, Engineering, Art and Mathematics) education in schools. Fablabs in [Vietnam] are also gradually building a production network linking individuals and startups to local suppliers, manufacturers and distributors who share the same vision: empowering the community, sharing knowledge, and open innovation. With a particular focus on developing products using technologies such as 3D printing, Robotics, Artificial Intelligence and Internet of Things, they are set to become prominent hubs for grassroots innovation in the era of Industry 4.0.

Looking forward, what might come out of these innovative spaces? Most likely, something uniquely Vietnamese with some international flavor—a mashup, if you will. Vietnamese culture is already influenced by the Korean (music such as K-pop), Japanese (literature such as manga), and American (movies) cultures. Ultimately, these pioneering intellectual and physical spaces can also spur the creation of incubators, accelerators, and other vehicles to break new ground and meet twenty-first-century challenges such as climate change, pollution, and job automation head-on.

It's important for Vietnam to leverage exponential technologies: Vietnam could lose 10.7 percent of its GDP by 2030 due to climate change in the form of heat being responsible for 5.7 percent of that loss. Rising temperatures could cost Vietnam USD $85 billion in lost productivity, a figure that could double by 2050, with outdoor workers more severely impacted. Meanwhile, air conditioning demand would also increase, which would put more strain on Vietnam's power infrastructure. Depending on whether it's green, renewable, and clean, increased electrical demand could push temperatures up even more in the form of pollution contributing to the greenhouse effect, as outlined by the *VnExpress*.[58]

In 2017, Vietnamese innovation was recognized during the United Nations President of the General Assembly's High-Level Summit on Innovation and Connectivity at the UN headquarters in New York City. During a presentation on innovation, a slide with Vietnamese farmers was displayed as an example of Vietnamese innovation. The farmers had lost access to gasoline, so they were unable to use their boat—until they converted it to solar power.

Besides designed and jury-rigged technologies, financial technology, or fintech, is poised to sweep Vietnam. The expression "cash is king" is even more apt in developing nations such as Vietnam. According to the World Bank, slightly less than 27 percent of Vietnamese consumers had a debit card in 2014—and almost 70 percent did not have a bank account. While these numbers have changed since then, with mobile payments on the rise and increased access to banking services, cash is still the preferred method of payment in Vietnam.[59]

Fintech choices for consumers in Vietnam are steadily growing, as there are already other services vying to transfer remittances into Vietnam, including Cash2VN (which uses Bitcoin as a transfer medium) and Sharemoney. And in 2016, homegrown MoMo, which offers mobile wallets for unbanked consumers (as well as peer-to-peer transfers), raised USD $28 million from Standard Chartered Private Equity and Goldman Sachs. This growing interest in digital financial services makes sense considering the optimistic economic projections for Vietnamese consumers in the next five years and beyond.

In particular, blockchain has shown promise in Vietnam—both as a medium and as a location to develop products and services based on the technology (commonly known as decentralized applications or "dapps"). In June 2016, BlockFin Asia, the first major blockchain and Bitcoin conference in Vietnam, was held in Ho Chi Minh City. The two-day event brought together prominent blockchain advocates from around the world to share insight and address some of the challenges and potential solutions for Vietnam's market.

In early 2018, the Ho Chi Minh City Customs Department revealed that over seven thousand Bitcoin mining rigs were imported by eight organizations and individuals, demonstrating the interest in new kinds of technology. (Bitcoin uses blockchain technology.[60]) Additionally, in March 2018, "more than 2,000 people attended the Blockchain Week conference, a two-day event held in Ho Chi Minh City and organized by Infinity Blockchain Labs," according to *Forbes*.[61] Though for every newsworthy development such as Kyber Network, a Singaporean-based startup with two Vietnamese cofounders raising USD $60 million in one day in September 2017 via an initial coin offering (ICO) for their smart contract-powered digital asset exchange,[62] there are more sobering developments, such as a team of seven Ho Chi Minh City–based scammers making off with USD

$660 million in ICO earnings.[63] It remains to be seen which kind of news will emerge more frequently from Vietnam—and the region.

In today's interconnected environment, Vietnam's business community (including startups) can leverage the best elements from the private sector to cocreate solutions and have the government scale them. However, scalability does not stop at Vietnam's borders. The silver lining is that Vietnam is not alone in its transformation—the entire region is undergoing these kinds of massive changes—and exponential technologies can also be applied in other parts of the world. Creating local solutions for local challenges ends up propagating beyond the initial local impact and contributes toward achieving the 2030 Agenda (Sustainable Development Goals implementation), referenced in the previous chapter.

Because of communication technologies such as the internet, it is possible for Vietnam to combine forces with other Southeast Asian nations to launch gamification prompts across ASEAN in order to drive talent to create innovative solutions for shared challenges à la the X PRIZE model. Imagine posing challenges relevant to the creation of smart cities, innovative jobs, cybersecurity, and ocean pollution, just to name a few. The winning technologies in their respective categories could then be open sourced across the region and pushed through global networks. As Peter Diamandis, founder and chairman of the X PRIZE Foundation, says, "The world's biggest problems are the world's biggest business opportunities."

Ultimately, technology—for now, in the form of smart phones—evens the playing field and provides access for Vietnamese consumers to participate in the digital economy in this Information Age. Thus, innovative solutions that are pioneered to promote financial inclusion and access to markets and capital in Vietnam can be exported to the region and other parts of the world—and vice versa. That is the beauty of Vietnam—its story is still being written, and exponential technologies will play a major role in its development arc as it strives for comprehensive prosperity.

CHAPTER 10

BEING A PART OF VIETNAM'S SUCCESS

IN THE FALL (often described as the most romantic time in Hanoi) of 2015, the Finland-Vietnam Innovation Partnership Program (IPP2) held its midterm Demo Day. A European investor had just arrived from the airport—having landed about an hour ago as part of his inaugural trip to Vietnam—so one of the event organizers began introducing him to various members of the community. "No," he began, "I don't see any potential for startups in Vietnam." Somehow, he had become an expert on Vietnam in less than twenty-four hours.

The next day, over lunch with other event organizers, this European investor sang a markedly different tune, admitting that there was more to Vietnam than he had originally thought. It was a remarkable turnaround, especially as he'd proclaimed the lack of potential with such conviction the day before. Overall, it's good that a day in Vietnam can make a believer out of a skeptic right out of the gate.

Around the same time, an American angel investor visited Hanoi, where he caused a lot of friction and angst during this initial visit. The trouble began with invitations that were sent out for a closed meeting—presumably to provide a safe space for nascent angel investors to ask questions and voice opinions freely. There was a mix-up regarding who should actually be present in the meeting—angel investors, aspiring angel investors, or those organizing angel investor communities?

As the workshop began in a conference room, there were former angel investors as well as institutional investors present—even though the event was now billed as "angels-only." Sometime after the meeting started, two cofounders of a local incubator stormed out—feeling insulted by being asked to leave by this American angel investor—since they were technically not angel investors. (One adviser to the incubator, a foreigner, had angel investor experience in Vietnam, and the group he was part of was actively trying to create an angel investor network.)

The puzzling part was this: the organization the cofounders represented had also coorganized the event the American angel had attended the day before. Eventually, two out of the three members returned to the room after settling down—but the foreign adviser had had enough of the American angel investor and proceeded to leave the building. The American angel investor attempted to apologize, but the damage was already done: alienating those whom you are sent to help. Overall, the abrasiveness and arrogance exhibited by the American angel investor was unsettling, considering he was a guest in country and had no prior experience in Vietnam.

The day before, at the aforementioned startup conference in Hanoi, there was another angel—a local—who was less than effective in planting the seeds for a robust angel investment community in Hanoi. At one point, he addressed the audience from the stage and proclaimed that "angel investing is just like regular investing…so just do it!" Sounds nice, but the evidence doesn't support this claim. In fact, the cardinal advice given to new angel investors is to be prepared to lose their investment.

The following year, this same angel investor publicly sought support for local startups from Facebook groups catering to expats in Vietnam.

As part of his pitch, he identified the value he saw in foreigners: "White faces, native English speakers provide a great impression to partners, customers." In other words, according to this local angel investor, the value-add of (white) foreigners is that they are not Vietnamese and can speak English. The energy is great, but the oversimplification of challenges and the objectification of a group of people isn't. (On the topic of oversimplication, one startup influencer in Central Vietnam offered this advice to a local founder: Don't accept anything less than USD $1 million to do a deal. So with that in mind, the founder reneged on an agreement with a foreign-operated innovation studio.)

Then there are some who mean well, and perhaps care about Vietnam, but are just out of their element. In late 2016, an American professor at a foreign university in Hanoi admitted that before he had been assigned to teach a class on it, he had never heard the word "intrapreneurship." I was stunned that he was so casual about his admission. Frankly, it's dangerous to pretend to be an expert in something when it's clearly not the case. In fact, more harm than good can be done, especially when Vietnamese students are paying good money to learn from, ostensibly, an expert.

We all start off learning about a subject at square one—but the learning curve is steep when one is learning about entrepreneurship and Vietnam at the same time. Cheerleading anything and everything isn't the best use of being a guest in a foreign country—or any platform, in general. Vietnamese people aren't oblivious: doing too much too soon can come across as sloppy and impacts the greater foreigner/expat community. Vietnamese look at a profile—which looks solid on paper—but then realize that the goods were mislabeled when it's time to execute. Then they apply the same lens to other foreigners in Vietnam, which negatively impacts the view of foreigners. But there are also some foreigners who seem to go out of their way to exploit their roles Vietnam—or perhaps they have been outside their home country for too long.

One American investor/operator in Vietnam seemed to have a new intern by his side at every startup event. During a night out with the local chief financial officer (CFO) of one of his portfolio companies, they appeared more like lovers quarreling instead of colleagues. As one Saigonese angel investor said about the two colleagues interacting, "Yeah, she's his CFO—the chief fucking officer."

Being in Vietnam as a foreigner is a double-edged sword, partly due to the automatic privileges and premiums mentioned in chapter 3. And it can warp one's sense of reality by creating misleading situations. In the right position, it can even be a net positive, depending on your perspective. For example, the head of one foreign business association, who has been in Vietnam for over a decade, admitted that he was (at least) partly interested in Vietnam because, to summarize, "this is a country where locals trust me more than their countrymen, just because I'm a foreigner." This was a response to a question about why he had decided to stay in Vietnam for so long. There was no hint in his response about Vietnam's trade/economic potential or an appreciation for the culture or anything else that one would expect from a business organization leader. (Still, the candor was appreciated.)

Then there are those who are insensitive to their host country's psyche and end up stereotyping half the country. In a group conversation at an event, the foreign head of a local accelerator cracked a flat joke about locals marrying foreigners in front of a Vietnamese startup executive: "Women are Vietnam's number one export, right?" Up until that point, the discussion had centered on what kind of applicants had been interested in the nascent program. The foreigner said that many of the foreign male applicants had local girlfriends, which they had cited as motivation for joining the current batch. Afterward, the Hanoian business executive admitted that he had not appreciated the attempt at humor.

And then there are those who have family or historical connections to Vietnam. Some Vietnamese Americans have said that they came to Vietnam for the benefits: "Why go to Silicon Valley and compete with the best in the world when I can come to Vietnam, already knowing the language and the culture?" That makes sense, and—anecdotally—if an expat in Vietnam makes it to two years in Vietnam, then that person either stays for the long haul or heads to a different place. Thus, there is a staggered mass exodus every two years—which means that the expat community present today was largely not around five or more years ago.

People seem to end up staying in Vietnam a lot longer than expected, perhaps due to the sunk-cost fallacy or the lifestyle. In many ways, being an expat in Vietnam is about survival: who can outlast, adapt, and add value in ways that locals and foreign companies will appreciate and are willing to pay for. At the same time, the decision to invest more into Vietnam can be difficult (especially for expat entrepreneurs). Another way to look at it is: How integrated should one be into Vietnamese society?

While there are benefits (business rights, visa, and so on) that come with a local spouse anywhere, there are other considerations for entrepreneurs/investors attempting to integrate into Vietnam beyond learning Vietnamese and moving into a newbusiness domain or industry—especially for older expats. Indeed, it can be hard to switch over from a lifestyle business to a scalable business model, especially in a new locale.

In particular, finding the right life balance in Vietnam can be challenging for many people. More often than not, there are public examples of extremes: behaviors, opinions, and consumption. For example, there is uninhibited nightlife in Saigon, while there are midnight closing times in Hanoi. Business meetings can last from two to three hours—even longer if the booze is flowing and the bonds are strengthening. Where does the line for business and personal relationships end? Sometimes it can be hard to distinguish whether it's a friend or a business associate who is picking up the check—and sometimes it's both.

There is a "small-town" feel at times—less so than in Vientiane or Phnom Penh, but it's not uncommon to run into the same circle of people in various establishments, or at least to meet people who know the same ones you do. A housewarming party in Hanoi is a reminder of how small the city is. For expats who want to be successful here and in greater Southeast Asia, Vietnam should be a long-term plan as soon as possible, to make the most out of the experience. There is no doubt that Saigon, Da Nang (Hội An included), and Hanoi attract different kinds of expats. But too often, a visible segment of expats seems to fall into a cycle of complacencies, vices, and/or distractions.

Out of these three cities, it's perhaps easiest to lose one's sense of self in the sprawling metropolis of Saigon; the loneliness of being an expat can contribute to a less-than-healthy lifestyle as well. Certainly, mistakes will be made both in business and social contexts in a new environment and setting: no one is perfect. The key is to learn from mistakes and avoid repeating them. Even when some people have reached their wit's end after being here for years, other opportunities have popped up that have compelled them to stay. But it's only because they've tried and failed previously that they were noticed—and had the reputation to be suitable for a new project. But what drives people to "leave Vietnam for a third time"? Or to stay in Vietnam for upward of a decade, never learning the language beyond a basic level?

The real opportunity here is to create and/or shape markets, which requires a deep and real investment to connect across cultures. Vietnam is still in "tree-growing" mode. Sure, one day there will be a harvest—but it takes time, capital, and other resources to educate consumers and stakeholders and to build/create newfound marketplaces. To that end, Vietnam needs more entrepreneurial talent to take smart risks, more STEAM (science, technology, engineering, art, and mathematics) talent that knows what it takes to bring a product to the global market, and more people who are interested in Vietnam from a respectful or cultural appreciation point of view instead of purely or largely a bia hơi[1] / bia ôm[2] focus. But, how to attract and incentivize such talent?

For starters, lower the risk of coming to Vietnam and doing business here (level the playing field and increase transparency), lower the barriers to raising capital here for startups (beyond incorporating in Singapore and keeping a team in Vietnam), and promote finding ways to leverage local talent when creating products and services that can be differentiated (aligned incentives).

Another major pitfall for expats is adopting local ways of thinking and doing things. It's very easy to complain and to succumb to some of the craziness that permeates interactions in the workplace and beyond. Staying rooted, being patient, and remaining steadfast during negotiations are valuable, much-needed qualities—especially when "hand-holding," as one Hanoian put it. However, also knowing when to quit due to time wasting, the expectation of charity, or unprofessional expat or local counterparts can save many headaches for everyone involved. It's definitely easier said than done and is a skill that takes time to develop.

Above all, expats should find that their tolerance for healthy and smart risks will have increased after living or working in Vietnam and greater Asia. Whether it's (legally) riding a motorbike to and from work in the middle of crazy traffic, dating (or eventually marrying) someone from a very different culture, or seizing a new opportunity, each experience will help shape confidence and character in future situations. There's a saying I once heard in Vietnam from a European commercial trade advisor with experience in both countries: "If you can get things done in Vietnam, you can get stuff done anywhere in the world...except for maybe India."

Living and working in a new country is a risk itself—why stop there? Vietnam is not perfect—no country is. Yet finding the good in situations and people is more a result of attitude than focusing on all current problems. Part of the trouble is that the more things change, the more they stay the same—especially here, just with fewer expats whom you know. In that sense, finding what's right about Vietnam can be harder than usual after some time in country. If you're in a city that you don't like, then move somewhere else. If you've tried a few cities and still aren't happy, then move to another country. This place isn't for everyone, and staying true to oneself and being ethical/moral seems to be a challenge for many, foreigners and locals alike. Nothing worthwhile is easy, and Vietnam's challenges are real and deep.

For those who stay in Southeast Asia long term and possess a strong sense of self-values, there are opportunities for the taking—whether as an outsider, a supportive ally, or maybe even as a valued member of a Vietnamese family.

GETTING READY

The first visit—or first year—in Vietnam is probably the hardest, as is the first time you do anything. Vietnam is a place for you if you want to solve real challenges with lasting impact—not if you want to build a better shopping list app. (But you can do that too.) Foreign entrepreneurs and investors should understand this distinction. Vietnam needs more startups—driven by investor demand—than the few thousand it currently has, so no one will turn you away if you want to copy a proven business model in the region and deploy it in Vietnam. Furthermore, in an interview with the *Financial Times*, Prime Minister Nguyễn Xuân Phúc shared to a reporter that "Vietnam aims to generate half of its economic output from the private sector within two years" which the interviewer interpreted as "giving a clear indication of the communist-ruled country's determination to make private enterprise the main engine of its economy."[3]

The "win-win-win" (if everyone involved isn't winning then you are the one losing) aspect of building something in Vietnam is that foreign entrepreneurs can work with local teams to build products for other markets—at a fraction of the cost compared to their home market. At the same time, local developers seeking international projects to add to their resumes can build up their confidence and hone their skills, then start their own projects when they are ready. Concurrently, more Vietnamese entrepreneurs can leave Vietnam to work with globally oriented entrepreneurs in places around the world. This is not brain drain if the entrepreneurs return with a deeper understanding of how to do international business in a different culture and with a newly developed foreign network in tow. And, of course, Vietnamese are crafting their own styles and making their own marks on how they see product design and implement product development.

People—entrepreneurs, investors, developers, designers, and so on—should go into Vietnam with eyes wide open and a healthy understanding of what the challenges are—and there are many. Anthony Liu, managing director of LKP Vietnam, came up with a general framework based on his experience in engineering projects in Vietnam: the 70% of 70% theory. Basically, any requirements presented to local implementors will be undertaken with the goal of accomplishing 70 percent of the scope—and they will only initially accomplish 70 percent of what they are aiming for. Thus, less than 50 percent is accomplished during the first attempt. (I experienced similar attitudes in system integration in Saigon.)

One European entrepreneur in Vietnam described how his office of ten female workers operated in the following way: "Fifty percent of the time they are on Facebook. Twenty percent of the time they are shopping online. Twenty percent of the time they are taking selfies and ten percent of the time they are doing real work."

Second to challenges are the excuses you will hear for everything (usually followed by a request to "please sympathize"). These excuses are not limited to Vietnam's private sector. One excuse sometimes heard from officials is that "Vietnam is a poor country." This comparison is made when analyzing Vietnamese metrics—usually in relation to the United States. However, Vietnamese are also quick to point out that Vietnam is a strong country when compared to its "younger brother"—that is, Laos. Unfortunately, you can't have it both ways. If there is no political will or capital to lead the way in tackling a particular problem, then the solution is to incentivize the private sector to make investments in clean tech or other areas and step aside. (While great in theory, this is harder to implement in general because of entrenched interests.)

As foreigners, we see slices of what is going on; we see things not as they are, but as we are. That being said, the path ahead for Vietnam will be longer *and* quicker than we realize, but Vietnam is not immune to going off track; it runs the risk of failure of vision (appreciating opportunities) or failure of imagination (considering risks). Combining the best of local and global assets can help undercut such risks—but only on a platform of mutual understanding. Some of the stronger teams emerging from Vietnam have a mix of locals and foreigners (including Overseas Vietnamese) as cofounders, or a foreigner leadership team with a strong local workforce. Usually, these foreigners have been working in Vietnam for several years at one or two companies before branching out on their own. And that's important time spent observing, learning, and refining your assumptions to get a sense of where the market is and where it may go. (The first private equity and venture capital funds in Vietnam were set up Vietnam in the early 2000s, so we are currently in the third wave of high-growth entrepreneurs.[4])

Despite local or international experiences, the language or cultural gap can be too great at times. Some local investors specifically target entrepreneurs who cannot speak English, as they are restricted to just Vietnamese-speaking investors. Unfortunately, these entrepreneurs are only limiting themselves. English is the language of doing business around the world. If investors can't understand a business model or don't have confidence in a team to clearly communicate their value proposition, chances are slim that they will invest.

Local company directors might counter that their foreign friends should be the link to outside markets and that they should be the ones to promote and share the products or services that Vietnamese companies can offer. Sadly, this argument doesn't hold weight if a company isn't even willing to invest in a decent English-language website or, for example, it insists on hiring its own web developer for the third time due to background relationships.[5]

Wide productivity and efficiency gaps still remain in Vietnam—take, for example, the customer service experience in Ho Chi Minh City compared to Hanoi, or try quantifying the productivity lost nationwide to social media. Facebook is wildly popular in Vietnam—with over 60 million accounts—and although LinkedIn is gaining popularity, most people are more comfortable doing business on Facebook. (Twitter is largely an afterthought or used to convey messaging to foreign audiences.)

Fast-growing Vietnamese companies need to decide if and when to go regional or beyond. Human capital, investment capital, and a vision for the company's future—and potential exit, if appropriate—will be key in achieving targets and founders' dreams. Looking ahead, as the AEC continues on a path toward full integration, will it be primarily an opportunity or a challenge for Vietnamese startups and SMEs?

Overall, those of us who work in private-sector development (PSD) require political stability to be able to do our work in Vietnam. No one should be afraid to speak his or her mind or have to worry about being placed under house arrest—but get ready to bite your tongue or moderate your comments online. Indeed, this is the development of two Vietnams—not in a physical sense, but in a spiritual manifestation. The Vietnam with so much promise and energized youth. And the Vietnam with a consistent population of bloggers under house arrest or under worse conditions. The Vietnam that recently repealed a ban on same-sex marriage and recognizes transgender identity rights. And the Vietnam whose farmers lose their land to development projects, often without adequate compensation despite their fervent protests.

Sometimes, daily interactions can be robotic in many ways, while other fleeting moments are instantly warm despite conversational partners asking the same ten basic questions as everyone else.[6] These dualities in Vietnam are as much opportunities as barriers to stable growth. Dissent, differing opinions, and critical thinking (in general, intellectual diversity) are all ways to advance the dialogue and to move any society forward. These are vital activities in the twenty-first century for any people and government to remain relevant in the continuous global dialogue.

At times in Vietnam, the vanity and the outmatched egos on display are hard to ignore or fathom—so leave yours at home. Yes, the whole world is brand conscious. However, one could argue that the Vietnamese (among other Asians) are more brand conscious than Westerners, because in Asia there is usually a direct correlation between price and quality. In the West, one can find good-quality items that might be less expensive than lower-quality items (for a variety of reasons—e.g., industry regulation, better quality control, more educated workforce, etc.).

There's a lot of new money in Asia, and one of the first things people with new money try to do is to emulate old money by consuming well-established luxury products and services: Louis Vuitton and Moët Hennessy products, Bentley vehicle purchases, fine wines, and so on. For example, a Land Rover Range Rover is USD $300,000 in Vietnam; the Evoque is USD $120,000 (due to taxes). Flaunting goods and experiences is how you show people you've made it in the Vietnamese context—that, plus taking care of loved ones in an opulent fashion. In addition, there are some social and "face-saving" pressures involved, which aren't as prevalent in the West. In other words, be prepared to see folks in Vietnam "keeping up with the Nguyễns,"[7] but to extremes.

If you are set on coming to Vietnam, get ready to drink and mete out large amounts of patience and grace. "I didn't know you could be an expat in Vietnam and not drink," said one New York–based investor who has visited Vietnam several times. Future waves of incoming entrepreneurs, investors, and coders will also face similar challenges of figuring out what is real, what is hype, and who is effective in country. Surprisingly, few expats have lived in both Hanoi and Ho Chi Minh City—and even fewer in Da Nang as well.

Overall, this book is meant to be a guide for foreign entrepreneurs and investors who are interested in setting up, living, or working in Vietnam. Hopefully, it has piqued the interest of people who may have never considered Vietnam before—Overseas Vietnamese, and also other foreigners, especially beyond the Western variety.

Trần Trí Dũng, a Hanoi-based consultant with the SWISS Entrepreneurial Program (managed by J. E. Austin Associates), expands on this concept:

> Everyone wants to avoid pitfalls. It is really a challenge to avoid pitfalls. The following three may be of help.
>
> 1. Don't make assumptions;
> 2. Don't set expectations; and
> 3. Feel free to ask questions.
>
> Problems and troubles are rooted from mismatches of expectations from both the guest and the host. Information is always information. There is no conflicting information. Conflicts happen when the guest and the host perceive the same information differently. A common pitfall is when "Yes" is not "Yes."
>
> Vietnamese are friendly, indeed. Therefore, a foreigner should never worry about making "idiot" questions. Vietnamese may laugh at your questions but they will be more than happy to explain you the truth and willing to help you get what you want. Sometimes, the foreigners get over-expectation. Sometimes they get under-expectation. This reminds the second of "no expectation."
>
> It is also a universal truth that the good and the bad exist together, wherever in the world you are. Don't judge people only with your perception, but ask many questions so you

can understand what is happening, and whether it is right or wrong.

Essentially, look for gaps and try to fill them. But when one identifies gaps or shortcomings, too often, Vietnamese respond to (constructive) criticism with "If you don't like it, then leave!" (Not everyone has this option, especially with family ties already established.) Thus, the opportunity costs are real—there is a lack of both professionalism and mentors underlying many interactions. Below are some suggestions to accelerate your understanding of a fascinating place:

1. Learn the local language. (You will save so much time and build relationships more quickly)
2. Learn the local business culture. (You will be able to avoid faux pas, as well as participate and contribute effectively and appropriately in business settings)
3. Learn the history. (The Chinese, the French, the Japanese, and the Americans—among others—have all directly influenced Vietnam's history at one point or another—how might that affect the Vietnamese perspective toward foreigners?)
4. Understand the "pulse" of the city and country. (What might the city you are in be like in a year? Or five years? What are the major ongoing infrastructure or development projects?)
5. Recognize opportunities and how to leverage them and your global network. (Do you see a product or service that Vietnamese consumers would want or need? Do you have a friend who has skills that would be valuable to a company in Vietnam? Make connections, both in person and for potential opportunities.)

While the creation of more Vietnam-focused funds in the near future is expected, as well as increased funding rounds and deal value in

Vietnam, one thing to keep in mind is that most startups in Vietnam (and in general) will fail—even those that have received institutional investment. But that's OK: failure is part of the personal and entrepreneurial journey. To quote Dropbox founder Drew Houston, "Don't worry about failure; you only have to be right once."

GETTING STARTED

The true future potential of Vietnam is embedded in its youth and in finding creative solutions to global problems with existing resources and an innovative mind-set—that is, frugal innovation.[8] Tapping into these strengths will unlock the full potential of the people and the country—and these keys are in Vietnamese hands. Anyone who has a vested interest in Vietnam should maintain high aspirations for young Vietnamese and even higher expectations for the future of Vietnam because of these strengths. Setting the stage for interactions between locals and foreigners is important, as there can be a lot of misreading and miscommunication between cultures, especially when there is a mismatch of expectations from the onset. It's important to point out that Vietnam itself is not homogenous—there are great differences (accents, attitudes, allowance for risk) between the north, south, and central areas of the country.

Overall, there are some very traditional aspects to consider in Vietnam: it's a patriarchal society where saving face is crucial, and most sensitive subjects are handled indirectly. Social events are dances of respect, camaraderie building, and copious amounts of alcohol. In the Vietnamese language, there are different ways to address people you are speaking to, depending on whether they are older or younger than you, your parents, and their position in society or the environment relative to yours. Thus, a situation that would be normal between colleagues in the West would be very different here, as age and relationships would come into play if there was ever a dispute.

What is less clear is how the nouveau riche—there was a 210 percent increase in wealth from 2007 to 2017[9]—will prioritize their lifestyle values beyond the point of survival. In other words, what will they do with their newfound power? (Vietnam experienced the third fastest-growing rate of Ultra High Net Worth population in the world from 2012-2017, according to the Wealth-X World Ultra Wealth Report 2018.[10])

As Vietnamese consumers explore new avenues of self-expression via fashion, culinary activities, and experiences, consumers may seek out novel products and services in an attempt to define their personas beyond the facets of brand and price point—both online and offline. Up-and-coming apps may hold the keys for the start of that journey: discovering and sharing something uniquely Vietnamese.

Naturally, key differences remain between the Western and Vietnamese ways of doing things, in the form of standards, expectations, culture, and expression. Yet, contrary to some misperceptions in the West, Vietnam is not trapped in the past: iPhones are everywhere, luxury retail brands such as Hugo Boss sell highly desired products in ornate shopping malls, and the first Rolls-Royce showroom opened in 2014 in Hanoi, where a USD $1.8 million car, the Oriental Sun, was sold on the first day of operations—in a country where the per capita GDP in 2016 was USD $2,170.[10]

Nationwide, many Vietnamese are natural-born entrepreneurs—and the youth are bursting with optimism, big dreams, and enthusiasm for new and progressive approaches to a variety of challenges ahead, both at home and abroad.

The fact remains that Vietnam is still a developing country with a per capita GDP of approximately USD $2,000; this means that there are many solutions yet to be created in a USD $238 billion economy that has not reached its full potential. In fact, Morgan Stanley Capital International (MSCI)[11] classifies Vietnam as a frontier economy—not an emerging economy—placing it in the ranks of Bangladesh and Sri Lanka in Asia.

At times, the pace of progress in Vietnam can be frustratingly slow, but things are changing nonetheless. Yet there is no doubt that Vietnam and greater Asia are poised for continued economic success in this century—some countries in the region are further along that trajectory than others.

Vietnam needs many actions and actors to become a well-functioning environment for startups and high-growth companies. This is a realistic and achievable goal, and many stakeholders are already working toward this vision: entrepreneurs, foreign governments, NGOs, elements of Vietnam's government, and others. Vietnam has many young people who are eager to learn, explore, and contribute in their way to recognized success.

Indeed, an effective tool for success in creating awareness of the Vietnam brand might be something as simple as one of Vietnam's most visible brands: the nón lá. The nón lá, or traditional conical hat, could be an emerging sign of Vietnamese startups on the global scene; at the 2015 SLUSH event in Helsinki, Finland, Vietnamese startup TraceVerified brought dozens of the cultural icon with company logos on them to hand out from its shared booth. It seemed to be a sound strategy to promote the startup, as the hats were a hit at the SLUSH after party. (Perhaps a "high-tech" nón lá version 2.0 will be available for future conference attendees; think along the lines of being solar-powered with a built-in battery charger or LED array.)

So if you plan to attend a startup event next year, don't be surprised if you happen to see some conical leaf hats at Web Summit, SLUSH, RISE, or maybe even at a similar event near you in the not-too-distant future.

Despite various orientations to Vietnam, one thing that most people can agree on is that Vietnam has an opportunity to follow in the footsteps of countries such as Japan and South Korea in terms of its potential for being an economic powerhouse. Vietnam also has the ability to forge its own path along the way, as Vietnam and the Vietnamese diaspora have a variety of strengths: resilience, improvisation, drive, and entrepreneurship (RIDE), to name a few. Today, Vietnam's role in the world is still taking shape, and a prosperous Vietnam is in the regional and global interest. It will require embracing new kinds of technology, supporting innovation, a long-term vision, investment in education, and a commitment to skills development to ensure continued success in the rapidly changing twenty-first century.

You can help. If you have an idea or concept, find a way to turn it into a product or service—and eventually a business via Vietnamese coders. If you are an expert in a particular vertical and want to help or be part of the next wave of Vietnamese tech entrepreneurs, come to Vietnam. If you're already in Vietnam, join a local meet up related to technology, startups, or entrepreneurship in your city. If there's no meet up or event in your city yet, organize one. If you have the capacity to advise/mentor/guide or lead a Vietnamese (or Vietnam-based) startup, put it out there on social media. (If you've never been, then visit Vietnam!)

The next generation of digital Vietnamese will come online soon—they are part of the Next Billion who will be connected to the internet and to the rest of the world. But Vietnam has elements of the Bottom Billion as well. Not only Vietnam, but the world, needs viable tools and solutions for both kinds of billions—and beyond.

Moving forward, my aim is twofold:

1. If you are a talented developer or entrepreneur (this means you) in Vietnam but don't have an idea or problem you are passionate about, then this book, hopefully, pointed you in the right direction; and
2. If you have a brilliant idea for a Vietnam–based startup (in one of the aforementioned five areas from chapter 7 or not), then reach out to someone in Vietnam to begin implementing it.

Vietnam needs people who create, who care, who don't easily develop bad habits, and who can help to raise the bar—not gravitate toward it. The incoming folks to Vietnam should set good examples and share best practices by helping to connect resources into Vietnam as a cultural bridge. But this means that the public sector needs to simplify processes and be more open—to discovery, to feedback, and to new perspectives.

What would be some of the rewards of such a mind-set shift? Well, some experts believe that Vietnam can reach 8 percent GDP growth if it tackles tough challenges such as inefficient productivity, preferential access to capital and contracts, SOE reform, nonperforming loans, and unskilled labor. During the 2016 Private Sector Forum mentioned in chapter 7, Dr. Sandeep Mahajan, then lead economist and program leader for Vietnam at the World Bank, pointed out that, "By 2035, Vietnam could be in the higher reaches of upper middle-income status (USD $22,000 GDP per capita PPP), moving toward becoming a prosperous, creative, equitable, and democratic society."

Toward the end of his presentation, Dr. Mahajan outlined the steps necessary to achieve the 2035 target of upper-middle-income status. Overall, Dr. Mahajan recommended a "reform agenda to boost productivity growth" that included giving "immediate priority to boosting productivity of [the] domestic private sector in several ways. Among them were "strengthening micro institutions of [the] market economy" by "[securing] private property rights" and "[strengthening] competition policy and its enforcement[.]" Dr. Mahajan also called for the "liberalizing and developing [of] factor markets," which included "[building] land markets by strengthening land registration, adopting market-based land valuations, and improving transparency of land transactions" and "[developing] a more diverse, stable, and inclusive financial sector."

A major recommendation of Dr. Mahajan's was to "restructure [the] SOE sector: adopt a commercial approach to state ownership, accelerate equitization, level the playing field for [the] private sector, [and] strengthen corporate governance."

Dr. Mahajan also suggested a look outward and to the future in order to "strengthen participation in global value chains" by "first—[enabling] a dynamic, competitive domestic private sector…[building] a modern, efficient services sector," and "improving connectivity within Vietnam and with trade partners."

As for the agricultural sector, Dr. Mahajan suggested commercializing and modernizing it by "address[ing] land fragmentation through functioning land markets" and by "[shifting] the government's role—from planning and managing to facilitating, supporting, regulating, [and] coordinating functions." Lastly, Dr. Mahajan recommended implementing "green agriculture policies: conserve fisheries and forests, incentivize more efficient use of water and other inputs, [and] build protective infrastructure."

It should be noted that the difference between 7 percent per capita GDP growth and 4 percent per capita GDP growth consistently over twenty years would result in a GDP per capita of USD $22,000 versus a GDP per capita of less than USD $12,000 by 2035 (in 2011 PPP). In 2014, Vietnam's GDP per capita (2011 PPP) was slightly less than USD $6,000.

If Vietnam can achieve these higher GDP growth rates, it will be investments in innovation and education that unleash the full potential of human capital in this Southeast Asian nation of soon-to-be one hundred million people.

If you are interested in being part of Vietnam's success story, you can start by being a friend to one of the more than one hundred thousand Vietnamese studying around the world outside Vietnam—or by remote mentoring startup teams originating from Vietnam (1776, an international startup incubator, has Union, a global web platform designed to do exactly this). If you are interested in learning more, reach out to anyone who has been quoted or profiled in this book. If you are in academia and can send more foreign students for a study tour or semester abroad, do so. If you are in the private sector and are looking for a reliable place to manufacture, develop a technology product, or enter into Vietnam's market, reach out.

Try to build bridges into Vietnam, and build networks around innovation and education with ties to Vietnam. If you have an idea for a solution to a challenge in Vietnam, speak out and share it. If you agree with anything in this book, share it on social media. If you disagree with anything (or everything) in this book, write about it on *Medium*—or write about your own experience in Vietnam thus far. (Or start a podcast or video blog on your own experiences in Vietnam.) The picture of the ecosystem comes more into focus with additional inputs or voices—as long as they contain clarity, purpose, and actionable insights. If you're a foreign entrepreneur in Vietnam, get on CB Insights, AngelList, Hacker News, and any other global platform to share your story, problems, failures, and successes. If you're Vietnamese, keep trying and keep moving forward into the future.

The bottom line is this: there is no reason why Vietnam can't meet high international standards and overcome the challenges of the future—and frankly, there is no other choice but to fully undertake the courageous journey ahead. As for what else is at stake, the choices made in these coming years of ever-increasing transition will be vital in creating a legacy for future generations of Vietnamese, a legacy that can't be bought: hope—not for themselves but for other countries facing similar challenges of economic, social, political, and cultural transformation ahead in this century. After all, the past doesn't define the future—the present does.

ACKNOWLEDGMENTS

PRIOR TO VISITING VIETNAM FOR the first time in 2011, my only exposure to the country had been in American history class in high school, where we examined US activities in Southeast Asia through the lens of containment of communism. To say this was a narrow examination of Vietnam would be an understatement. Thus, I had the opportunity to learn more about the country that was at the crux of a pivotal time during twentieth century history, although this was not my original intent for spending time in Vietnam. My time in Vietnam has also helped me to appreciate the Vietnamese diaspora's generational trajectory in ways I did not before. For that I am grateful, because I better appreciate this global community, some of whom are my compatriots.

This book is the culmination of many interactions and interviews with locals, "returnees," Việt Kiều, and other foreigners in Vietnam. In many ways, this is the book that I wish I had had when I first arrived in Vietnam. Most importantly, it's from the heart. For some relevant subjects, I don't believe I am qualified to comment or represent since I am not Vietnamese. Though I tried to navigate as best as I could through uncomfortable and necessary topics, the future of the country is ultimately up to the Vietnamese people to decide and create.

I value every interaction I've had in Vietnam—whether or not the outcome was the desired one. When I first visited Vietnam for work in 2011, I didn't know what I didn't know about the local or regional markets. Most of my experience was the result of trial and error, formulating hypotheses, and asking friends—mostly locals—what they thought. Some projects I worked on didn't bear the fruit we expected while others enabled me to learn deeply about myself, society, and aligned interests. I learned how to manage risks that we simply don't have in a formal and structured environment like many Western markets. Since my first visit, I've worked alongside Saigonese, I've worked with Việt Kiều, and I have done business with Hanoians. And I have worked with public-sector actors (programs supported by the governments of Vietnam, the United States, Finland, etc.) as well as private-sector advocates (local and international investors, entrepreneurs, and developers) in Vietnam to further the development of the enterprise ecosystem with a variety of foreigners. Thank you to everyone who has been a colleague, counterpart, friend, cofounder, or confidant along the way.

It wasn't until 2013 that I moved to Ho Chi Minh City. In my first year, I tried to soak up as much information as possible via experience, reading, and speaking with people who had been in Vietnam longer than I had. My first year in Saigon was difficult, and I am thankful that I learned about Vietnam first as an employee (of a New York–based firm), then as a consultant, and later as an entrepreneur.

When I moved to Hanoi in 2014, it was like relearning about Vietnam all over again. What surprised me was that Hanoi felt like home for me in a way that Saigon never did. But at the same time, I was and remain a guest in Vietnam—and a stakeholder, perhaps, for as long as I am a guest.

Vietnam is a nation of survivors—I admire the people because of their ability to withstand and adapt. I hope to see more people thrive in Vietnam and in Southeast Asia. People sometimes ask me if or why I love Vietnam. I don't. For I do not believe that I can ever have the same feelings about Vietnam that a citizen or native son or daughter of Vietnam does.

However, I respect Vietnam, and I believe respect is more important in this context than love.

My published writings on Vietnam have mostly explored cross-cultural issues, business, and recent news and events, all in an attempt to better understand Vietnam, its people, and cultures. For every point made in this text, there is an equal counterpoint. (Most of my time in Vietnam has been spent in almost exclusively urban areas, so unless specifically noted, I am not referring to rural areas throughout the text.)

Although I do not have any historical or familial ties to Vietnam, I ended up spending more time in Vietnam than I expected. After a year and two projects in Saigon, I wanted to better understand the differences across the country, so I moved to Hanoi, where I lived for more than two years. Finally, I moved to Da Nang in 2017 in order to experience the central Vietnamese style and approach to life.

After all this time in different parts of the country, I believe Vietnam has a bright future, and I'll always be a friend to Vietnamese people at home and around the world. This book would not have been possible without many people's efforts, not only my own. In particular I wish to express my heartfelt gratitude to Dr. Everett Myers, Tyra Nguyễn, Barnaby D. Hewitt, and Ms. Hà for your support at different points along the way. I am especially grateful to Stephen P. Conroy, for our varied and encompassing conversations inside and outside of Vietnam; thank you. Furthermore, I would like to express my gratitude to my beta readers, in particular Iris Leung, Rachel Bui, and Mai Le; to those quoted in the book; to my editor, Ray Dittmeier; and to Naren Aryal, Daniel Wheatley, the book's project manager, and the entire team at Mascot Books. Moreover, I would like to express my appreciation for Donny Trương's superb book, *Vietnamese Typography*, which was helpful in selecting an appropriate font (Minion) for my book; check out www.vietnamesetypography.com for more information.

Thank you as well to Dr. John F. Kikoski, Dr. Balbir B. Bhasin, Jon Baer, Dr. Anders Corr, James Grundvig, Dr. Justin Gifford, Andrew Romans,

Christopher M. Schroeder, John Hagel III, and Bill Hayton for reviewing my book proposal and/or spending time answering my questions about the publishing process. Last but not least, thank you to Giang Lam for agreeing to write the book's foreword and for sharing your knowledge and perspective of Vietnam with me.

As always, thank you to my family: Mom, Dad, and David, for your unyielding support.

Finally, thank you to everyone who answered any number of my endless questions about anything and everything in Vietnam. Any shortcomings are entirely my own.

REFERENCES

CHAPTER 1: WHY VIETNAM?

1 The Russian Federation in lieu of the Soviet Union.
2 Ha Phuong, "Welcome to the US, Vietnamese Students," *VnExpress International*, December 4, 2016, https://e.vnexpress.net/news/business/data-speaks/welcome-to-the-us-vietnamese-students-3513338.html.
3 *Bloomberg* claims that the US was surpassed by China in 2017.
4 Bruce Einhorn and Mai Ngoc Chau, "Vietnamese Factories Hum at Full Capacity Despite Trump Snub," Bloomberg, January 24, 2017, https://www.bloomberg.com/news/articles/2017-01-24/vietnam-still-attracts-investors-as-trump-deals-trade-setback.
5 "The Other Asian Tiger." *The Economist.* August 04, 2016. Accessed September 26, 2018. https://www.economist.com/leaders/2016/08/04/the-other-asian-tiger.
6 Ngoc Hoi Nguyen, "Socialist Oriented Market Economy Undeniable—National Defence Journal," *National Defence Journal*, October 19, 2015, http://tapchiqptd.vn/en/events-and-comments/socialist-oriented-market-economy-undeniable/8207.html.
7 "Poverty in Viet Nam," Asian Development Bank, https://www.adb.org/countries/viet-nam/poverty.
8 "Poverty in Viet Nam."
9 For more information on poverty in Vietnam, please see the Climbing the Ladder Poverty Reduction and Shared Prosperity in Vietnam Report: http://documents.worldbank.org/curated/en/206981522843253122/Climbing-the-ladder-poverty-reduction-and-shared-prosperity-in-Vietnam.
10 Minh Nga, "Vietnam's Economy Grows 6.8 Percent in 2017, Hitting 10-Year High," *VnExpress International*, December 27, 2017, https://e.vnexpress.net/news/business/data-speaks/viet-nam-s-economy-grows-6-8-percent-in-2017-hitting-10-year-high-3690861.html.
11 "Vietnam Young Entrepreneurs Association," Vietnam Young Entrepreneurs Association, http://www.we-apec.com/directory/vietnam-young-entrepreneurs-association.
12 Quan Hoang Vuong, "Vietnam's Political Economy in Transition (1986–2016)," Stratfor, May 27, 2014, https://www.stratfor.com/the-hub/vietnams-political-economy-transition-1986-2016.

13 Phuong Nguyen, “Phuong Nguyen: Vietnam's Reformers Struggle to Find the Right Way Forward,” *Nikkei Asian Review*, January 12, 2017, https://asia.nikkei.com/magazine/TUNE-UP-TIME-FOR-VIETNAM/On-the-Cover/Phuong-Nguyen-Vietnam-s-reformers-struggle-to-find-the-right-way-forward.
14 “The World Factbook,” Central Intelligence Agency, https://www.cia.gov/library/publications/the-world-factbook/geos/vm.html.
15 And even as members of peacekeeping missions since 2014.
16 Elisabeth Rosen, “How Young Vietnamese View the Vietnam War,” *The Atlantic*, April 30, 2015, https://www.theatlantic.com/international/archive/2015/04/youth-vietnam-war-fall-saigon/391769/.
17 “Viet Nam Schools in a Class of Their Own,” Asian Development Bank, December 15, 2016, https://www.adb.org/news/features/viet-nam-schools-class-their-own.
18 Harry A. Patrinos, “Which Region in the World Has the Smartest Kids? According to the OECD, It's East Asia,” East Asia and Pacific on the Rise, January 12, 2017, http://blogs.worldbank. org/eastasiapacific/which-region-world-has-smartest-kids-according-oecd-it-s-east-asia.
19 Ralf Matthaes, “The Changing Reality of Retail,” CBRE Vietnam, http://www.cbrevietnam.com/wp-content/uploads/2012/12/TNS-CBRE-Importance-of-branding-on-retail.pdf.
20 Aparna Bharadwaj et al., “Vietnam and Myanmar: Southeast Asia's New Growth Frontiers,” Boston Consulting Group, December 17, 2013, https://www.bcgperspectives.com/content/articles/consumer_insight_growth_vietnam_myanmar_southeast_asia_new_growth_frontier/.
21 “Vietnam's Middle Class Projected to Double by 2020,” *VnExpress International*, October 27, 2016, http://e.vnexpress.net/news/business/vietnam-s-middle-class-projected-to-double-by-2020-3489724.html.
22 Knight Frank Research, *The Wealth Report 2017*, 11th ed. (Knight Frank LLP), 2017, https://content.knightfrank.com/research/83/documents/en/the-wealth-report-2017-4482.pdf.
23 Nguyen, Giang Kieu. “New Airline Set to Join Vietnam's Congested Skies.” Bloomberg.com. July 31, 2018. Accessed September 26, 2018. https://www.bloomberg.com/news/articles/2018-07-31/new-airline-set-to-join-vietnam-s-congested-skies-and-airports
24 Nguyen, Giang Kieu. “New Airline Set to Join Vietnam's Congested Skies.”
25 “Long Thanh Airport Project Likely Years Behind Schedule,” *Viet Nam News*, updated January 20, 2016, http://vietnamnews.vn/economy/281429/long-thanh-airport-project-likely-years-behind-schedule.html#GHDOikVJWDMpQtmB.97.
26 “Newest Adjustment on Tan Son Nhat Airport Expansion Project Sends Investors into Frenzy,” Viet Nam Net, updated May 9, 2017, http://m.english.vietnamnet.vn/fms/business/178015/newest-adjustment-on-tan-son-nhat-airport-expansion-project-sends-investors-into-frenzy.html#.
27 Xuan Thang Nguyen, “New Arguments about the Ongoing Development of the Socialist-Oriented Market Economy in Vietnam,” *Political Theory*, January 18, 2017, http://lyluanchinhtri.vn/home/en/index.php/last-highlights/item/434-new-arguments-about-the-ongoing-development-of-the-socialist-oriented-market-economy-in-vietnam.html.
28 Matt Phillips, “Communist Vietnam Just Adores Global Capitalism—and It's Easy to See Why,” *Quartz*, February 26, 2015, https://qz.com/352192/vietnam-just-adores-global-capitalism/.
29 “Vietnam's 2016 FDI Inflow Hits Record High of $15.8 Bln-govt.” Reuters. December 28, 2016. Accessed September 26, 2018. https://www.reuters.com/article/vietnam-economy-fdi-idUSL4N1EG1XP
30 “Vietnam Attracts Nearly US$35.9 Billion in FDI in 2017.” Great Ideology of Karl Marx with the Revolution of Vietnam - Nhan Dan Online. December 23, 2017. Accessed September 26, 2018. http://en.nhandan.org.vn/business/item/5732302-vietnam-attracts-nearly-us$35-9-billion-in-fdi-in-2017.html
31 “Vietnam's 2016 FDI Inflow Hits Record High of $15.8 Bln—Govt,” Reuters, December 28, 2016, http://www.reuters.com/article/vietnam-economy-fdi-idUSL4N1EG1XP.
32 Nguyen, Khanh. “Foreign Direct Investment (FDI) – 10 Years' Reflection and Real Estate Development.” JLL. August 07, 2018. Accessed September

26, 2018. http://www.joneslanglasalle.com.vn/vietnam/en-gb/news/452/foreign-direct-investment-10-years-reflection-and-real-estate-development
33 "Video: The Factors Influencing Reshoring Trends," Cushman and Wakefield, November 29, 2016, http://www.cushmanwakefield.com/en/research-and-insight/2016/business-process-outsourcing-location-index-2016/.
34 *The Economist*. October 2016. Accessed September 26, 2018. https://events.economist.com/events-conferences/asia/vietnam-summit-2016/
35 Agence France-Presse, "Reboot: Adidas to Make Shoes in Germany Again—But Using Robots," *The Guardian*, May 24, 2016, https://www.theguardian.com/world/2016/may/25/adidas-to-sell-robot-made-shoes-from-2017.
36 "Buoyed By US Firms, Vietnam Emerges As an Asian Manufacturing Powerhouse," *Washington Post*, May 21, 2016, https://www.washingtonpost.com/politics/buoyed-by-us-firms-vietnam-emerges-as-an-asian-manufacturing-powerhouse/2016/05/21/6f117876-1b6a-11e6-b6e0-c53b7ef63b45_story.html?utm_term=.2b90314280bf.
37 Bain, Marc. "To See How Asia's Manufacturing Map Is Being Redrawn, Look at Nike and Adidas." Quartz. May 10, 2018. Accessed September 26, 2018. https://qz.com/1274044/nike-and-adidas-are-steadily-ditching-china-for-vietnam-to-make-their-sneakers/
38 Nguyen, "Phuong Nguyen: Vietnam's Reformers Struggle."
39 Robert, "APEC—Window for Vietnam to Reach the World," Talk Vietnam, November 11, 2010, https://www.talkvietnam.org/2010/11/apec-window-for-vietnam-to-reach-the-world/.
40 "EU-Vietnam FTA Needs to Balance Interests: Deputy PM," VietnamPlus, November 21, 2017, https://en.vietnamplus.vn/euvietnam-fta-needs-to-balance-interests-deputy-pm/122102.vnp.
41 "Thousands of Goods Items to Enjoy Zero Percent Tariff in 2018," Viet Nam Net, January 1, 2018, http://m.english.vietnamnet.vn/fms/business/193429/thousands-of-goods-items-to-enjoy-zero-percent-tariff-in-2018.html#.
42 Eckardt, Sebastian, Deepak Mishra, and Viet Tuan Dinh. "Vietnam's Manufacturing Miracle: Lessons for Developing Countries." Brookings. April 17, 2018. Accessed September 26, 2018. https://www.brookings.edu/blog/future-development/2018/04/17/vietnams-manufacturing-miracle-lessons-for-developing-countries/
43 "Samsung Contributes 22.7% to Country's Exports," *Viet Nam News*, updated January 11, 2017, http://vietnamnews.vn/economy/349485/samsung-contributes-227-to-countrys-exports. html#ArVlDWRUemfP14Jz.97.
44 "Samsung Electronics to Expand Production in Vietnam," *Tuoi Tre News*, April 22, 2018, https://tuoitrenews.vn/news/business/20180422/samsung-electronics-to-expand-production-in-vietnam/45218.html.
45 "Jll's Latest City Momentum Index Identifies the World's Most Dynamic Cities," JLL, http://www.jll.com/cities-research/City-Momentum.
46 Melissa Cheok, "These Asian Cities Will Grow the Fastest in the Next Five Years," Bloomberg, August 09, 2017, https://www.bloomberg.com/news/articles/2017-08-08/indian-cities-to-see-fastest-growth-in-asia-over-five-years.
47 "VN Ranks Third among Fastest-Growing Global Stock Markets," *Viet Nam News*, updated November 27, 2017, http://vietnamnews.vn/economy/418324/vn-ranks-third-among-fastest-growing-global-stock-markets.html#JE8BDi9rIDyvRTij.97.
48 Minh Đăng, "Thị Trường Chứng Khoán 29/12: VN Index Tăng 48% Năm 2017, Vượt Đỉnh 10 Năm Lên 984 Điểm," *VietnamBiz*, December 29, 2017, http://vietnambiz.vn/thi-truong-chung-khoan-2912-vn-index-tang-48-nam-2017-vuot-dinh-10-nam-len-984-diem-41657.html.
49 The VN-Index was previously up around 1,000 in 2007 before crashing to 200.
50 "Top 3 Industries Gain Highest Profitability Rates in 2017," *Vietnam Investment Review*, January 02, 2018, http://www.vir.com.vn/top-3-industries-gain-highest-profitability-rates-in-2017-55200.html.
51 Lilian Karunungan and Yvonne Man, "What Emerging-Market Pioneer Mark Mobius Would Do With $100,000," Bloomberg, December 06, 2017, https://www.bloomberg.com/news/articles/2017-12-06/what-emerging-market-pioneer-mark-mobius-would-do-with-100-000.

52 “Video: Mark Mobius on His Top Pick, Vietnam, and Xi-Trump Summit,” Reuters, October 31, 2017, https://www.reuters.com/video/2017/10/31/mark-mobius-on-his-top-pick-viet-nam-and?videoId=372889481.
53 Thi Bich Ngoc Nguyen, “Franklin Templeton's Mark Mobius Commits $3b for Investments in Vietnam,” DealStreetAsia, October 22, 2015, https://www.dealstreetasia.com/stories/franklin-templetons-mark-mobius-commits-3b-investment-in-vietnam-16668/.
54 Mark Mobius, “Vietnam's Transformation,” Franklin Templeton Investments, June 5, 2017, http://mobius.blog.franklintempleton.com/2017/01/05/vietnams-transformation/.
55 “Vietnam's Climate Change Laws,” *Climate Change News*, March 21, 2013, http://www. climatechangenews.com/2013/03/21/vietnams-climate-change-laws/.
56 Marianne Smallwood, “Areas of Vulnerability to Sea-Level Rises in Vietnam's Mekong Delta,” GIS at Tufts, http://sites.tufts.edu/gis/files/2013/02/Smallwood_Marianne.pdf.
57 “Keeping the Floods at Bay and Building Resiliency in Can Tho, Vietnam,” World Bank, December 9, 2014, http://www.worldbank.org/en/news/feature/2014/12/09/keeping-the-floods-at-bay-and-building-resiliency-in-can-tho-vietnam.
58 World Bank, Transforming Vietnamese Agriculture: Gaining More from Less, Washington, DC: Vietnam Development Report, 2016, https://www.researchgate.net/profile/Steven_Jaffee/publication/305399137_Transforming_Vietnamese_Agriculture_Gaining_More_for_ Less_-_Vietnam_Development_Report_2016/links/5943778ea6fdccb93ab289b9/Transforming-Vietnamese-Agriculture-Gaining-More-for-Less-Vietnam-Development-Report-2016.pdf.
59 Gray A. Williams et al., “Meeting the Climate Change Challenge: Pressing Issues in Southern China and SE Asian Coastal Ecosystems,” Regional Studies in Marine Science 8 (July 7, 2016), http://dx.doi.org/10.1016/j.rsma.2016.07.002.
60 Hoang Huong, “Vietnam's ‘Rice Bowl’ Is Sinking,” A More Vulnerable World, November 25, 2015, https://climate.earthjournalism.net/2015/11/25/vietnams-rice-bowl-is-sinking/.
61 “Thermal Power Plants Next to HCM City Raise Concerns About Pollution,” Viet Nam Net, March 23, 2017, http://english.vietnamnet.vn/fms/environment/174953/thermal-power-plants-next-to-hcm-city-raise-concerns-about-pollution.html.
62 Huong Pham, “Air Pollution in Vietnam Cities Hit Unhealthy Levels: Government Study,” *VnExpress International*, September 30, 2016, http://e.vnexpress.net/news/news/air-pollution-in-vietnam-cities-hit-unhealthy-levels-government-study-3476529.html.
63 “Viet Nam,” Environmental Performance Index, https://epi.envirocenter.yale.edu/epi-country-report/VNM.
64 “Air Quality in Vietnam,” Green ID, http://en.greenidvietnam.org.vn//app/webroot/upload/files/Status%20air%20quality%20Q1%202017_V3.pdf.
65 “VN Air Quality Bad Over Half the Year,” *Viet Nam News*, April 26, 2017, http://vietnamnews.vn/environment/pollution/375352/vn-air-quality-bad-over-half-the-year.html#OWM4dxMu5edZbMAk.97.
66 Pham, “Air Pollution in Vietnam Cities Hit Unhealthy Levels.”
67 Justin Worland, “Air Pollution: World Bank Says Costs Total in Trillions,” *Time*, September 09, 2016, http://time.com/4484027/air-pollution-economic-toll-world-bank/.
68 Vietnamnet.vn. “HCM City Seeks Ways to Curb CO2 Emissions from Vehicles - News VietNamNet.” Vietnam Net Bridge. August 31, 2018. Accessed September 26, 2018. http://english.vietnamnet.vn/fms/environment/207822/hcm-city-seeks-ways-to-curb-co2-emissions-from-vehicles.html
69 “Thermal Power Plants Next to HCM City Raise Concerns About Pollution.”
70 “600 Trained to Serve Cat Linh—Ha Dong Railway,” Viet Nam Net, February 24, 2017, http://english.vietnamnet.vn/fms/society/173316/600-trained-to-serve-cat-linh-ha-dong-railway.html.
71 “Cost Increases on Hanoi Metro Line 2,” Viet Nam Net, April 25, 2017, http://english. vietnamnet.vn/fms/business/177220/cost-increases-on-hanoi-metro-line-2.html.

72 "French Consortium to Deliver Hanoi Metro Line 3," *Global Rail News*, January 17, 2017, https://www.globalrailnews.com/2017/01/17/french-consortium-to-deliver-hanoi-metro-line-3/.
73 "2nd Station of Vietnam's First Metro Line Breaks Ground," Tuoi Tre News, December 24, 2014, http://tuoitrenews.vn/society/24925/2nd-station-of-vietnams-first-metro-line-breaks-ground.
74 "2nd Station," Tuoi Tre News.
75 "Ho Chi Minh City Subway Project Faces $726mn Cost Overrun," *Tuoi Tre News*, October 06, 2015, http://tuoitrenews.vn/business/30828/ho-chi-minh-city-subway-project-faces-726mn-cost-overrun.
76 "HCMC Seeks Contractor for Metro Line No 2," *Viet Nam News*, February 19, 2016, http://vietnamnews.vn/society/282531/hcmc-seeks-contractor-for-metro-line-no-2.html.
77 That's 857 miles, for the Americans. :)
78 Karl Lester M. Yap and Nguyen Dieu Tu Uyen, "In Asia's Infrastructure Race, Vietnam is Among the Leaders," Bloomberg, March 23, 2017, https://www.bloomberg.com/news/articles/2017-03-22/in-asia-s-infrastructure-race-vietnam-is-among-the-leaders.
79 Minh, Anh. "Vietnam Eyes Power Imports from China, Laos - VnExpress International." VnExpress International – Latest News, Business, Travel and Analysis from Vietnam. August 10, 2018. Accessed September 26, 2018. https://e.vnexpress.net/news/business/vietnam-eyes-power-imports-from-china-laos-3790465.html
80 Hai Vo and Son Trung, "Vietnamese Mega-Cities Scouring for Mega-Funding on Infrastructure Drive," *VnExpress International*, May 16, 2017, http://e.vnexpress.net/news/news/vietnamese-mega-cities-scouring-for-mega-funding-on-infrastructure-drive-3585582.html.
81 Atsushi Tomiyama, "Vietnam Looks Abroad for Infrastructure Investors," *Nikkei Asian Review*, April 12, 2017, https://asia.nikkei.com/Politics-Economy/International-Relations/Vietnam-looks-abroad-for-infrastructure-investors.
82 AFP, "Vietnam's Creaking Education System Pushes Students Overseas," *Daily Mail Online*, January 21, 2015, http://www.dailymail.co.uk/wires/afp/article-2919749/Vietnams-creaking-education-pushes-students-overseas.html.
83 Atsushi Tomiyama, "Social Media Lets Vietnamese Vent Like Never Before," Nikkei Asian Review, January 12, 2017, http://asia.nikkei.com/magazine/TUNE-UP-TIME-FOR-VIET-NAM/On-the-Cover/Social-media-lets-Vietnamese-vent-like-never-before?page=2.
84 "Top 10 Countries with the Most Engineering Graduates," Interesting Engineering, February 22, 2016, http://interestingengineering.com/top-10-countries-with-the-most-engineering-graduates/.
85 "The Long View: How Will the Global Economic Order Change by 2050?" PricewaterhouseCoopers LLP, February 2017, https://www.pwc.com/gx/en/world-2050/assets/pwc-the-world-in-2050-full-report-feb-2017.pdf.
86 "The Atlas of Economic Complexity by @HarvardCID." The Atlas of Economic Complexity. May 3, 2018. Accessed September 26, 2018. atlas.cid.harvard.edu/rankings/growth-projections
87 "Spotlight on the New Wealth Builders," The *Economist* Intelligence Unit Perspectives, https://www.eiuperspectives.economist.com/sites/default/files/TheEIU_spotlight_new_wealth_builders.pdf.
88 "Vietnam Retail Sales Will Nudge US$2 Trillion," Inside Retail Asia, November 29, 2017, https://insideretail.asia/2017/11/29/vietnam-retail-sales-will-nudge-us2-trillion/#daily.
89 Atsushi Tomiyama, "Vietnam Retail Sales Hit Record $130bn in 2017," *Nikkei Asian Review*, January 10, 2018, https://asia.nikkei.com/Business/Consumers/Vietnam-retail-sales-hit-record-130bn-in-2017.
90 "Vietnam Among Top 30 Attractive Emerging Retail Markets," VOV—The Voice of Vietnam Online, June 29, 2016, http://english.vov.vn/trade/vietnam-among-top-30-attractive-emerging-retail-markets-323867.vov.

91 "Global Innovation Index 2017 Report Now Available," The Global Innovation Index, https://www.globalinnovationindex.org/home.
92 Miguel Chanco, "Innovation," Twitter, June 16, 2017, https://twitter.com/mc_economist/status/875653639309713408.
93 "Viet Nam," World Economic Forum, http://reports.weforum.org/global-competitiveness-index-2017-2018/countryeconomy-profiles/#economy=VNM.
94 "Ease of Doing Business in Vietnam," World Bank, http://www.doingbusiness.org/data/exploreeconomies/vietnam#dealing-with-construction-permits.
95 In early 2018 it was revealed that the World Bank would have to redo the rankings going back four years. At the time of publication, it's unclear what impact this revelation would have on Vietnam's rankings.
96 "PM: High Logistic Costs Place Burden on Businesses." VOV - VOV Online Newspaper. April 17, 2018. Accessed September 26, 2018. https://english.vov.vn/economy/pm-high-logistic-costs-place-burden-on-businesses-372779.vov
97 Arvis, Jean-Francois, Lauri Ojali, Christina Wiederer, Ben Shepherd, Anasuya Raj, Karlygash Dairabayeva, and Tuomas Kiiski. *Connecting to Compete 2018 Trade Logistics in the Global Economy The Logistics Performance Index and Its Indicators.*Report. 2018. Accessed September 26, 2018. https://openknowledge.worldbank.org/bitstream/handle/10986/29971/LPI2018.pdf?sequence=1&isAllowed=y
98 Kentaro Iwamoto, "Thailand and Vietnam Jump in Business-Friendliness Ranking," *Nikkei Asian Review*, November 01, 2017, https://asia.nikkei.com/Politics-Economy/Policy-Politics/Thailand-and-Vietnam-jump-in-business-friendliness-ranking?n_cid=NARAN012.
99 Vi Vu, "Guess How Many People Are Jamming into Saigon? Hint: It's as Bad as Tokyo," *VnExpress International*, August 17, 2017, https://e.vnexpress.net/news/news/guess-how-many-people-are-jamming-into-saigon-hint-it-s-as-bad-as-tokyo-3628742.html.
100 Malcolm W. Browne, "Overcrowded Vietnam Is Said to Face Catastrophe," *New York Times*, May 08, 1994, http://www.nytimes.com/1994/05/08/world/overcrowded-vietnam-is-said-to-face-catastrophe.html?pagewanted=all.
101 "Infographic: Top Cities and Urbanization in ASEAN," ASEAN UP, July 05, 2017, https://aseanup.com/infographic-top-cities-urbanization-asean/.
102 Masao Kakihara, "Mobile Apps in APAC: 2016 Report," Think with Google, December 13, 2016, https://apac.thinkwithgoogle.com/intl/en/articles/mobile-apps-in-apac-2016-report.html.
103 Tomiyama, "Social Media Lets Vietnamese Vent Like Never Before." https://asia.nikkei.com/Politics/Social-media-lets-Vietnamese-vent-like-never-before.
104 Quy, Nguyen. "Vietnam Demands Facebook Fix Wrong Depiction of Its Sovereignty - VnExpress International." VnExpress International – Latest News, Business, Travel and Analysis from Vietnam. July 02, 2018. Accessed September 26, 2018. https://e.vnexpress.net/news/news/vietnam-demands-facebook-fix-wrong-depiction-of-its-sovereignty-3771725.html.
105 Phuong Linh Nguyen, "Apple's Sales Boom in Communist Vietnam," Reuters, April 24, 2014, http://www.reuters.com/article/us-apple-vietnam-idUSBREA3N1DC20140424.
106 Joseph Waring, "Smart Phone Shipments Jump 57% in Vietnam," Mobile World Live, March 13, 2015, https://www.mobileworldlive.com/devices/news-devices/smart phone-shipments-jump-57-vietnam/.
107 "Mobile Phones in Vietnam," Euromonitor International, October 2017, http://www. euromonitor.com/mobile-phones-in-vietnam/report.
108 "Mobile Cellular Subscriptions (Per 100 People)," World Bank, http://data.world-bank.org/indicator/IT.CEL.SETS.P2.
109 James Hookway, "Vietnam's Mobile Revolution Catapults Millions into the Digital Age," *Wall Street Journal*, June 12, 2015, https://www.wsj.com/articles/vietnams-mobile-revolution-catapults-millions-into-the-digital-age-1434085300.

110 "Internet in Vietnam Remains at Snail's Pace Due to Cable Repair Delays," *VnExpress International*, March 27, 2017, http://e.vnexpress.net/news/news/internet-in-vietnam-remains-at-snail-s-pace-due-to-cable-repair-delays-3561616.html.
111 "VN Sees Promising 4G Future," *Viet Nam News*, April 02, 2016, http://vietnamnews. vn/economy/294735/vn-sees-promising-4g-future.html#gxRqsxYXtKOamgCg.97.
112 "Race Is On as Vietnam Grants First 4G Service Licenses," *Nikkei Asian Review*, October 21, 2016, https://asia.nikkei.com/Business/AC/Race-is-on-as-Vietnam-grants-first-4G-service-licenses.
113 "VinaPhone Becomes First Network to Launch 4G Service in Vietnam," *VnExpress International*, November 4, 2016, http://e.vnexpress.net/news/business/vinaphone-becomes-first-network-to-launch-4g-service-in-vietnam-3494122.html.
114 "Following BKAV, Viettel Aims to Make Luxury Smart Phone," Viet Nam Net, April 24, 2017, http://english.vietnamnet.vn/fms/science-it/177001/following-bkav-viettel-aims-to-make-luxury-smartphone.html.
115 Full disclosure: I worked with one of their subsidiaries.
116 "Vietnam's Top Conglomerate Vingroup to Foray into Smartphones." Reuters. June 12, 2018. Accessed September 26, 2018. https://www.reuters.com/article/us-vingroup-smartphones/vietnams-top-conglomerate-vingroup-to-foray-into-smartphones-idUSKBN1J80CE.
117 Quynh Nguyen, "Viettel to Expand to Indonesia and Nigeria," *Vietnam Economic Times*, April 28, 2017, http://vneconomictimes.com/article/business/viettel-to-expand-to-indonesia-and-nigeria.
118 "Vietnam Telecom Infrastructure Market Forecast and Opportunities, 2012–2022—Key Players Are Viettel, MobiFone, Vinafone, Vietnamobile, and GTel," Yahoo! Finance, May 01, 2017, https://finance.yahoo.com/news/vietnam-telecom-infrastructure-market-forecast-104000004. html.
119 Trung Hai Ngo, "Urban Development Strategy for Vietnam Cities System to 2050," International Conference on Eco2 Cities, and Workshop for East Asia Pilot Eco2 Cities, October 20–23, 2010, http://siteresources.worldbank.org/INTURBANDEVELOPMENT/Resources/336387-1270074782769/6925944-1288991290394/Day1_P8_9_VIAP.pdf.
120 For more information on rural Vietnam, please see the Growth, Structural Transformation, and Rural Change in Viet Nam A Rising Dragon on the Move Report: https://global.oup.com/academic/product/growth-structural-transformation-and-rural-change-in-viet-nam-9780198796961?cc=us&lang=en&#.

CHAPTER 2: FIRST IMPRESSIONS

1 Phuong Ha, "Vietnam Finishes Third in Southeast Asia Race for Tourist Dollars," *VnExpress International*, May 18, 2017, http://e.vnexpress.net/news/business/data-speaks/vietnam-finishes-third-in-southeast-asia-race-for-tourist-dollars-3586338.html.
2 Roberto Crotti and Tiffany Misrahi, eds., *The Travel and Tourism Competitiveness Report 2017* (Geneva: World Economic Forum, 2017), http://www3.weforum.org/docs/WEF_TTCR_2017_web_0401.pdf.
3 "Backpacking Vietnam Part 1: Shocked and Scammed in Hanoi," July 11, 2014, video, 9:18, posted by Because We Camp, https://www.youtube.com/watch?v=vcGpgNYJjho.
4 Nomadic Matt, "Why I'll Never Return to Vietnam," Nomadic Matt, September 19, 2010, https://www.nomadicmatt.com/travel-blogs/why-ill-never-return-to-vietnam/.
5 Anna Karsten, "Why I Won't Be Visiting Hanoi Again," Anna Everywhere, February 21, 2015, http://annaeverywhere.com/hanoi/.

6 "Mark Bowyer Founder of Rusty Compass." AsiaLIFE Cambodia. October 7, 2015. Accessed September 26, 2018. https://www.asialifemagazine.com/vietnam/mark-bowyer-founder-of-rusty-compass/.
7 "Very Few Foreign Visitors Return to Vietnam: Travel Association," *Tuoi Tre News*, July 20, 2016, http://tuoitrenews.vn/business/35968/very-few-foreign-visitors-return-to-vietnam-travel-association.
8 Tim Russell, "Simple Truth: Vietnam Just Not 'Serious About Tourism,'" *Thanh Nien News*, June 22, 2013, http://www.thanhniennews.com/commentaries/simple-truth-vietnam-just-not-serious-about-tourism-1976.html.
9 Dr. Stephanie Jones and Rafael Masters, *Opening Up to International Investment and Diversification—A Case Study of Vietnam*, report, Maastricht School of Management, August 2016, https://www.msm.nl/resources/uploads/2016/09/MSM-WP2016-7-1.pdf.
10 Vietnamnet.vn. "Foreign Arrivals to HCM City up 14 times over 25 Years - News VietNamNet." Vietnamnet NEW. August 17, 2018. Accessed September 26, 2018. http://english.vietnamnet.vn/fms/travel/206956/foreign-arrivals-to-hcm-city-up-14-times-over-25-years.html.
11 In 2016, the first finishing school opened up in Hanoi.
12 Vikram Mansharamani, "Sizzling Saigon: Here Comes the Middle Class!" Vikram Mansharamani, August 12, 2015, http://www.mansharamani.com/articles/sizzling-saigon-here-comes-the-middle-class/.
13 Article 18 of Vietnam's 2013 Amended Constitution has more information about the role of Overseas Vietnamese.
14 "Trump's Immigration Rules Threaten Remittances to Vietnam," *VnExpress International*, March 13, 2017, http://e.vnexpress.net/news/business/data-speaks/trump-s-immigration-rules-threaten-remittances-to-vietnam-3554066.html.
15 Full disclosure: I was interviewed during this broadcast.
16 Even today, I am learning about Vietnam, every day.
17 Vietnam is urbanizing at a rate of 3.4 per cent per year.
18 "Submarine Cable That Feeds Vietnam with Internet Disrupted Again," *Tuoi Tre News*, January 05, 2015, http://tuoitrenews.vn/business/25171/submarine-cable-that-feeds-vietnam-with-internet-disrupted-again.
19 The strongest US cultural exports are Hollywood and Silicon Valley, in the author's opinion.
20 "Vietnam Joins Alcohol Consumption Global Top Ten List," *Viet Nam News*, September 14, 2016, http://vietnamnews.vn/society/342723/viet-nam-joins-alcohol-consumption-global-top-ten-list.html#gkQrquBymR7Gj8mR.97.
21 "Vietnam Beats US in New 4G Speed Survey, Ranks Second in Southeast Asia," *VnExpress International*, February 21, 2018, https://ampe.vnexpress.net/news/business/data-speaks/vietnam-beats-us-in-new-4g-speed-survey-ranks-second-in-southeast-asia-3713755.html.

CHAPTER 3: VIETNAM UP CLOSE

1 Those who are not white may face other discrimination challenges while in Vietnam.
2 "Chapter 1: The American Brand," in *Global Opposition to US Surveillance and Drones, but Limited Harm to America's Image*, July 14, 2014, http://www.pewglobal.org/2014/07/14/chapter-1-the-American-brand/.
3 "Vietnamese Still Have a Favorable View of the US, but Trump Is Another Story," *VnExpress International*, June 27, 2017, http://e.vnexpress.net/news/news/vietnamese-still-have-a-favorable-view-of-the-us-but-trump-is-another-story-3605329.html.

4 Hoang Nguyen, "Fancy a Four Flowers or Ginger Fried Pork Pizza?" BBC News, May 22, 2017, http://www.bbc.com/news/business-39961772.
5 "Our Story," Lovepop, accessed February 28, 2018, https://www.lovepopcards.com/pages/our-story.
6 Vo Hai, "Hanoi Considers Ditching War-Time Loudspeakers," *VnExpress International*, January 12, 2017, http://e.vnexpress.net/news/news/Hanoi-considers-ditching-war-time-loudspeakers-3527608.html.
7 From 2018 through 2021, a UNDP Regional Project "Promoting a Fair Business Environment in ASEAN" is active in Vietnam, funded by the UK Prosperity Fund. Vietnam is one of the priority countries for addressing corruption challenges in the private sector. Source: http://www.vn.undp.org/content/vietnam/en/home/presscenter/speeches/2018/DraftAnti-CorruptionLaw.html.

CHAPTER 4: A MIND-SET SHIFT

1 Put away your Western assumptions and tap into your inner fortune teller, lucky numbers (2, 6, 8, and 99), and zodiac calendar.
2 "Coworking Spaces Becoming More Popular in Vietnam," Viet Nam Net, January 03, 2018, http://m.english.vietnamnet.vn/fms/business/189324/co-working-spaces-becoming-more-popular-in-Vietnam.html#.
3 "Saigon Steps Up Its Game in Battle for the Sidewalks," *VnExpress International*, February 23, 2017, http://e.vnexpress.net/news/video/news/saigon-steps-up-its-game-in-battle-for-the-sidewalks-3545906.html.
4 "Doan Ngoc Hai Barred from Leading Campaign; Disorder Returns to Saigon Sidewalks," *Tuoi Tre News*, May 21, 2017, http://tuoitrenews.vn/society/41086/doan-ngoc-hai-barred-from-leading-campaign-disorder-returns-to-saigon-sidewalks.
5 Huu Cong, "Saigon's Sidewalk Cleanup Pioneer Asks for 'Carte Blanche' to Plow Ahead," *VnExpress International*, August 4, 2017, http://e.vnexpress.net/news/news/saigon-s-sidewalk-cleanup-pioneer-asks-for-carte-blanche-to-plow-ahead-3622870.html.
6 "Ông Đoàn Ngọc Hải Nộp Đơn Từ Chức," Tuoi Tre Online, January 8, 2018, https://tuoitre.vn/ong-doan-ngoc-hai-nop-don-tu-chuc-20180108141035089.htm.
7 Ngon, Thien. "Saigon's Captain Sidewalk Withdraws Resignation Letter - VnExpress International." VnExpress International – Latest News, Business, Travel and Analysis from Vietnam. May 19, 2018. Accessed September 26, 2018. https://e.vnexpress.net/news/news/saigon-s-captain-sidewalk-withdraws-resignation-letter-3750168.html.
8 Bowyer, Mark. "Saigon's Pavements - Yes, They're Still Getting Worse." A Traveller's Guide to Vietnam's Buddhist Crisis of 1963 - Rusty Compass Travel Blog. August 6, 2018. Accessed September 26, 2018. https://www.rustycompass.com/blog/saigons-pavements-yes-theyre-still-getting-worse-303#.W4x8tc5Kipo.
9 Tran Quang, "How Vietnam's Street Vendors Are Getting Round the Sidewalk Cleanup," *VnExpress International*, April 3, 2017, http://e.vnexpress.net/news/video/travel-life/how-Vietnam-s-street-vendors-are-getting-round-the-sidewalk-cleanup-3564364.html.
10 Michael G. Vann, "Of Rats, Rice, and Race: The Great Hanoi Rat Massacre, an Episode in French Colonial History," *French Colonial History* 4 (2003), http://freakonomics.com/media/vannrathunt.pdf.
11 Vann, "Of Rats."
12 Vann, "Of Rats."

13 These days, rats are a frequent sight at night in Hanoi—but now they also have an extensive maze of electrical wires to navigate throughout the city.
14 "11 Amerasian Kids Leave Vietnam and Happily Embrace Their U.S. Families." PEOPLE.com. October 18, 1982. Accessed September 26, 2018. https://people.com/archive/11-amerasian-kids-leave-vietnam-and-happily-embrace-their-u-s-families-vol-18-no-16/.
15 Raphelson, Samantha. "One Man's Mission To Bring Home 'Amerasians' Born During Vietnam War." NPR. July 12, 2018. Accessed September 26, 2018. https://www.npr.org/2018/07/12/628398153/one-mans-mission-to-bring-home-amerasians-born-during-vietnam-war.
16 Callery, T. Grant. "Children of War: The Problems of Amerasian Children in Vietnam." *Case Western Reserve Journal of International Law*6, no. 1 (1973): 4-32. Accessed September 26, 2018. https://scholarlycommons.law.case.edu/cgi/viewcontent.cgi?article=2121&context=jil.
17 Ken Burns and Lynn Novick, *Episode 4: Resolve—The Vietnam War: A Film by Ken Burns and Lynn Novick*, PBS video, 12:00. August 25, 2017. http://www.pbs.org/kenburns/the-vietnam-war/episodes/episode-4/.
18 Nicholas Kristof, "Graduate of the Year," *New York Times*, May 24, 2014, https://www.nytimes.com/2014/05/25/opinion/sunday/kristof-graduate-of-the-year.html.
19 Nicholas Kristof, "From Somaliland to Harvard," *New York Times*, September 12, 2015, https://www.nytimes.com/2015/09/13/opinion/sunday/nicholas-kristof-from-somaliland-to-harvard.html.
20 Nga Trang Tuyet Nga, "Q&A with Vietnam's Inspiring Social Entrepreneur of the Year," World Economic Forum, March 29, 2017, https://www.weforum.org/agenda/2017/03/q-a-with-vietnam-s-inspiring-social-entrepreneur-of-the-year/.
21 Johnny Lin, "How to Make $80,000 Per Month on the Apple App Store," Medium, June 10, 2017, https://medium.com/@johnnylin/how-to-make-80-000-per-month-on-the-apple-app-store-bdb943862e88.
22 Mai Nguyen, "Vietnamese Researcher Shows iPhone X Face ID 'Hack,'" Reuters, November 15, 2017, http://mobile.reuters.com/article/amp/idUSKBN1DE1TH.
23 A counterpoint would be that these reforms should have been implemented earlier and that Đổi Mới was really Đổi Cũ, that is, a "change to old" or a return to the natural state of the marketplace after disastrous post-war policies.
24 In the words of several Vietnamese who have shared opinions with your author.
25 Based on interviews and conversations with government officials.
26 Often referred to as "E&I."
27 Quora, "Nondisruptive Creation Could Be the Path to Success Entrepreneurs Are Looking For," *Forbes*, September 29, 2017, https://www.forbes.com/sites/quora/2017/09/29/nondisruptive-creation-could-be-the-path-to-success-entrepreneurs-are-looking-for/#5952e709211a.
28 "The Bloomberg Innovation Index," Bloomberg, accessed February 28, 2018, https://www.bloomberg.com/graphics/2015-innovative-countries/.
29 "Vietnam, South Korea Agree to Do $100 Billion in Bilateral Trade By..." Reuters. March 23, 2018. Accessed September 26, 2018. https://www.reuters.com/article/us-vietnam-southkorea-moon/vietnam-south-korea-agree-to-do-100-billion-in-bilateral-trade-by-2020-idUSKBN1GZ0GX.
30 Or at the very least, greater incentives for cooperating with other ministries—or consolidating them on a headcount basis.
31 Whether you believe them is a different story; at least if stated, one can hold actors to standards.
32 Soccer, for the Americans.
33 "Vietnam Captain Says Stunning U23 Asian Cup Run Thanks To 'Crazy' Fans Back Home," *VnExpress International*, January 25, 2018, https://e.vnexpress.net/news/news/vietnam-captain-says-stunning-u23-asian-cup-run-thanks-to-crazy-fans-back-home-3703832.html.

CHAPTER 5: CATALYZING GROWTH IN VIETNAM

1 Previously, it had just been importing models from Malaysia into Vietnam.
2 "ELSA Raises 3.2M For Its A.I.-Powered English Pronunciation Assistant," TechCrunch, March 7, 2018, https://techcrunch.com/2018/03/06/elsa-raises-3-2m-for-its-a-i-powered-english-pronunciation-assistant/.
3 Full disclosure: I have previously had a business relationship with this agency through GKTA Group.
4 Full disclosure: My brother, David, was part of OnOnPay's digital marketing team in 2015.
5 Bobby Liu, "The Topica Founder Institute Mafias," Medium, August 17, 2016, https://medium.com/@bobbyliu/the-topica-founder-institute-mafias-e0cf96311ee5.
6 Nguyễn is the cofounder of WeFit, a fitness app.
7 "Vietnam Steps Up Removal of Tariff Barriers When Joining AEC," Viet Nam Net, January 24, 2016, http://english.Vietnamnet.vn/fms/business/150302/VietNam-steps-up-removal-of-tariff-barriers-when-joining-aec.html.
8 "ASEAN Economic Community," ASEAN, accessed February 28, 2018, http://asean. org/asean-economic-community/.
9 "Mekong Innovative Startups in Tourism - Tourism and Travel Tech Accelerator." MIST. Accessed September 26, 2018. http://mist.asia/.
10 Woetzel, Jonathan, et al. "Outperformers: High Growth Emerging Economies and the Companies that Propel Them." Report. September 2018. Accessed October 5, 2018. https://www.mckinsey.com/~/media/McKinsey/Featured Insights/Innovation/Outperformers High growth emerging economies and the companies that propel them/MGI-Outperformers-Executive-summary-Sep-2018.ashx.
11 Truong Sanh, "Female Entrepreneurs Take Saigon Crowdfunding Event by Storm," *VnExpress International*, April 27, 2017, http://e.vnexpress.net/news/business/female-entrepreneurs-take-saigon-crowdfunding-event-by-storm-3576901.html.
12 "Freeport McMoran's DreamBuilder," Thunderbird School of Global Management, accessed February 28, 2018, https://thunderbird.asu.edu/programs/dreambuilder.
13 Neil Fraser, "Teaching in Vietnam," Neil's News, February 26, 2017, https://neil.fraser. name/news/2017/02/26/.
14 Marion Vigot, social media post, https://www.facebook.com/marion.vigot/posts/10155217090274071.
15 As noted in a roundtable Du Học Sinh discussion in November 2016.
16 "Open Doors," IIE: The Power of International Education, accessed February 28, 2018, http://www.iie.org/Research-and-Publications/Open-Doors/Data/US-Study-Abroad/All-Destinations/2012-14.
17 "More Vietnamese Students Study Abroad, but Few Foreigners Enroll in VN," Viet Nam Net, November 10, 2016, http://english.Vietnamnet.vn/fms/education/166725/more-Vietnamese-students-study-abroad-but-few-foreigners-enroll-in-vn.html.
18 "Vietnam Center: Study Abroad," Loyola University Chicago, accessed February 28, 2018, https://www.luc.edu/studyabroad/vietnam.shtml.
19 "Vietnam: The Brockport Vietnam Program," College at Brockport: State University of New York, accessed February 28, 2018, https://brockport.studioabroad.com/index.cfm?Fuse-Action=Programs.ViewProgram&Program_ID=10096.
20 "VinUniversity Project," Cornell University, accessed February 28, 2018, https://business.cornell.edu/faculty-research/vin-university/.
21 "FAQ," Knowmads Hanoi, accessed February 28, 2018, http://www.knowmads.vn/faq. html.
22 I don't want to diminish the dramatic transformation for Vietnamese society over the past several decades. Eighty-eight percent of Vietnamese respondents—the highest percentage across thirty-eight countries—to a 2017 Pew Research Center poll indicated that life today was better than fifty years ago. This makes perfect sense if you recall

that in 1967 Vietnam was in the midst of war and has only had peace for a short time compared to its historical timeline. Source: http://www.pewglobal.org/2017/12/05/worldwide-people-divided-on-whether-life-today-is-better-than-in-the-past/.

CHAPTER 6: THE BEGINNINGS OF A STARTUP NATION

1 "Vietnam Start-ups Need More Investment." VOV - VOV Online Newspaper. April 26, 2018. Accessed September 26, 2018. https://english.vov.vn/economy/vietnam-start-ups-need-more-investment-373496.vov.
2 "Mùa Xuân Khởi Nghiệp," Nhân Dân, January 1, 2016, http://www.nhandan.com.vn/cuoituan/item/28417502-mua-xuan-khoi-nghiep.html.
3 "Off to a Good Start, but Startup Education Falls Short," Viet Nam News, April 10, 2017, http://vietnamnews.vn/opinion/in-the-spotlight/374342/off-to-a-good-start-but-startup-education-falls-short.html#hWlFvmqdJ3LqIRMt.97.
4 "More Administrative Procedures Cut to Support Foreign Firms," Viet Nam Plus, January 22, 2018, https://en.vietnamplus.vn/more-administrative-procedures-cut-to-support-foreign-firms/125299.vnp.
5 "Gov't Cuts MoIT Regulations," *Viet Nam News*, January 17, 2018, http://vietnamnews. vn/economy/421274/govt-cuts-moit-regulations.html#b0UTdXu2L66IRfLP.97.
6 "Enterprises Have to Pay Much on Administrative Procedures: Government's Report." Vietnamnews.vn. August 18, 2018. Accessed September 26, 2018. https://vietnamnews.vn/society/464076/enterprises-have-to-pay-much-on-administrative-procedures-governments-report.html#09v546teGQsobXtR.97.
7 "Vietnam Releases Report on Administrative Procedure Compliance." Great Ideology of Karl Marx with the Revolution of Vietnam - Nhan Dan Online. August 17, 2017. Accessed September 26, 2018. http://en.nhandan.com.vn/business/item/6506702-vietnam-releases-report-on-administrative-procedure-compliance.html.
8 Vietnamnet.vn. "Ministry of Finance Proposes to Cut 51.4% of Business Conditions - News VietNamNet." Vietnam Net Bridge. August 15, 2018. Accessed September 26, 2018. http://english.vietnamnet.vn/fms/business/206847/ministry-of-finance-proposes-to-cut-51-4--of-business-conditions.html.
9 "Vietnam to Cut Costs, Rules for Firms," Viet Nam Net, December 10, 2017, http://m. english.vietnamnet.vn/fms/business/191824/vietnam-to-cut-costs-rules-for-firms.html#.
10 Its economy did not look so different from Vietnam's.
11 A kind of ode to Vietnam's Đổi Mới policy, enacted in 1986.
12 Agence France-Presse, "Vietnam Courts Japanese High-Tech Investment," *The Nation*, January 17, 2017, http://www.nationmultimedia.com/news/breakingnews/30304297.
13 "Policy Brief No. 50: Robots and Industrialization in Developing Countries," UNCTAD, October 2016, http://unctad.org/en/PublicationsLibrary/presspb2016d6_en.pdf.
14 James Manyika et al., "Digital America: A Tale of the Haves and Have-Mores," McKinsey and Company, December 2015, http://www.mckinsey.com/industries/high-tech/our-insights/digital-america-a-tale-of-the-haves-and-have-mores.
15 Michael Chui, James Manyika, and Mehdi Miremadi, "Where Machines Could Replace Humans—and Where They Can't (Yet)," McKinsey and Company, July 2016, http://www.mckinsey. com/business-functions/digital-mckinsey/our-insights/where-machines-could-replace-humans-and-where-they-cant-yet.
16 Tim Worstall, "If Foxconn's Chinese Factories Are Now Automating Then Those Apple Jobs Are Never Coming Back," *Forbes*, December 31, 2016, https://www.forbes.com/sites/timworstall/2016/12/31/

if-foxconns-chinese-factories-are-now-automating-then-those-apple-jobs-are-never-coming-back/#4c05549836d9.

17 Christopher Alessi, "Kuka Deal Signals China's Robot Fixation," *Wall Street Journal*, May 18, 2016, https://www.wsj.com/articles/china-is-largest-fastest-growing-market-worldwide-for-industrial-robots-1463584169.

18 "Political Students Ask the Prime Minister How to Start a Business," *VnExpress International*, October 16, 2016, http://vnexpress.net/tin-tuc/giao-duc/sinh-vien-chinh-tri-hoi-thu-tuong-cach-khoi-nghiep-3484487.html.

19 "Bachelors, Masters Constitute 20% of Unemployed People in Vietnam," *Tuoi Tre News*, December 27, 2015, http://tuoitrenews.vn/society/32459/bachelors-masters-constitute-20-of-unemployed-people-in-vietnam.

20 Atsushi Tomiyama, "Vietnam's University Student Blues: I Graduated, But...," *Nikkei Asian Review*, July 12, 2016, https://asia.nikkei.com/Politics-Economy/Economy/Vietnam-s-university-student-blues-I-graduated-but.

21 "Growing Demand for Vocational Training in Vietnam," ICEF Monitor, May 24, 2016, http://monitor.icef.com/2016/05/growing-demand-vocational-training-vietnam/.

22 "VN Has 110,100 Startups This Year," Viet Nam Net, December 29, 2016, http://english. vietnamnet.vn/fms/business/170334/vn-has-110-100-startups-this-year.html.

23 "Businesses Fail Despite Economic Recovery," Viet Nam Net, May 9, 2016, http://english.vietnamnet.vn/fms/business/155964/businesses-fail-despite-economic-recovery.html.

24 "265 Businesses Close Doors Every Day," Viet Nam Net, April 1, 2017, http://english. vietnamnet.vn/fms/business/175792/265-businesses-close-doors-every-day.html/.

25 "New Business Registration in March Hits 6-Year High," Nhân Dân, March 28, 2017, http://en.nhandan.com.vn/business/item/5093902-new-business-registration-in-march-hits-6-year-high.html.

26 Minh, Anh. "Vietnam's Q1 Economic Growth Hits Decade High - VnExpress International." VnExpress International – Latest News, Business, Travel and Analysis from Vietnam. April 05, 2018. Accessed September 26, 2018. https://e.vnexpress.net/news/business/data-speaks/vietnam-s-q1-economic-growth-hits-decade-high-3728891.html.

27 "Vietnam Sees 11,262 New Enterprises Established in July." Hanoi Times. Accessed September 26, 2018. http://www.hanoitimes.vn/economy/2018/07/81e0ca9b/vietnam-sees-11-262-new-enterprises-established-in-july/.

28 Vietnam. Ministry of Planning and Investment. General Statistics Office. *Number of Enterprises Temporarily Ceased Operations by Kinds of Activity*. https://www.gso.gov.vn/Modules/Doc_Download.aspx?DocID=22733.

29 "Vietnam to Cut Costs, Rules for Firms," Viet Nam Net, December 10, 2017, http://m. english.vietnamnet.vn/fms/business/191824/vietnam-to-cut-costs-rules-for-firms.html#.

30 "Vietnam to Cut Costs, Rules for Firms."

31 Edmund Malesky, *The Viet Nam Provincial Competitiveness Index: Measuring Economic Governance for Private Sector Development, 2016 Final Report* (Hanoi: Viet Nam Chamber of Commerce and Industry and United States Agency for International Development, 2017).

32 "The Inclusive Growth and Development Report 2017," World Economic Forum, January 16, 2017, https://www.weforum.org/reports/the-inclusive-growth-and-development-report-2017.

33 "Venture Capital Funnel Shows Odds of Becoming a Unicorn Are Less than 1%," CB Insights, March 29, 2017, https://www.cbinsights.com/research/venture-capital-funnel-2/.

34 These are also the initials of Vietnam's most revered war hero, General Võ Nguyên Giáp.

35 Fram^, a Swedish-Vietnamese firm, IPOed on Nasdaq First North in 2017.

36 Ellis Hamburger, "Indie Smash Hit 'Flappy Bird' Racks Up $50K Per Day in Ad Revenue," The Verge, February 05, 2014, https://www.theverge.com/2014/2/5/5383708/flappy-bird-revenue-50-k-per-day-dong-nguyen-interview.

37 Alyson Shontell, "The Life and Sudden Death of 'Flappy Bird': How a Guy Making

38 $50,000 Per Day Grew to 'Hate' His Own Game," *Business Insider*, February 10, 2014, http://www. businessinsider.com/why-flappy-birds-shut-down-2014-2.

39 Lan Anh Nguyen, "Exclusive: Flappy Bird Creator Dong Nguyen Says App 'Gone Forever' Because It Was 'An Addictive Product,'" *Forbes*, February 11, 2014, https://www.forbes. com/ sites/lananhnguyen/2014/02/11/exclusive-flappy-bird-creator-dong-nguyen-says-app-gone-forever-because-it-was-an-addictive-product/#4bc5982d6476.
40 "Non-Observed Economy to Be Measured in 2018," Voice of Vietnam Online, January 16, 2018, http://english.m.vov.vn/economy/nonobserved-economy-to-be-measured-in-2018-366773.vov#ref-https://t.co/GjEyp60Fcg?amp=1.
41 "Vietnam Loses $300 Million a Year Due to Tobacco Smuggling," *VnExpress International*, December 11, 2016, http://e.vnexpress.net/news/business/economy/vietnam-loses-300-million-a-year-due-to-tobacco-smuggling-3511502.html.
42 "International Hunt for Vietnamese-American Smuggler," *Tuoi Tre News*, December 14, 2013, http://tuoitrenews.vn/society/16004/print?undefined.
43 61.3 percent in 2017.
44 "Vietnam's Public Debt Stands at 61.3% in 2017: Finance Ministry," Viet Nam Net, January 9, 2018, http://english.vietnamnet.vn/fms/business/193575/vietnam-s-public-debt-stands-at-61-3-in-2017-finance-ministry.html.
45 "Falling Oil Prices Adversely Affect Vietnam Economy," *VOV Online Newspaper*, September 06, 2015, http://english.vov.vn/economy/falling-oil-prices-adversely-affect-vietnam-economy-300298.vov.
46 "WB Warns Vietnam Against Growing Budget Deficit," *Vietnam Investment Review*, July 19, 2016, http://www.vir.com.vn/wb-warns-vietnam-against-growing-budget-deficit.html.
47 "Public Debt Exceeds 62 Percent of GDP, Vietnam Walks Tightrope," Viet Nam Net, March 23, 2016, http://english.vietnamnet.vn/fms/business/152589/public-debt-exceeds-62-percent-of-gdp-vietnam-walks-tightrope.html.
48 "Vietnam's Productivity Is 15 Times Lower Than Singapore's," *Tuoi Tre News*, September 5, 2014, http://tuoitrenews.vn/society/22179/ vietnams-productivity-is-15-times-lower-than-singapores.
49 "Vietnam's Labor Productivity Increases Nearly 24% in Five Years," Viet Nam Net, January 3, 2016, http://english.vietnamnet.vn/fms/society/149471/vietnam-s-labor-productivity-increases-nearly-24-in-five-years.html.
50 A. J. G. Simoes and C. A. Hidalgo. "The Economic Complexity Observatory: An Analytical Tool for Understanding the Dynamics of Economic Development." Workshops at the Twenty-Fifth AAAI Conference on Artificial Intelligence. (2011).
51 "The Future of ASEAN: Viet Nam perspective" https://www.pwc.com/vn/en/publications/vietnam-publications/the-future-of-asean-vietnam.html.
52 E. B. Boyd, "Exclusive: Secretary of State Kerry Talks about the Power of Entrepreneurship," *Fast Company*, June 26, 2016, http://www.fastcompany.com/3061288/change-agents/ exclusive-secretary-of-state-kerry-talks-about-the-power-of-entrepreneurship.
53 "Google CEO's Vietnam Visit Gives Hope to Local Startups," *Tech Wire Asia*, December 23, 2015, http://techwireasia.com/2015/12/ google-ceos-vietnam-visit-gives-hope-to-local-startups/.
54 "Vietnam's Internet Market the Most Dynamic in the World," Viet Nam Net, May 22, 2016, http://english.vietnamnet.vn/fms/science-it/156786/vietnam-s-internet-market-the-most-dynamic-in-the-world.html.
55 Alisée de Tonnac, "Why Talent Is Everywhere," July 10, 2017, video, 32:04, posted by BPMredaktion, https://www.youtube.com/watch?v=PwAnaEciSL4.
56 "Industrial Park Occupancy Rate Reaches 73%." Vietnamnews.vn. August 14, 2017. Accessed September 26, 2018. https://vietnamnews.vn/economy/381720/industrial-park-occupancy-rate-reaches-73.html#Dv26XRgDVrmopVCJ.97.
57 "Da Nang VN's Most Liveable City: Asia Institute," *Viet Nam News*, December 30, 2016, http://vietnamnews.vn/life-style/348956/da-nang-vns-most-liveable-city-asia-institute. html#e3YVEdYMS33PmRr9.97.

58 Naotaka Owada, "Vietnam Engineering Talent Favored by Japan Software Developers," *Nikkei Asian Review*, September 04, 2014, https://asia.nikkei.com/magazine/20140904-TA-TA-GROUP/Business/Vietnam-engineering-talent-favored-by-Japan-software-developers.
59 "Company History," TMA Solutions, accessed February 28, 2018, http://www.tmasolutions.com/company-history.
60 Sean Coughlan, "Asia Tops Biggest Global School Rankings," BBC News, May 13, 2015, http://www.bbc.com/news/business-32608772.
61 "Vietnam's Startup Scene—Not Just Building Tech but Developing It—Video," CNET, July 29, 2015, https://www.cnet.com/videos/vietnams-startup-scene-not-just-building-tech-but-developing-it/.

CHAPTER 7: CHALLENGES AND OPPORTUNITIES

1 Still, the government of Vietnam exerts strong influence over the press, civil society, and the private sector—formally and through a licensing regime, nebulous legislation, and other gatekeeping measures.
2 Atsushi Tomiyama, "Social Media Lets Vietnamese Vent like Never Before," *Nikkei Asian Review*, January 12, 2017, http://asia.nikkei.com/magazine/TUNE-UP-TIME-FOR-VIET-NAM/On-the-Cover/Social-media-lets-Vietnamese-vent-like-never-before.
3 "Internet Once Feared to Threaten National Security," Viet Nam Net, April 20, 2017, accessed March 30, 2018, http://english.vietnamnet.vn/fms/special-reports/176878/internet-once-feared-to-threaten-national-security.html.
4 James Hookway, "5 Five Things about the Internet in Vietnam," *Wall Street Journal*, June 12, 2015, https://blogs.wsj.com/briefly/2015/06/12/5-five-things-about-the-internet-in-vietnam/.
5 "Vietnamese Government Wants Homegrown Social Networks to Replace Facebook," *VnExpress International*, April 19, 2017, http://e.vnexpress.net/news/news/vietnamese-government-wants-homegrown-social-networks-to-replace-facebook-3572504.html.
6 Hoang Thuy, "Vietnam Cuts Domestic Server Requirement for Foreign Firms from Cyber-Security Bill," *VnExpress International*, January 11, 2018, https://ampe.vnexpress.net/news/news/vietnam-cuts-domestic-server-requirement-for-foreign-firms-from-cyber-security-bill-3697069.html.
7 Logan, Sarah, and Cecelia Nguyen. "Facebook and Vietnam's New Cybersecurity Law." The Interpreter. July 26, 2018. Accessed September 26, 2018. https://www.lowyinstitute.org/the-interpreter/facebook-and-vietnams-new-cybersecurity-law.
8 Minh Nga, "Half of Vietnamese Get News from Social Media, Survey Finds," *VnExpress International*, January 13, 2018, https://ampe.vnexpress.net/news/business/data-speaks/most-vietnamese-get-news-from-social-media-survey-finds-3698212.html.
9 James Hookway, "Introducing Force 47, Vietnam's New Weapon against Online Dissent," *Wall Street Journal*, December 31, 2017, https://www.wsj.com/articles/introducing-force-47-vietnams-new-weapon-against-online-dissent-1514721606.
10 Created in August 2008.
11 Furthermore, no one should be afraid of speaking his or her mind or have to worry about targeted retribution for legitimate concerns and needs that are being unmet.
12 "AIC Comments on Draft Decree Amending Decree 72," Asia Internet Coalition, November 8, 2016. https://www.aicasia.org/2016/11/08/aic-comments-on-draft-decree-amending-decree-72/.

13 My Pham, "Vietnam Urges Firms to Stop YouTube and Facebook Ads in Protest over Fake Content," Reuters, March 16, 2017, http://www.reuters.com/article/us-vietnam-google-idUSKBN16N110.

14 "Bill Demanding Google, Facebook Install Domestic Servers Raises Eyebrows in Vietnam," *VnExpress International*, November 3, 2017, https://e.vnexpress.net/news/news/bill-demanding-google-facebook-install-domestic-servers-raises-eyebrows-in-vietnam-3665331.html.

15 Nguyen Ha, "Google under Pressure from Vietnam to Open Rep Office to Boost Internet Control," *VnExpress International*, January 19, 2018, https://e.vnexpress.net/news/news/google-under-pressure-from-vietnam-to-open-rep-office-to-boost-internet-control-3700964.html.

16 "Vietnam Says Facebook Has Pledged to Prevent Anti-Government and 'Offensive' Content," Fortune, April 27, 2017, http://fortune.com/2017/04/27/vietnam-facebook-antigovernment-offensive-content/?xid=time_socialflow_twitter.

17 "Vietnamese Internet Users Baffled as Popular Facebook Pages Vanish," *VnExpress International*, March 20, 2017, http://e.vnexpress.net/news/news/vietnamese-internet-users-baffled-as-popular-facebook-pages-vanish-3557943.html.

18 Nguyen Ha, "Google under Pressure from Vietnam to Open Rep Office to Boost Internet Control," *VnExpress International*, January 19, 2018, https://e.vnexpress.net/news/news/google-under-pressure-from-vietnam-to-open-rep-office-to-boost-internet-control-3700964.html.

19 "Sustainable Development." IISD. July 12, 2018. Accessed October 11, 2018. https://www.iisd.org/topic/sustainable-development.

20 Bao Yen, "Vietnam Needs to Change Approach to Solving Environment Disputes: UNDP," *VnExpress International*, February 1, 2018, https://ampe.vnexpress.net/news/news/environmental-injustice-left-largely-unresolved-in-vietnam-undp-3705857.html.

21 At least one local blogger was arrested and accused in 2017 of "using the internet to spread some propaganda videos and writings that are against the government of the Socialist Republic of Vietnam." ("Vietnam: Police Arrest Activist for Sharing 'Anti-Government Propaganda,'" *Asian Correspondent*, January 22, 2017, https://asiancorrespondent.com/2017/01/vietnam-police-arrest-activist-tran-thi-nga-for-sharing-anti-government-propaganda/.) From January 2018 to October 2018, more than 55 dissidents or bloggers had been arrested.

22 "Background," Vietnam Private Sector Forum, August 2016, http://vpsf.vn/pages/intro.

23 "ADB Applauds Vietnam on Reducing Deficit," Vietstock, September 30, 2017, http://en.vietstock.vn/2017/09/adb-applauds-vietnam-on-reducing-deficit-37-295375.htm.

24 Tuan, Viet. "Vietnam to Cut Civil Servants by 5,510 next Year - VnExpress International." VnExpress International – Latest News, Business, Travel and Analysis from Vietnam. August 16, 2018. Accessed September 26, 2018. https://e.vnexpress.net/news/news/vietnam-to-cut-civil-servants-by-5-510-next-year-3793110.html.

25 Full disclosure: I worked with a member of his family on two separate projects in 2013 and 2014.

26 "Coal," in *International Energy Outlook 2016* (Washington, DC: US Energy Information Administration, 2016).

27 "Vietnam—Power Generation," Export.gov, July 18, 2017, https://www.export.gov/article?id=Vietnam-Power-Generation.

28 Mark Clifford, Janet Pau, and Joanna Sobolewsk, *Decarbonization: Opportunities in ASEAN*, February 2017, http://www.asiabusinesscouncil.org/docs/Decarbonization.pdf.

29 Yudha Siregar, "Boosting Electrification Ratio: Lessons from Vietnam," ASEAN Center for Energy, July 15, 2016, http://www.aseanenergy.org/blog/boosting-electrification-ratio-lessons-from-vietnam/.

30 "CO2 Emissions (Metric Tons Per Capita)," World Bank, accessed February 28, 2018, http://data.worldbank.org/indicator/EN.ATM.CO2E.PC?locations=VN.

31 Camila Domonoske, "2 Degrees, $100 Billion: The World Climate Agreement, by the Numbers," NPR, December 12, 2015, accessed March 31, 2018, http://www.npr.org/sections/

thetwo-way/2015/12/12/459502597/2-degrees-100-billion-the-world-climate-agreement-by-the-numbers.
32 "Viet Nam Pledges $1 Million to GCF at COP 21," Green Climate Fund, December 4, 2015, http://www.greenclimate.fund/-/vietnam-pledges-1-million-to-green-climate-fund-at-cop-21.
33 *Vietnam Power Development Plan for the Period 2011–2020*, accessed February 28, 2018, http://gizenergy.org.vn/media/app/media/legal documents/GIZ_PDP 7 rev_Mar 2016_Highlights_IS.pdf.
34 Thi Khanh Nguy, "Vietnam Is Ripe for a 21st-Century Energy Policy," Institute for Energy Economics and Financial Analysis, May 24, 2016, http://ieefa.org/vietnam-ripe-21-century-energy-policy/.
35 Ha Phuong, "Mapped: Hydropower Plants Across Vietnam," *VnExpress International*, November 13, 2017, https://e.vnexpress.net/infographics/data-speaks/mapped-hydropower-plants-across-vietnam-3669538.html.
36 AFP, "Floods, Landslides Kill 37 in Vietnam, Scores Missing," Yahoo!, October 12, 2017, https://www.yahoo.com/amphtml/news/floods-landslides-kill-37-vietnam-scores-missing-044021518.html.
37 Thanh Nguyen and Nhung Nguyen, "Confessions of a Hydropower Calamity in Vietnam," *VnExpress International*, October 15, 2017, https://e.vnexpress.net/projects/confessions-of-a-hydropower-calamity-in-vietnam-3655314/index.html.
38 IRENA, *REthinking Energy 2017: Accelerating the Global Energy Transformation* (Abu Dhabi: International Renewable Energy Agency, 2017), 2017, http://www.irena.org/DocumentDownloads/Publications/IRENA_REthinking_Energy_2017.pdf.
39 Kevin Watkins, *The Human Development Report 2007/2008* (NYC: United Nations Development Programme, 2008), accessed February 28, 2018, http://hdr.undp.org/sites/default/files/hdr_20072008_summary_english.pdf.
40 "Vietnam," CGIAR Research Program on Climate Change, Agriculture, and Food Security, accessed February 28, 2018, https://ccafs.cgiar.org/vietnam.
41 Michael Taylor, "Hanoi Enjoyed Just 38 Days of Clean Air in 2017: Report," Reuters, January 30, 2018, https://mobile.reuters.com/article/amp/idUSKBN1FJ164.
42 "Sea-Level Rise Could 'Displace Millions,'" IRIN, May 20, 2011, http://www.irinnews.org/report/92763/vietnam-sea-level-rise-could-displace-millions.
43 Alex Perera, "Southeast Asia's Clean Energy Economy Blazes Ahead," World Resources Institute, May 9, 2017, http://www.wri.org/blog/2017/05/southeast-asias-clean-energy-economy-blazes-ahead.
44 "Vietnam Plans Major Solar Power Growth," Viet Nam Net, November 5, 2017, http://m.english.vietnamnet.vn/fms/business/189649/vietnam-plans-major-solar-power-growth. html#.
45 "About Us," Regulatory Indicators for Sustainable Energy, accessed February 28, 2018, http://rise.esmap.org/about-us.
46 "Vietnam," Happy Planet Index, accessed February 28, 2018, http://happyplanetindex. org/countries/vietnam.
47 "World's Population Increasingly Urban with More than Half Living in Urban Areas," United Nations, July 10, 2014, http://www.un.org/en/development/desa/news/population/world-urbanization-prospects-2014.html.
48 Eduardo Klien and Yoriko Yasukawa, "Asia's Population Is Ageing Fast. Here's What We Can Learn," World Economic Forum, September 5, 2016, https://www.weforum.org/agenda/2016/09/asia-pacific-ageing-what-we-can-learn.
49 Linh Tong, "Vietnam Struggling with Ageing Population," East Asia Forum, January 25, 2017, http://www.eastasiaforum.org/2017/01/25/vietnam-struggling-with-aging-population/.
50 United Nations Population Fund, *The 2014 Viet Nam Intercensal Population and Housing Survey: Population Sex-Age Structure and Related Socio-Economic Issues in Viet Nam* (Ha Noi, 2016), accessed February 28, 2018, http://vietnam.unfpa.org/sites/default/files/pub-pdf/PD_English_Monograph_Age & Sex Structure of population 2014_2016.pdf.

51 Tu Hoang, "WB: Vietnam Urbanization among Fastest in Region," *Saigon Times*, January 27, 2015, http://english.thesaigontimes.vn/39250/WB-Việt Nam-urbanization-among-fastest-in-region-.html.
52 Brian Spaen, "In 2 Years, Renewables Will Be Cheaper than Fossil Fuels," Green Matters and World Economic Forum, January 17, 2018, https://www.weforum.org/agenda/2018/01/renewables-will-be-equal-or-cheaper-than-fossil-fuels-by-2020-according-to-research.
53 Tan Dung Nguyen, "Decree No. 96/2015/ND-CP of October 19, 2015," Vietnam Law and Legal Forum, December 24, 2015, http://vietnamlawmagazine.vn/decree-no-96-2015-nd-cp-of-october-19-2015-5149.html.
54 "Vietnam Enterprise Law 2014," Vietnam Law in English, November 26, 2014, http://vietnamlawenglish.blogspot.com/2015/05/vietnam-enterprise-law-2014.html.
55 "The Landscape for Impact Investing in Southeast Asia." The GIIN. August 2, 2018. Accessed September 26, 2018. https://thegiin.org/research/publication/landscape-southeast-asia.
56 Ruth Umoh, "BlackRock's Push for 'Social Responsibility' Highlights This Major Shift among Corporations," CNBC, January 23, 2018, https://www.cnbc.com/2018/01/23/blackrocks-push-for-social-responsibility-shows-shift-in-companies.html.
57 Yuta Uebayashi, "Japan, Vietnam to Cooperate on TPP," *Nikkei Asian Review*, January 17, 2017, https://asia.nikkei.com/Politics-Economy/International-Relations/Japan-Vietnam-to-cooperate-on-TPP.
58 Thi Khanh Nguy, "Vietnam Needs a 21st Century Electricity Plan," RenewEconomy, May 23, 2016, http://reneweconomy.com.au/75848/.
59 Thi Khanh Nguy, "Vietnam Is Ripe for a 21st-Century Energy Policy," Institute for Energy Economics and Financial Analysis, May 26, 2016, http://ieefa.org/vietnam-ripe-21-century-energy-policy/.
60 "Booklet: Debunking Renewable Energy Myths in Vietnam," Green Innovation and Development Center (GreenID), November 15, 2016, http://en.greenidvietnam.org.vn/view-document/5858f720a7f8219b4b8b4569.
61 Jenna R. Jambeck et al., "Plastic Waste Inputs from Land into the Ocean," *Science* 347, no. 6223 (February 13, 2015): doi:10.1126/science.1260352.
62 The Corruption Perceptions Index (CPI), released by Transparency International, ranks Vietnam at 107th out of 180 economies based on perceptions of experts and businesspeople.
63 "About 3 Million Workers Need Accommodations by 2020." VOV - VOV Online Newspaper. August 02, 2018. Accessed September 26, 2018. https://english.vov.vn/society/about-3-million-workers-need-accommodations-by-2020-380360.vov.
64 "Vietnamese Love for Parents: It's Filial Affection, but Not Duty," *Tuoi Tre News*, December 04, 2017, https://tuoitrenews.vn/news/features/20171204/vietnamese-love-for-parents-its-filial-affection-but-not-duty/42988.html.
65 Son Luong, "Ho Chi Minh City to Switch to Mobile Apps to Build E-Governance," *Tuoi Tre News*, February 22, 2018, https://tuoitrenews.vn/news/society/20180222/ho-chi-minh-city-to-switch-to-mobile-apps-to-build-egovernance/44204.html.
66 In early 2018, Hanoi initiated the State Capital Management Committee to oversee the equitization of USD $220 billion worth of government assets. "Vietnam Sets Up $220 bln Committee to Boost Privatization," Reuters, February 5, 2018, https://www.reuters.com/article/vietnam-privatisation/vietnam-sets-up-220-bln-committee-to-boost-privatisation-idUSL4N1PV40R.
67 United Nations, "Transforming Our World: the 2030 Agenda for Sustainable Development," United Nations, October 15, 2015, http://www.un.org/ga/search/view_doc.asp?symbol=A/RES/70/1&Lang=E.
68 Kopf, Dan. "Vietnam Is the Most Globalized Populous Country in Modern History." Quartz. October 02, 2018. Accessed October 06, 2018. https://qz.com/1409407/vietnam-is-the-most-globalized-populous-country-in-modern-history/.

CHAPTER 8: BUILDING A SOLID FOUNDATION

1 United Nations, "Sustainable Development Goals," United Nations, accessed February 28, 2018, http://www.un.org/sustainabledevelopment/sustainable-development-goals/.
2 United Nations, "Sustainable Developmental Goals."
3 H. E. *Trương Tấn Sang*, "Statement at the United Nations Summit to Adopt the Post-2015 Development Agenda," United Nations, September 25, 2015, https://sustainabledevelopment.un.org/content/documents/20321vietnam.pdf.
4 *Trương Tấn Sang*, "Statement at the United Nations."
5 "Vietnam: Sustainable Development Knowledge Platform." United Nations. June 2018. Accessed September 26, 2018. https://sustainabledevelopment.un.org/memberstates/vietnam.
6 Thuy, Bich. "Vietnam Launches Action Plan to Reach Agenda 2030 Goals." Vietnam Investment Review - VIR. July 09, 2017. Accessed September 26, 2018. http://www.vir.com.vn/vietnam-launches-action-plan-to-reach-agenda-2030-goals-50473.html.
7 Full disclosure: I was a cofounder of Augmented Ventures, which was part of a consortium with HATCH! in 2016. In early 2016, I left the firm.
8 Hao Tran, "Huong Nguyen on Collaborative Workspaces and Emerging Entrepreneurialism in Vietnam," Vietcetera, accessed February 28, 2018, http://vietcetera.com/huong-nguyen-on-collaborative-workspaces-and-emerging-entrepreneurialism-in-vietnam/.
9 "Local Acquisitions—Alibaba and Ant Financial's Choice of Expansion in Asean," *ASEAN Today*, December 31, 2017, http://www.aseantoday.com/2017/12/how-alibaba-and-ant-financial-increase-their-presence-in-asean/.
10 "Nothing is more precious than Independence and Liberty."—Hồ Chí Minh, who quoted parts of the American Declaration of Independence at Ba Đình Square on September 2, 1945: "All men are created equal; they are endowed by their Creator with certain inalienable Rights; among these are Life, Liberty, and the pursuit of Happiness."
11 See here for more details: http://www.chinhphu.vn/portal/page/portal/English/strategies/strategiesdetails?categoryId=30&articleId=10057712.
12 See here for additional details: http://www.chinhphu.vn/portal/page/portal/English/strategies/strategiesdetails?categoryId=30&articleId=10054959.
13 "International Forum on Sustainable Infrastructure: Integrating Climate Resilience and Natural Capital into Transport Infrastructure Planning and Design," GMS Environment Operations Center, accessed February 31, 2018, http://www.gms-eoc.org/events/forum-on-sustainable-infrastructure-.
14 GMS Environmental Operations Center, "International Forum."
15 *The Official Launch of The Viet Nam Provincial Governance and Public Administration Performance Index (PAPI) 2017*. Presentation PDF. http://papi.org.vn/eng/wp-content/uploads/2018/04/2017PAPI_LaunchingPresentation_ENG.pdf.
16 United Nations Development Programme, "The Viet Nam Provincial Governance and Public Administration Performance Index (PAPI) 2012," UNDP, May 12, 2013, http://www.vn.undp.org/content/vietnam/en/home/library/democratic_governance/PAPI-2012.html.
17 Long Giang, Cuong Nguyen, and Anh Tran, "Does PAPI Monitoring Improve Local Governance? Evidence from a Natural Experiment in Vietnam," *International Journal of Development Issues* 16, no. 1 (2017), https://doi.org/10.1108/IJDI-05-2016-0028.
18 Reuters, "Vietnamese Leader Halts Work on Steel Plant Over Threat of Chemical Spill," *New York Times*, April 16, 2017, https://www.nytimes.com/2017/04/16/business/vietnamese-leader-halts-work-on-steel-plant-over-threat-of-chemical-spill.html.
19 "Trucchigraphy—The Vietnamese Paper Art That Wows Global Audience," *Tuoi Tre News*, December 25, 2017, https://tuoitrenews.vn/news/lifestyle/20171225/trucchigraphy-the-vietnamese-paper-art-that-wows-global-audience/43312.html.
20 "Sea-Level Rise Could 'Displace Millions,'" IRIN, May 20, 2011, http://www.irinnews.org/report/92763/vietnam-sea-level-rise-could-displace-millions.

21 "Vietnam: Sustainable Development Knowledge Platform." United Nations. June 2018. Accessed September 26, 2018. https://sustainabledevelopment.un.org/memberstates/vietnam.
22 "Sea-Level Rise," IRIN.
23 Full disclosure: former client.
24 Jones, Olivia. "What We Learned: The 2016 Vietnam GIX." May 4, 2016. www.tuck.dartmouth.edu/mba/blog/what-we-learned-the-2016-vietnam-gix.
25 Rob Cox, "Vietnam Is a Bad Example to Newly Emerging Markets," Reuters, October 01, 2012, http://blogs.reuters.com/breakingviews/2012/10/01/vietnam-is-a-bad-example-to-newly-emerging-markets/.
26 "Infographic: Science, Technology and Innovation in Vietnam," World Bank, November 24, 2014, http://www.worldbank.org/en/news/feature/2014/11/24/infographic-science-technology-and-innovation-in-vietnam.
27 Claire Honore Hollweg, Tanya Smith, and Daria Taglioni, *Vietnam at a Crossroads: Engaging in the Next Generation of Global Value Chains* (Washington, DC: World Bank Group, 2017), http://documents.worldbank.org/curated/en/808541488967692813/Vietnam-at-a-crossroads-engaging-in-the-next-generation-of-global-value-chains.
28 "Vietnam Launches Innovation Network to Tap Diaspora Expertise - VnExpress International." VnExpress International – Latest News, Business, Travel and Analysis from Vietnam. August 20, 2018. Accessed September 26, 2018. https://e.vnexpress.net/news/news/vietnam-launches-innovation-network-to-tap-diaspora-expertise-3794880.html.
29 "HCM City Sees High Investment from Overseas Vietnamese," DTI News, March 31, 2017, http://dtinews.vn/en/news/017004/50199/hcm-city-sees-high-investment-from-overseas-vietnamese.html.
30 Mohamed A. El-Erian, "The Future of Economic and Financial Globalization," *Journal of International Affairs*, March 15, 2017, https://jia.sipa.columbia.edu/future-economic-and-financial-globalization.
31 Stéphanie Thomson, "Jack Ma: America Has Wasted Its Wealth," World Economic Forum, January 18, 2017, https://www.weforum.org/agenda/2017/01/jack-ma-america-has-wasted-its-wealth.
32 Michael J. Mauboussin and Alfred Rappaport, "Reclaiming the Idea of Shareholder Value," *Harvard Business Review*, July 01, 2016, https://hbr.org/2016/07/reclaiming-the-idea-of-shareholder-value.
33 John Boudreau, "The Biggest Winner from TPP Trade Deal May Be Vietnam," Bloomberg, October 9, 2015, https://www.bloomberg.com/news/articles/2015-10-08/more-shoes-and-shrimp-less-china-reliance-for-vietnam-in-tpp.
34 "CPTPP Brings Vietnam Direct Economic Benefits and Stimulate Domestic Reforms, WB Report Says," World Bank Group, March 9, 2018, http://www.worldbank.org/en/news/press-release/2018/03/09/cptpp-brings-vietnam-direct-economic-benefits-and-stimulate-domestic-reforms-wb-report-says.
35 Thao Nguyen, "Vietnam's Internet Governance Policies: Opportunities for Developing a Competitive Digital Economy," Harvard Kennedy School, May 2013, https://www.hks.harvard.edu/centers/mrcbg/publications/awp/awp16.
36 "Decree 60 Opens Business Doors, but Barriers Still Exist," Viet Nam Net, July 26, 2015, http://english.vietnamnet.vn/fms/business/136723/decree-60-opens-business-doors-but-barriers-still-exist.html.
37 "Decree Guiding the Law on Investment," PwC Legal Vietnam NewsBrief, December 9, 2015, https://www.pwc.com/vn/en/publications/2015/pwc-legal-vietnam-newsbrief-decree-118-guiding-law-on-investment.pdf.
38 "Circular 155/2015/TT-BTC Regarding Information Disclosure on Securities Markets," PwC Vietnam NewsBrief, January 8, 2016, https://www.pwc.com/vn/en/publications/2016/pwc_vietnam_newsbrief_information_diisclosure_on_securities_markets_under_circular_155_2015_tt_ btc_en.pdf.

39 "Resolution 19 Improves Competitiveness," VietnamPlus, June 23, 2016, http://en.vietnamplus.vn/resolution-19-improves-competitiveness/95145.vnp.
40 T. S. Pham Thi Thu Hang, "Resolution 35 Brings 'Fire' Reforms to Ministries and Localities," VCCI, January 2, 2017, http://e.vcci.com.vn/details-3694-Resolution-35-brings-fire-reforms-to-ministries-and-localities.html.
41 For more on corruption, that is, abusing public office for private gain, see the Growing Out of Corruption post on VoxDev: https://voxdev.org/topic/institutions-political-economy/growing-out-corruption.
42 "Charting a Course for Trade and Economic Integration in the Asia-Pacific," Asia Society Policy Institute, accessed February 28, 2018, http://asiasociety.org/policy-institute/charting-course-trade-and-economic-integration-asia-pacific.
43 Cutler, Wendy, Charles Finny, Peter Grey, Kim Jong-Hoon, and Shotaro Oshima. "Shifting Trade Winds: US Bilateralism and Asia-Pacific Economic Integration," Asia Society, accessed January 2018. http://asiasociety.org/sites/default/files/2018-01/Trade Issue Paper Final 1.19.18.pdf.
44 UNDESA, "Committee of Experts on Public Administration, 16th Session," United Nations, accessed February 28, 2018, https://publicadministration.un.org/en/CEPA/session16.
45 John Hagel III, "What Are Platforms and Systems, and Why Are They So Important?" World Economic Forum, February 17, 2017, https://www.weforum.org/agenda/2017/02/what-are-platforms-and-systems/.
46 Assuming the age limits are adhered to.
47 Vietnam has a retirement age of sixty for males and fifty-five for females, whereas the age limit for a Politburo member to stay into next term is sixty-five—although exceptions can be, and are, made.
48 On the other hand, I've met with young members of the Vietnamese-American community who have told me that they care more about what is going on in Vietnam than in the Vietnamese-American community. More specifically, that they feel close to Vietnam and want to go to contribute, a sentiment that may clash with their parents' perspectives.
49 "Elon Musk : How to Build the Future." *YouTube* (video blog), September 15, 2016. Accessed September 26, 2018. https://youtu.be/tnBQmEqBCY0?t=23s.
50 Julie Bort, "LinkedIn Founder Reid Hoffman Has a Formula That Anyone Can Use to Be Happier and More Successful," *Business Insider*, September 26, 2016, http://www.businessinsider.com/reid-hoffman-formula-for-happiness-2016-9.
51 "Thomas Friedman, Columnist for the *NYTimes*, on How Technological Accelerations Are Shaping Our World," January 12, 2017, video, 1:16:01, posted by UChi Pol, https://www.youtube.com/watch?v=1oOTK-y0SrI&feature=youtu.be&t=59m30s.
52 "Dialogue with the Author of 'The World Is Flat,'" Diplomatic Academy of Vietnam, May 15, 2014, http://www.dav.edu.vn/en/news/1086-dialogue-with-the-author-of-the-world-is-flat.html.
53 Formerly known as the Institute of International Relations (IIR), it serves as training grounds for Vietnam's Ministry of Foreign Affairs.
54 "Viet Nam: How to Build a Data Revolution | Video Vox." Seven Things I Learned about the Transition from Communism | VOX, CEPR Policy Portal. Accessed September 26, 2018. https://voxeu.org/content/viet-nam-how-build-data-revolution.

CHAPTER 9: LOCALIZING GLOBAL SOLUTIONS

1 Quynh Trang, "Vietnam's 30 Biggest Firms Reluctant to Publish Transparent Information," *VnExpress International*, April 26, 2017, https://e.vnexpress.net/news/business/vietnam-s-30-biggest-firms-reluctant-to-publish-transparent-information-3576451.html.

2 "Sustainability Influences Purchase Intent of Vietnamese Consumers," Nielsen, April 25, 2015, http://www.nielsen.com/content/dam/nielsenglobal/vn/docs/PR_EN/Vietnam_CSR%20release_EN.pdf.

3 However, it's unclear how much more they'd be willing to pay—and how sustained such practices would be.

4 Thomson Reuters Sustainability, "EXECUTIVE PERSPECTIVE: Banking with Impact," Discover Thomson Reuters, May 19, 2017, https://blogs.thomsonreuters.com/sustainability/2017/05/19/executive-perspective-banking-with-impact/.

5 "CEO Guide to the Sustainable Development Goals," SDG Business Hub, accessed February 28, 2018, http://sdghub.com/ceo-guide/.

6 I reached out to the organization in May 2017 but have not heard back.

7 CDP, accessed February 28, 2018, https://www.cdp.net/en.

8 "Our Impact," Edge Strategy, accessed February 28, 2018, https://web.archive.org/web/20170711202104/http://www.edge-cert.org/our-impact/facts-figures-2/.

9 Leah McGrath Goodman, "If Women Are So Good at Managing Money, Why Are So Few of Them Doing It?" *Newsweek*, January 26, 2016, http://www.newsweek.com/2016/02/05/hedge-fund-women-419481.html.

10 "Women on Corporate Boards Globally," Catalyst, March 16, 2017, http://www.catalyst.org/knowledge/women-corporate-boards-globally.

11 "Invest in Other Women," Ellevate, accessed February 28, 2018, https://www.ellevatenetwork.com/invest/invest-in-other-women.

12 And one of four official dollar billionaires in Vietnam, according to *Forbes*.

13 Katia Savchuk, "Vietnam's Budget Airline Founder Is Southeast Asia's Only Woman Billionaire," *Forbes*, March 8, 2017, https://www.forbes.com/sites/katiasavchuk/2017/03/08/vietnams-budget-airline-founder-is-southeast-asias-only-woman-billionaire/.

14 Banerji, Angara, Albe Gjonbalaj, Sandile Hlatshwayo, and Anh Van Le. "F&D Article." IMF. September 2018. Accessed September 26, 2018. https://www.imf.org/external/pubs/ft/fandd/2018/09/female-labor-force-participation-in-vietnam-banerji.htm.15 Vol. 55, No. 3. http://www.imf.org/external/pubs/ft/fandd/2018/09/female-labor-force-participation-in-vietnam-banerji.htm.

15 "Women in Charge: Mastercard Index Reveals How Countries Are Progressing to Empower Women Entrepreneurs." MasterCard Social Newsroom. March 7, 2018. Accessed September 26, 2018. https://newsroom.mastercard.com/press-releases/women-in-charge-mastercard-index-reveals-how-countries-are-progressing-to-empower-women-entrepreneurs/.

16 "GEM 2017 / 2018 Global Report," Global Entrepreneurship Monitor. Accessed October 11, 2018. https://www.gemconsortium.org/report/50012.

17 Rastogi, Vaishali, Mariam Jaafar, Nerijus Zemgulys, and Chananya Ranangban. Report. September 2017. Accessed September 26, 2018. http://image-src.bcg.com/Images/BCG-Moving-Toward-Gender-Diversity-SEA-Sep-2017_tcm93-177639.pdf.

18 *Women in the Boardroom: A Global Perspective*, 5th ed. (2017), accessed February 28, 2018, https://www2.deloitte.com/content/dam/Deloitte/cn/Documents/about-deloitte/deloitte-cn-cg-women-in-the-boardroom-5ed-en-170612.pdf.

19 "How the Gender Pay Gap Varies in South-East Asia," *Financial Times*, March 23, 2018, https://www.ft.com/content/1f62b27a-2ddf-11e8-9b4b-bc4b9f08f381.

20 Jessica Davis Pluess and Peder Michael Pruzan, *Women's Empowerment in Global Value Chains*, report, accessed February 28, 2018, https://www.bsr.org/reports/BSR-Report-Womens-Empowerment-Supply-Chains.pdf.

21 "The Higg Index," Sustainable Apparel Coalition, accessed February 28, 2018, http://apparelcoalition.org/the-higg-index/.
22 "Home," IIX Foundation, accessed February 28, 2018, https://iixfoundation.org/.
23 "An UPSHIFT Journey: From Kosovo to Vietnam," UNICEF Connect, February 23, 2016, https://blogs.unicef.org/innovation/an-upshift-journey-from-kosovo-to-vietnam/.
24 "What Are the Principles for Responsible Investment?" PRI, accessed February 28, 2018, https://www.unpri.org/about/the-six-principles.
25 Ceyla Pazarbasioglu, "A New Role for Development Banks?" World Bank, May 15, 2017, http://blogs.worldbank.org/voices/new-role-development-banks.
26 Clive Harris, "How MDBs Are Raising Their Game on Infrastructure Development," World Bank, April 20, 2017, http://blogs.worldbank.org/ppps/how-mdbs-are-raising-their-game-infrastructure-development.
27 "The Global Guidelines Project," Ecology and Infrastructure International, accessed February 28, 2018, http://www.ecologyandinfrastructure.com/guidelines/.
28 "SNV Vietnam Joins the Vietnam Sustainable Energy Alliance," SNV, accessed February 28, 2018, http://www.snv.org/update/snv-vietnam-joins-vietnam-sustainable-energy-alliance.
29 "The Provincial Competitiveness Index (PCI) 2017 Launch," Vietnam Chamber of Commerce and Industry, accessed March 22, 2018, http://pci2017eng.pcivietnam.vn/uploads/pci2017/PCI2017_Press-Release.pdf.
30 "Home." VIOD - Vietnam Institute of Directors - VIOD - Vietnam Institute of Directors. Accessed September 26, 2018. http://viod.vn/about-us/about-viod/.
31 Ben Beers, "What Our Data Is Telling Us about Emerging Social Entrepreneurs," Echoing Green, April 6, 2017, http://www.echoinggreen.org/ideas/what-our-data-telling-us-about-emerging-social-entrepreneurs.
32 Richard Florida and Melanie Fasche, "The Rise of the Urban Creative Class in Southeast Asia," Martin Prosperity Institute, January 18, 2017, http://martinprosperity.org/content/the-rise-of-the-urban-creative-class-in-southeast-asia/.
33 "Vietnam's Trade Deficit with Thailand to Balloon." VOV - VOV Online Newspaper. August 21, 2018. Accessed September 26, 2018. https://english.vov.vn/trade/vietnams-trade-deficit-with-thailand-to-balloon-381633.vov.
34 Colliers International Research, "HCMC Quarterly Knowledge Report | Q4 2016," LinkedIn SlideShare, accessed February 28, 2018, https://www.slideshare.net/ColliersVietnam/hcmc-quarterly-knowledge-report-q4-2016.
35 "Ho Chi Minh City's Economic Growth to Slow This Year," *VnExpress International*, September 26, 2016, http://e.vnexpress.net/news/business/ho-chi-minh-city-s-economic-growth-to-slow-this-year-3474304.html.
36 "Without Registered Trademarks, Businesses Lose Markets," Viet Nam Net, August 9, 2016, http://english.vietnamnet.vn/fms/business/161447/without-registered-trademarks-businesses-lose-markets.html.
37 Dennis Price, "Build on Regional Strengths to Support Local Entrepreneurs," ImpactAlpha, August 3, 2017, https://news.impactalpha.com/build-on-regional-strengths-to-support-local-entrepreneurs-7c4c62cea73a.
38 "Work with Us," Endeavor, accessed February 28, 2018, https://endeavor.org/work-with-us/.
39 Quang Mai Duy, "[Topica Founder Institute] Vietnam Startup Funding 2015 Report," LinkedIn SlideShare, January 8, 2016, http://www.slideshare.net/quangmd/topica-founder-institute-vietnam-startup-funding-2015-report.
40 Quang Mai Duy, "Vietnam Startup Deals Insight 2016," LinkedIn SlideShare, March 29, 2017, https://www.slideshare.net/quangmd/vietnam-startup-deals-insight-2016.
41 For reference, in 2015 there were sixty-seven deals with a total value of USD $137 million.
42 Topica Founder Institute, "Vietnam Startup Deals Insight 2017," LinkedIn SlideShare, February 9, 2018, https://www.slideshare.net/topicafounderinstitute/vietnam-startup-deals-insight-2017-87618940.

43 Justin Wood, "ASEAN at 50: What Does the Future Hold for the Region?" World Economic Forum, May 9, 2017, https://www.weforum.org/agenda/2017/05/asean-at-50-what-does-the-future-hold-for-the-region.
44 Dieu Tu Uyen Nguyen, "Vietnam Turns to Its Neighbors after Trump Kills Trade Deal," Bloomberg, January 26, 2017, https://www.bloomberg.com/news/articles/2017-01-25/vietnam-turns-to-neighbors-as-trump-strikes-blow-to-trade-deal.
45 Sue-Lin Wong, "China Launches New AIIB Development Bank as Power Balance Shifts," Reuters, January 16, 2016, http://www.reuters.com/article/us-asia-aiib-investment-idUSK-CN0UU03Y.
46 Issaku Harada, "AIIB Hits Its First-Year Lending Target," *Nikkei Asian Review*, January 26, 2017, http://asia.nikkei.com/magazine/20170126/Politics-Economy/AIIB-hits-its-first-year-lending-target.
47 Jane Perlez and Yufan Huang, "Behind China's $1 Trillion Plan to Shake Up the Economic Order," The New York Times, May 13, 2017, https://www.nytimes.com/2017/05/13/business/china-railway-one-belt-one-road-1-trillion-plan.html?_r=0.
48 Minh Vu Truong, "The Geopolitics of Infrastructure: ASEAN's China Challenge," Asia Maritime Transparency Initiative, February 13, 2017, https://amti.csis.org/geopolitics-infrastructure-asean-china/.
49 "Freight Farms Expands into Vietnam," Trifecta Ecosystems, December 6, 2017, accessed February 28, 2018, http://trifectaecosystems.com/news/freight-farms-expands-vietnam/.
50 "SAP Social Sabbatical Empowers Vietnam Organizations to Drive Sustainable Operating Models for Social Good," Stockhouse, April 28, 2017, http://www.stockhouse.com/news/press-releases/2017/04/28/sap-social-sabbatical-empowers-vietnam-organizations-to-drive-sustainable.
51 Jenny Soffel, "What Are the 21st-Century Skills Every Student Needs?" World Economic Forum, March 10, 2016, https://www.weforum.org/agenda/2016/03/21st-century-skills-future-jobs-students/.
52 Master's Thesis; Andrew Rowan. "Global Managerial Strategy in a Novel and Disruptive 21st Century: Pitfalls to Avoid, Opportunities to Seize."
53 Vo Hai, "Hanoi Offers $200,000 Prize to Solve Worsening Traffic Jams," *VnExpress International*, January 12, 2017, https://e.vnexpress.net/news/news/hanoi-offers-200-000-prize-to-solve-worsening-traffic-jams-3527593.html.
54 Eric Johnson, "Grab wants to go way beyond ride-hailing in Asia, co-founder Hooi Ling Tan says." Recode, August 1, 2018. https://www.recode.net/2018/8/1/17639380/grab-hooi-ling-tan-ride-hailing-asia-platform-payments-groceries-kara-swisher-decode-podcast.
55 Phan Anh, "55,000 Coal Stoves Plague Hanoians with Toxic Smog," *VnExpress International*, March 18, 2018, https://e.vnexpress.net/news/news/55-000-coal-stoves-plague-hanoians-with-toxic-smog-3724344.html.
56 Ryo Seo-Zindy, "Emerging Digital Production and Innovation Networks in Southeast Asia," Researching DIFN, March 03, 2017, https://difn.wordpress.com/2017/03/03/emerging-production-and-innovation-networks-in-southeast-asia/.
57 Pham Huong, "Hanoi Sweats through Hottest Day in Decades," *VnExpress International*, June 2, 2017, https://e.vnexpress.net/news/news/hanoi-sweats-through-hottest-day-in-decades-3594106.html.
58 Uber accepted cash in Vietnam from late 2015 until early 2018, where it saw the highest rates of credit card declines in Southeast Asia in 2015 when new customers tried to sign up.
59 Kevin Helms, "Cryptocurrency Mining Soars in Vietnam—Over 7000 Rigs Imported," *Bitcoin News*, January 03, 2018, https://news.bitcoin.com/cryptocurrency-mining-soars-vietnam-7000-rigs-imported/.
60 Casey Hynes, "Vietnam May Soon Emerge As One of Southeast Asia's Blockchain Innovation Hubs," *Forbes*, March 27, 2018, https://www.forbes.com/sites/chynes/2018/03/27/why-vietnam-could-emerge-as-a-blockchain-innovation-hub/#4e4a08802cc5.

61 "Vietnamese Startups, Entrepreneurs Warm Up to ICOs," *Fintechnews Singapore*, September 30, 2017, http://fintechnews.sg/12369/vietnam/vietnam-ico/.
62 John Biggs, "Exit Scammers Run Off with $660 Million in ICO Earnings," TechCrunch, April 13, 2018, http://techcrunch.com/2018/04/13/exit-scammers-run-off-with-660-million-in-ico-earnings/.

CHAPTER 10: BEING A PART OF VIETNAM'S SUCCESS

1 Literally means "fresh beer," but the experience of drinking with vast quantities of people on small stools together is implied.
2 Otherwise known as a "girlie bar."
3 John Reed, "Vietnam Looks to Bolster Private Sector Output," *Financial Times*, March 27, 2018, https://www.ft.com/content/eade23c2-30ef-11e8-b5bf-23cb17fd1498.
4 For more information on the pre-VC environment in Vietnam, see this report: http://documents.worldbank.org/curated/en/639591468131388763/pdf/367390PSDP1No141EN.pdf.
5 A real example.
6 How old are you, are you married, where do you come from, and so on?
7 The most common family name in Vietnam, pronounced "win."
8 Navi Radjou, "Creative Problem-Solving in the Face of Extreme Limits," TED, October 2014, http://www.ted.com/talks/navi_radjou_creative_problem_solving_in_the_face_of_extreme_limits#t-14579.
9 Sally French, "Wealth in This Asian Country Grew by 210% in the Last 10 Years—And It's Not China," MarketWatch, January 29, 2018, https://www.marketwatch.com/story/wealth-in-this-asian-country-grew-by-210-in-the-last-10-years-and-its-not-china-2018-01-29.
10 https://www.wealthx.com/wp-content/uploads/2018/09/Wealth-X_WUWR_2018.pdf?utm_source=https%3A%2F%2Fwww.wealthx.com%2Fwp-content%2Fuploads%2F2018%2F09%2FWealth-X_WUWR_2018.pdf.
11 "Vietnam—GDP Per Capita (Current US$)," World Bank, accessed February 28, 2018, https://data.worldbank.org/indicator/NY.GDP.PCAP.CD?locations=VN.
12 "Market Classification," MSCI, accessed February 28, 2018, https://www.msci.com/market-classification.

ABOUT THE AUTHOR

Andrew P. Rowan is an American entrepreneur who has lived and worked in Hanoi, Ho Chi Minh City, and Da Nang since 2013. As the founder and director of GKTA Group, he established a partnership with the €11 million Finland-Vietnam Innovation Partnership Program (IPP2), which accelerates growth for Vietnam-based startups, with support from the governments of Vietnam and Finland.

Recognized as a leading expert on entrepreneurship, startups, and economic development, Andrew has collaborated on innovation initiatives in Vietnam with the US Embassy in Hanoi, as well as with Vietnam's Ministry of Science and Technology. He graduated with honors from Sacred Heart University and holds a master's degree in international business from Hult International Business School. His work or writings have been featured in *Tech in Asia*, *e27*, and *Tech Wire Asia*, among other international publications. A skilled moderator and panelist, Andrew has presented on entrepreneurship and innovation topics at New York University; the University of California, Davis; and the Rochester Institute of Technology. Andrew is a member of the New York Conference on Asian Studies (NYCAS) and the New York Southeast Asia Network (NYSEAN). Born in Mount Vernon, New York, he is a graduate of Horace Greeley High School in Chappaqua, New York.

INDEX

A

B

C

Đ

E

F

G

H

I

J

K

L

M

N

O

P

R

S

T

U

V

W

X

Y

Z